Stephen Eckett
on
Online Investing

Stephen Eckett
on
Online Investing

by

Stephen Eckett

HARRIMAN HOUSE LTD

43 Chapel Street
Petersfield
Hampshire
GU32 3DY
GREAT BRITAIN

Tel: +44 (0)1730 233870
Fax: +44 (0)1730 233880
email: enquiries@global-investor.com
web site: www.global-investor.com

First published in Great Britain in 2002

Copyright Harriman House Ltd

The right of Stephen Eckett to be identified as the author has been asserted by
him in accordance with the Copyright, Designs and Patents Act 1988.

ISBN 1 897 59714 2

British Library Cataloguing in Publication Data
A CIP catalogue record for this book can be obtained from the British Library.

Printed and bound by Ashford Colour Press Ltd, Gosport, Hampshire

CONTENTS

1. Computers and the internet

2. Investing Basics

3. Data Sources

4. Fundamental Analysis

5. Technical Analysis

6. Trading

7. US Markets

8. International Markets

9. Derivatives and Betting

10. Miscellaneous

Appendices

Index

Introduction

When Interactive Investor went public in February 2000, the company had no earnings and negligible turnover. Soon after floating it had a market capitalisation of over £800m, equivalent to around £1,000 per registered user. Nine months after that, in November 2000, themutual.net bought the client database of the defunct TheStreet.co.uk for just £2 per user. Did someone say bubble?

Despite the woes of dotcom companies, the internet is becoming increasingly important, especially in matters of investment. According to ComPeer, by the end of 2001 online trades accounted for 31 per cent of execution-only share trading, and there were 350,000 online investors. If anything, this statistic understates the significance of the internet, since many investors use it for research purposes but not for trading. For many, investing in the markets would be nigh on impossible without the sophisticated analysis tools and low charges the internet offers.

So, the internet is now mainstream. That doesn't stop it being intensely frustrating at times, even when performing the simplest tasks. Why is that? It may be the fact that as modern life speeds up, our own skills fail to keep pace: investors with a deep knowledge of the financial markets know little about computers, and vice versa. Or it may be the tendency of IT companies to focus on product innovation but not on user support. Whatever the reason, if you've spent a couple of fruitless hours searching online for Vodafone's closing price last Tuesday, you're irked, not to say downright angry.

The purpose of this book is not to wax lyrical about the internet or to bemoan its shortcomings. It was written to solve problems and to answer questions, like -

- Where can I find a list of the stocks in the FTSE 100 Index?
- Is there a web site that gives the beta values of shares?
- Which sites offer free real-time share prices?
- How do I download data from a web page into a spreadsheet?

For a few years I've written a column for *Investors Chronicle*, answering just these sorts of questions. This book is a compilation of the most common queries, but with updated answers.

There are over 200 questions covering the broad universe of investing. In addition, the appendix includes a comprehensive directory of 400 web sites which I have found helpful, entertaining or otherwise of interest in my own investing. Where appropriate, I have referred to specific web pages on these sites, rather than just general links to a home page.

In tune with modern times, and also the topic dealt with here, there is a web site to support the book: `www.global-investor.com/onlineinvesting`. From there you can download 11 spreadsheets that I have created to illustrate answers in the text.

I hope you find the book useful. There's no doubt that investing online is the future of investing; but it would be better to reach that future with less hassle. After all, the internet, like all technology, is supposed to make our lives easier.

Stephen Eckett

About the author

Stephen Eckett has worked for a number of years in the financial industry with Baring Securities, Bankers Trust and S.G. Warburg, in London, Hong Kong and Tokyo. He is a co-founder and Director of Global-Investor.com, the financial education company. He also writes for a number of financial journals and is the author of the award-winning book, *Investing Online*.

1   Computers and the internet

- Computer basics
- Internet connections
- Web browsing shortcuts
- Performance tips
- Keyboard shortcuts
- Importing data
- Downloads into Excel
- Internet Explorer add-ons
- Search engine optimisation
- Troubleshooting

Computer support

Q My computer keeps 'freezing', sometimes in the middle of trading, which is a nuisance. Do you know what the problem is, and can you suggest a solution?

A It is difficult to answer questions like this without knowing more about the particular configuration of your computer. However, I can give a few general tips:

Firstly, make sure you buy a good computer from a reputable producer and distributor. If you have a local computer shop, it may be sensible to buy from there rather than online if it offers a good after-sales service. The online price may be cheaper, but saving a hundred quid is a false economy if it means you get inadequate support afterwards.

Secondly, it's a good idea to regularly scan and defragment the hard drive. Further information on this can be found in Windows Help (`Start key > Help`): search under ScanDisk and Defrag. It's also worthwhile giving your computer a full service occasionally at **PCPitstop**. Useful background articles on computers can be found at **HowStuffWorks** and **TechTutorials**.

If you have a specific problem, first look for a solution in the Windows Help (see above). If that doesn't help, try the **Microsoft online help**, which has recently been greatly improved. If the problem concerns a non-Microsoft program (unusual, but it sometimes happens), try the program maker's web site for support; for example, support for WinZip can be found on WinZip's web site. It may also be worth searching the newsgroups, although this can be very hit or miss, and only for the dedicated geek.

If the whole computer thing leaves you bemused and frustrated, you might like to try **PC Medics**, which is an independent company offering a rapid response support for PC users.

L HowStuffWorks: www.howstuffworks.com

Microsoft (online help): support.microsoft.com

Newsgroups: groups.google.com

PC Medics: www.pc-medics.co.uk

PCPitstop: www.pcpitstop.com

Tech Tutorials: www.techtutorials.com

WinZip: www.winzip.com

Q I am thinking of buying a laptop computer. Is it possible to connect these to the internet just like desktop machines?

A Yes, there are several ways to connect a laptop to the internet. Many laptops now come with a modem built in, in which case it is merely a matter of connecting a telephone cable direct to the computer. If there is no built-in modem, then you need to buy a PCMCIA card modem (a small, credit-card sized device) and plug it into the computer.

Alternatively, you could **connect your laptop to a desktop machine** so that they share one internet connection. If you're using Windows the simplest method is to set up a *peer-to-peer network* between the two computers, which doesn't require any complicated LAN software. (For further information on Windows Peer-to-Peer networking see the **Microsoft** web site, or a page dedicated to **Windows95 Peer-to-Peer Networking**).

There are several ways that two or more networked computers can **share an internet connection**, but the best I've found is using a magic box from 3COM called a *LAN Modem*. This little box is one of the greatest inventions of the last 100 years: it simultaneously acts as a network hub (controlling the data flow of all the networked computers), but is also a modem for connecting to the internet (over ordinary analogue or ISDN lines). With this box in place, two or more computers can simultaneously access the net – great for small offices or homes with wired families. I also find that a further advantage of networking a laptop to my desktop machine is that when I'm trading I can have both monitors displaying information simultaneously; and because I keep the two hard drives synchronised, one computer acts as a complete back-up machine for the other.

Mobile internet

Of course, the great advantage of laptops is the ability to be truly wired and mobile. While in theory it is possible to connect a laptop to phone sockets anywhere, in practice the experienced laptop road warrior knows it's rarely that simple. For a start, phone sockets are not available everywhere, and where you can find one, the line might be prohibitively expensive (in the case of a hotel) or the socket resolutely hostile to a UK-designed plug (if you're abroad).

The solution to this is to connect the laptop to a cellular telephone; I connect mine to a Nokia using an infra-red link, and on the whole this works well. But it does increase the complexity of the whole connection. The Gods must be smiling: your laptop must have enough juice in the batteries, your telephone receiving a signal, your ISP working and not engaged etc. But if you get a kick out of dealing on Nasdaq while sitting on a train in the English countryside, this is for you.

L Microsoft: www.microsoft.com

Windows95 Peer-to-Peer Networking:

www.corp-reflection.com/pub/peer/

Apple Macs

Q I am a Mac user and currently use Sharescope through a Windows emulation program. I find this cumbersome and wondered if you know of any investment software that runs effectively under the Mac operating system?

A I must admit to rather ignoring Mac-users in this column. The trouble is that most investment software producers are fairly small operations and they naturally target the larger client base of PC users, so many programs are not compatible with the Mac operating system.

However, according to Russell Bird of **Paritech**, as long as the Mac is fairly new (with the G4 processor), then PC programs like **Metastock** should run fairly well using Virtual PC. And things should improve with the introduction of the new OSX operating system. However, Russell says it may still be difficult getting a stock history database converted to a format that works on a MAC.

Two programs to check out that were written specifically for Macs are **Pro Analyst** and **ProTA**. Both work with UK market data.

Hopefully, in the future, differences between PCs and Macs will further erode. And in the case of investment programs, it's likely that these will migrate totally online to become web services – at which point they almost automatically become cross-platform, accessible equally by users of Macs, PCs or Linux machines.

L Metastock: www.equis.com

Paritech: www.paritech.co.uk

Pro Analyst: trendsoft.com/ProAnalyst/

ProTA: www.beesoft.net

4

Using more than one ISP

Q You have written before about using more than one ISP. I am hesitant to sign up to a second ISP in case the software I download somehow corrupts or overwrites my present communication procedure. Is this likely to happen and is the process straightforward?

A This is quite a common question, and unfortunately there is no easy answer. Much depends on your own computer system and the specific ISPs being used. I think the best I can do is to describe my own set-up, and hope that this is generally useful.

When signing up to a new ISP, whenever possible, I **avoid using their installation disk**, which is usually quite aggressive in changing various configuration files on your computer. Better is to click on `My Computer` (Windows only), then `Dial-Up Networking`, then `Make New Connection`, and input the telephone number of the new ISP directly, along with your new username and password. Other parameters can also be input directly, such as the email server address. All this information should be available from the ISP.

Having set up the new ISP facility on the computer (whether manually, or using an installation disk), when I want to connect to the ISP, again I go to the `Dial-Up Networking` box in `My Computer`, and select the ISP connection directly from there.

Even better than using the `Dial-Up Networking` box, it is better to add short-cuts to the ISP connections in the `Start` menu.

Throughout the day I monitor the performance of my ISP connection using `tracert` (see page 15 for more on this), and if things start slowing down, I log-off and reconnect using a different ISP.

5

Connection charges

Q Since starting to trade online, my phone charges have shot up. Is there a way to set up my system so that I am only connected when I periodically 'refresh' the on-screen data?

A Much depends on your specific computer set up, your internet connection, and what type of browser you are using. But below are a few ideas that might help.

If there are big web pages that I want to read, I load the page into the browser, and then log off from the internet - the web page will stay on the screen. To log off from the internet without losing the browser, double-click on the icon (two little terminals flashing) in the bottom right `System Tray` of Windows, and manually select `Disconnect`. Note, this procedure may be a little different (or not possible) if using a service such as AOL or CompuServe. If there are lots of pages that I want to read, I save the web pages to the hard disk on my computer, log off from the internet, and then read the pages offline. The key to the success of this operation is to be very precise in choosing where you actually save the files on your hard disk, so they can be found again easily in Windows Explorer.

If there is one web page that I am interested in (perhaps a page showing the prices of all FTSE 100 stocks), I load that page, and log off from the internet - the page will stay on the screen, even though the connection has been broken. Later, when I want to refresh the page, I'll simply hit the `F5` function key on the keyboard, and the computer will connect to the internet and update the page automatically.

Beyond the above, you might like to think about investing in an ISDN line. Better still would be an ADSL line, or cable connection (if you have cable to your house).

Download speeds

Q Several companies have contacted me recently offering their annual reports etc. via the internet instead of through the post. Last night I downloaded the 28 page annual report of Qualcomm Inc. from the company's site which occupied my computer for more than 25 minutes. Do I need a faster modem or internet connection?

A The **Qualcomm** annual reports can be downloaded from the investor relations section (click Financial Publications) of the company's web site. The 2000 report is approximately 3.3MB in size, which is fairly hefty.

A standard modem rated at 56Kb transfers data at a speed of approximately 56,000 bits per second (equivalent to roughly 7KB, or 7,000 bytes, per second); which would download 3.3MB (equivalent to roughly 3,300KB) in about 471 seconds. But modems don't always work at their optimum speed if you have a poor line connection.

On a PC running Windows you can check your effective connection speed by double clicking the two little terminals icon in the bottom right system tray. If this displays a connection speed of, say, just 28,000 bits/sec, the download of the Qualcomm report could take twice the time calculated above.

However, there are some steps which you can take to improve performance:

• First, make sure you have a **56Kb (or better) modem**; they are so cheap now that not upgrading from an old modem is a false economy in most cases.

• Second, consider using **more than one ISP**; throughout the day the performance of different ISPs fluctuates, and it can be useful to switch between them to optimise your connection speed.

• Lastly, if the connection speed is as fast as it can be, and the download is still taking a long time, you can always download the file **in the background**. To do this, instead of left clicking on the report's hyperlink, right-click and (for Internet Explorer) select Save target as…, which enables you to save the file direct to your hard disk, but frees the browser up to continue looking at other web sites in the meantime.

L Qualcomm (investor relations): www.qualcomm.com/cda/IR/

7

Downloading very large files

Q Being a MetaStock fan for a number of years I was eager to follow your recommendation with regard to their www.echarts.com web site. Unfortunately you have to download a program called 'Real Player 8 basic version'. This is free but the download time is two hours and fifty-four minutes. At that rate the Pony Express would be quicker!

A I have written about download speeds before, and suggested some simple steps to speed things up. However effective those steps are though, large files still take a very long time to download.

There may be a different way round the problem. If you want to download a fairly standard internet file, there's a chance that the file you want will be included on the cover CD of one of the monthly internet magazines. Get a copy of one of these magazines (the best are *Internet* and *.net*), load the CD into your computer and there should be a choice of programs to install.

For example, installing *Real Player* might take two minutes from a CD, compared to two hours + if you download it over the internet. This is no good if you want to download a finance-specific file (e.g. the annual report of Qualcomm), but should work for general programs such as: *MS Internet Explorer, Netscape, Real Player, Macromedia Flash, and Adobe Acrobat Reader.*

8

Q Can you explain what broadband, 'always on' internet connections are, and who provides them?

A Broadband simply means accessing the internet at fast speed - 500Kbps (kilo bits per second) or greater, which is about ten times faster than an ordinary *dial-up* connection. With an *always on* connection, you don't have to dial-up afresh to the internet every time you want to use it. There are three main broadband internet options:

Cable modem

The first is via a *cable modem*, using a previously installed cable service. The two major UK cable providers (**Telewest** and **NTL**) recently announced an alliance to market broadband internet via cable (to counter BT's ADSL service – more of which below). Telewest and NTL combined have 90,000 clients using their cable broadband internet services, from a total of 9m homes (covering 37% of UK and Ireland) currently *broadband-enabled*. The intention is to increase coverage to 11.6m homes by end 2002.

The cost of a cable broadband internet is a £50 installation fee and around £33 per month (although this drops to £25 per month if other cable services are also subscribed to). However, not everyone who has cable has yet the option of broadband internet (the cable companies are trying to roll this out as fast as possible), and not everyone has any cable service at all yet (availability of cable broadband internet can be checked at the **NTL broadband site)**.

ADSL

Some people in remote rural areas will never have cable, and they will have to fall back on the old copper wires of the telephone system. The last few years has seen great progress in squeezing ever better performance out of those expensively installed wires. This has culminated in the current ADSL (*Asynchronous Digital Subscriber Line*) technology, which rivals that of existing cable broadband internet with speeds of around 512Kbps. Again, not everyone has access to this (check the **BT Openworld** web site to see if you do). As yet only about 50% of BT exchanges support ADSL, although at the beginning of August 2001 BT announced they intend to increase this to 80-90% in the next year. Constraints on ADSL accessibility include limits on the capacity of individual exchanges, and the user's distance from their local exchange.

The BT ADSL service charges £30 per month (and coming down all the time) and has a £150 installation fee. There are also some 20 or so other companies that offer ADSL. One of these is **Easynet** which although charging £79 per month claims their service is more appropriate for small office use, rather than the BT ADSL which is targeted at consumers.

There are now 80,000 ADSL users in the UK – a similar figure to the total cable broadband usage. With recent initiatives announced by both BT on the ADSL side, and Telewest and NTL on cable, the Battle of Broadband Internet is underway.

Satellite

The final option for broadband internet is a *satellite* connection. This is an exciting technology which for some time has offered the hope of high-speed internet connection to remote places that may never get cable or even ADSL. The technology is tried and tested, and a recent development has even allowed two-way satellite connections (previously users had to download data via the satellite link, and upload via an ordinary telephone line).

At the moment, the main users of satellite are not ordinary consumers but businesses. Companies that regularly need to transfer very large files, or who are in multimedia (e.g. broadcasting concerts) can use satellite transfer over proprietary networks and attain high levels of speed and reliability.

The problem for consumers is that not many companies offer a satellite service. Some have tried in the past - for instance, Europe Online and Easynet - but both have since discontinued the service. Neverthless, the demand is there and it's reasonable to suppose that new services will fill it before too long.

Last thought on broadband

Don't forget that your experience of surfing the web will depend on more than just having a broadband internet connection. Your effective speed will also be determined by the activity on the remote web server, the general prevailing congestion on the internet and the speed of your own computer.

Broadband internet is obviously the future for all of us (whether we want it or not), and we can expect its use to grow quickly. To some, £30 per month may seem a lot; to others it may merely represent the saving in charges on one online stock deal over the old offline rate. Having said that, I still use ISDN and find that perfectly fast enough for all investment purposes in the UK.

```
BT Openworld: www.btopenworld.com

Easynet: www.easydial.co.uk

NTL: www.ntl.com

NTL (broadband site): www.broadband-cable.co.uk

Telewest: www.telewest.co.uk
```

Wireless modems

Q How long will it be before you can get a laptop with built in WAP which doesn't need a separate telephone to connect to the internet?

A WAP was designed for small portable devices, and a portable computer is not, in this context, 'small'. If you have a portable computer, the task is to connect it to the internet, which, once achieved, will be superior to the functionality-restricted WAP. Personally, I usually travel with a laptop computer and a mobile phone. The former connects to the phone with an infra-red link, and a connection to the internet is easily made.

So, at the moment, I would recommend connecting to the internet while on the move by using a mobile phone. However, if for some reason you don't want to use a mobile phone, it is possible to use a *wireless modem* – a PCMCIA modem for a portable computer with an aerial that connects direct to a mobile network. When researching hardware questions such as this, there are many resources on the web, the best of which is probably **CNET**. On the CNET site there is a link to `Hardware`, then to `Modems`, and then to `Wireless modems`, where they list wireless modems from BreezeCOM, Novatel and Sierra. The major disadvantage of these wireless connections is that speed is drastically restricted due to the current speed of data transfer over mobile networks. These modems claim speeds of 19.2 Kbps, but I think in the UK effective wireless speeds may be as low as 9.6 Kbps. So, while fine for email, they are too slow for surfing the web.

Bluetooth

A new standard for wireless computing is **Bluetooth**. Recently I've been experimenting with connecting a laptop computer to a mobile phone using Bluetooth technology instead of an infra-red connection. I'm having mixed results. A problem as yet is that the Bluetooth technology does not seem to be standardised. Another problem to watch out for is that Windows XP does not yet support Bluetooth.

L Bluetooth: www.bluetooth.com

CNET: www.cnet.com

11

Digital Television and WAP

Q I have a computer, but wonder if there are any advantages in using digital television or WAP on a mobile telephone for finding information on shares?

A Digital television suffers from two disadvantages compared to a computer. Firstly, the **screen resolution** on a television is not as good as on a computer, which means that less information can be presented and what there is is not very pleasant to look at. There's a big difference between watching a film on a TV screen, and scrutinising a share price chart.

Secondly, **interaction** with a digital TV is more awkward than that it is with a computer. Yes, there are hand-held remotes with a few coloured buttons on them, but they are not as intuitive to use as a keyboard and mouse. Navigation is primitive.

Currently, there are not many financial services available on digital TV anyway. Obviously, in the future computers and television will merge into one box. But in the *near* future, growth areas for digital TV are likely to be home shopping and online betting, while computers connected to the internet will remain the medium of choice for share investors.

Turning to *WAP*, there is nothing available on WAP that cannot be found on the internet via an ordinary computer. There are now lots of financial WAP services on offer, but the take-up by clients has been poor. One reason for this is undoubtedly the fiddly interface of a mobile telephone. Also, investors' obsession with real-time tracking of the value of their portfolios has probably waned with the recent dismal performance of the market.

Opening multiple browser windows

Q In a recent article you told a reader to access a web page by selecting 'open in new window', as this would enable him to read it off-line. Can you elaborate?

A Visit any of the major financial web sites, and you'll find numerous links to different news stories, commentary and data. If you want to look at just one link, you position your mouse over it, and click the left button. Simple.

If you want to read lots of the linked articles, you could follow the same procedure: click on the first link, read the article, click back to the home page, and go on to the next one. The trouble is that it may take several minutes to explore each link, and all the time you are incurring telephone charges.

A more efficient method is to position the mouse over a link and then click the *right* mouse button. A small sub menu will appear on the screen, with a number of options. In both Netscape and IE (Internet Explorer), near the top of the menu is the option, `Open in new window`. If you click on this, a new browser window will open, and the link's target page will be loaded into the new window. Depending on the resolution of your screen and whether the new window opens up maximised (to occupy the whole screen), it may not be immediately obvious that a new window has actually opened up – if the original window becomes hidden behind the new one just opened. To check, look at the Windows menu bar (containing the `Start` button at the foot of the screen); if there are two buttons with the Netscape or IE logo, it means you now have two browser windows open.

Having right-clicked on a link (to open it in a new window), you can then return to the home page quickly using `alt-tab` (or clicking the browser button in the Windows bottom bar), select another link and right-click again. Then immediately - without waiting for the new page to download - return to the home page, select another link and right-click that . . and carry on opening new windows. The number of new windows you can open is limited only by your computer's memory – most computers should be able to open five or more windows with no problem.

The advantage of the procedure just outlined is that, if you are quick, all the web pages can be downloading simultaneously in the background – to download 10 articles may take just 20 seconds. Having done that, you can log off from the internet (i.e. stop the telephone charges), but you will still have all the downloaded web pages in the various browser windows open. You can then read the web pages 'offline' at your leisure.

The procedure just described explains how to open new windows from links that already exist on a web page. That won't be the case if you are looking at Yahoo, and want to open a window for Ample - the Yahoo page won't have such a link. In this case, from the browser top menu bar select, `File > New > Window` or, far better, hold the `Control` key down on the keyboard and tap the letter `N`. A new window will open, and the URL of the web site (in this case, `www.iii.co.uk`) can be typed direct into the new window's `Location box`.

Opening multiple browser windows is the single most useful trick I can think of when investing online. Without it, surfing the net would be slow and frustrating. With it, there's no reason why – outside of very rare circumstances – the net should ever seem slow.

Switching quickly between programs

Q You've referred a few times to something called 'alt-tabbing' – what is this?

A Alt-tabbing is a method of switching quickly between programs on PCs running Windows.

When you have multiple programs running under Windows, small buttons (representing the programs) are displayed on the Windows `Task Bar` at the bottom of the screen. Clicking these buttons with the mouse will select the current active program, and display the program's window to the fore.

However, a far more effective way of window switching is `alt-tabbing`. This involves holding the keyboard `Alt` key down with your left thumb, and then tapping the `Tab` key with a finger (while still depressing the `Alt` key). Do this once and a menu will pop-up in the middle of the screen, showing all the programs currently running on your computer. Subsequently, each time you tap the `Tab` key (with the `Alt` key still depressed) a program is highlighted in rotation. Lift your thumb off the `Alt` key, and the program currently highlighted in the pop-up box will come to the front of your screen. This enables very rapid switching between windows - and programs. It is not specific to internet browsers and is a standard Windows technique.

With a little practice, this procedure becomes second nature: rolling the thumb and forefinger on and off the `alt-tab` keys switches quickly back and forth between two or more windows. When I am trading, I commonly have eight or more browser windows open simultaneously (e.g. the input order form of an online broker, ADVFN Level II quotes, an AFX news page, a bulletin board page and several charting pages). With all those windows open, I will be continually `alt-tabbing` between pages.

14

Speeding up web browsing

Q I use a number of different web site for trading and research, but loading the pages and moving between the sites can be agonisingly slow. How can I speed things up?

A The best way to improve the viewing of web sites is to **open multiple windows** in your web browser program. This allows your computer to load a number of pages at once, and you can be looking at one of them while the others load in the background (see page 13 for more on this).

As far as slowness is concerned, it is often caused by the 'sheer weight of traffic' on the internet. There's no easy way around this, but **using more then one ISP may offer a solution**. Just as it can sometimes be good to use the M25 (I'm talking hypothetically here of course), and at other times to nip down a country lane, so it can be better to use individual ISPs at different times because internet traffic bottlenecks are always changing. Personally, I use four ISPs (two or three should normally be sufficient), and during an ordinary trading day I switch from one to another as the service from any particular ISP deteriorates.

But how do you know if the bottleneck is caused by your ISP? What you need to realise is that when you are looking at a web site the data is being relayed across many different computers in transit from the web site to your own computer. If a web site is slow, it could be the fault of any one computer in the chain of communication.

Fortunately, there is a tool which can help you identify which one - the command `tracert` on Windows machines (other operating systems usually have an equivalent). To use this command, open a `DOS Windows` box (found in `Start > Programs`), type `tracert www.yahoo.com`, and click `OK`. The program sends three small packets of data in turn to each of the computers on the route to the Yahoo web site, and displays how long in milliseconds it takes for the data to be bounced back. The one that takes the longest is the rogue machine.

This method can be used for any web site that seems to be loading slowly. For example, if you have trouble connecting to the BBC site, the problem might be with the BBC web server itself, a problem with your ISP, or a problem with some other connecting computer en route. To find where the problem is try

`tracert www.bbc.co.uk`

So, before next calling your ISP and rhetorically asking them why you are paying them money for a rotten service when there are now free services around, it might be an idea to check that your slow web connection is actually caused by this ISP!

Further information on the Tracert command can be found on page 16.

Q Can you give any tips to a 'newbie' on how to make browsing more efficient?

A Using the internet can sometimes (frequently!) be a frustrating experience, and previously I've mentioned a few tips that can help make it less fraught. Here are the Top Ten Tips in one place:

- **Open multiple windows** of your browser to enable viewing and downloading of many web pages simultaneously. This is probably the single most important recommendation I can make. If I had to browse the web with just one window, I'd give up today.

- **Use keyboard short-cuts**, instead of the mouse. The mouse is fine for beginners, but inefficient in a fast-paced trading environment. To learn more about keyboard short-cuts, bring up the `Windows Help` box, and search for `shortcut keys` in the index.

- **Create a structured file library** on your hard disk, using multiple sub-folders. Save web pages in an organised fashion (never just hit `File > Save`, without first thinking where you want to save the file), and later use the `Windows Explorer Find` facility to retrieve documents.

- **Use the Site Map,** not the home page, to navigate around large web sites.

- **Directly edit the url in your browser location box** to access pages. For example, the URL `http://uk.finance.yahoo.com/q?d=v1&s=VOD&m=L` is the address of a page on Yahoo giving price data for Vodafone. If you want to see the equivalent data for Barclays Bank, you don't have to use Yahoo's search box to find it. Simply type the EPIC code for Barclays (BARC) in place of VOD, click 'Go', and hey presto! - you'll be on the right page - in other words, you'll be on: `http://uk.finance.yahoo.com/q?d=v1&s=BARC&m=L`.

- **Use the Tracert command** to identify the cause of a slowdown if web pages are loading slowly. (Further information on this utility can be found at the Microsoft web site - input `tracert` to the Search box on the home page).

- **Use more than one ISP**. This is sensible not just from a risk diversification viewpoint, but also because it's useful to be able to switch between ISPs during the day, as they are all subject to different bottlenecks and slow periods from time to time.

- **Protect your real identity** on the internet. Don't be afraid to use a fictitious name, combined with use of an anonymous email service such as `www.hotmail.com`, `www.yahoo.com` or `www.bigfoot.com`.

- **Elect to receive news by email** rather than having to view web sites, where this service is offered to you. It's easier to read text in an email than poorly designed web pages; and also doesn't require reading while online incurring telephone charges.

- **Back-up, back-up, back-up!**

Bookmark efficiency

Q I've been using the internet for over two years now, and during that time have bookmarked many web pages that I've come across. But my list of bookmarks is getting very long. Is there a clever way to manage these?

A The traditional way to mark a web page is to add it to the browser's `Favourites` (or `Bookmarks` in Netscape). This enables you to return later to the web page without having to remember the exact address. There are a few techniques to make this process more efficient. Firstly, **sub-dividing the bookmark list into folders**. For example, one folder could contain web sites with stock tips, another could be focused on company research, and another on the US markets. A quick method of bookmarking a page in IE is to drag the icon in the top location box over the `Favourites` button, which will expand automatically, and then drop the icon into a specific folder. Although, it has to be said, this being Microsoft, this little feature-ette also seems to have a tendency to crash the program.

Another tip in managing bookmarks is to **edit the title** that appears in the bookmark list. When you first bookmark a page, this title is taken directly from the web page itself, and is not always very helpful. For example, a page with the general title, *Equities*, might be better re-named, say, UK *equities – top 10 most active* (editing can be done in: `Favourites > Organise Favourites`).

There's also a huge range of free software and shareware that can be downloaded from the web to help manage bookmarks more effectively. To find these, visit **Download.com**, **Tucows** or **ZD Net** and input the keyword *bookmark* into the search engine. Download.com lists over 100 such programs, including the popular SpotOn, which creates 'tours' of web sites – useful if you visit the same investment web sites everyday.

L Download.com: www.download.com

Tucows: www.tucows.com

ZD Net: www.zdnet.com/downloads/

Building your own bookmark page

Q I read on a bulletin board that someone had created their own bookmark page for investing. Is this is easy to do?

A Yes. At first glance it sounds like a rather sad, geeky activity. After all, life's too short to start learning how to write web pages, right? But 10 years ago, writing letters using a word processor was also considered the preserve of trained specialists. Today, almost anyone can use Word to write a letter, and when you come to save a document you are even offered the option of saving it in HTML format (i.e. as a web page).

An example of the type of page I use can be seen on **this book's web site**. This page contains over 100 links to UK financial web pages, which I find more efficiently presented on one web page than in the browser's awkward bookmark facility. A feature of these links is that they are subdivided into many categories, and that the links target specific pages within a web site, rather than merely the home page.

If you want you can download the page I've created and use it as a starting point for your own customised bookmark page. To download, select `File > Save As` from the browser menu bar, and then designate a sensible directory to save the file in (e.g. C:\invest). After saving, it's a good idea to create a quick way of opening the file in the future. One is to open Windows Explorer, find the downloaded file, `links-v2.htm`, and drag the file from the window onto the Windows Desktop while holding down the `Ctrl` key on the keyboard – this creates a *short-cut* to open the file.

The next stage is to edit the file to customise it exactly as you want. This can be done using a simple text editor or a proper HTML editor. In the case of the former, Notepad can be used, although a far better text editor is **EditPlus**. Even Word can be used, if you remember to save the file as type *Text*, and not as a Word document.

Having opened the file, you'll be looking at HTML code in the raw – a bit of a shock if it's your first time. However, look closely, and you'll soon see what's going on and be able to edit it, without necessarily understanding everything in detail.

You might be thinking, why bother fiddling around with HTML code when the browser bookmark system seems to work OK? But there are quite a few advantages in creating your own links page. One is that the same page can easily be used by different computers and browsers, or shared with other people. And if you already have some web space (e.g. from your ISP), the links page can be uploaded to that, and then used whether you are at home, at work, or travelling.

L EditPlus: www.editplus.com
This book's web site: www.global-investor.com/onlineinvesting

Refreshing web pages

Q I've noticed that some web pages seem to reload themselves automatically, while others don't. Is it possible to see which pages are going to reload, without just waiting to see if it happens?

A Yes. This is an important topic, as in a trading situation **it's vital to know if the data before you is current, or a few minutes old**. To recap, web pages are not like Reuters screens. With Reuters, you can sit back and data is fed continuously to the screen automatically. Web pages work differently: they make one request to the remote server to download and display data, and then, effectively, disconnect from the remote server.

For example, if you visit the Yahoo web site, and click around a few pages, you might think that you are 'logged on to Yahoo'. But you aren't. When you click on one of the links to go to another page, your computer sends a request to download that file from the Yahoo server, but as soon as the new page has been downloaded there is no longer any connection between your computer and Yahoo. In effect, Yahoo doesn't know you exist at that time. For this reason, the internet is called a 'state-less system'.

Some pages, however, do update themselves automatically.

For example, if you look at the home page of **Bloomberg** and then select `View > Source` from the browser's menu bar (for Internet Explorer), the underlying HTML code for the web page will be displayed. Ignoring all the gobbledegook, somewhere around the tenth line you will find -

<META http-equiv="REFRESH" content="300">

This is HTML code instructing the browser program to reload the web page after (in this case) 300 seconds. This is sensible for a financial page of course, as its content may well be changing all the time, and Bloomberg doesn't want people looking at a page that is out of date. So, load the Bloomberg page, sit back, and it will automatically refresh itself every five minutes. By contrast, if you look at the source code for the BBC news sites there is no Refresh command – if you leave your computer on and go away for a three week holiday, the same page will be there when you get back.

If the Refresh command is so useful why doesn't every web site use it?

Some web sites may not be aware of the facility; other web sites, such as the BBC, may feel that their sites are busy enough already, without having their servers repeatedly hit every few seconds with browsers updating pages.

Bear in mind that where web sites *do* use the Refresh command, their motives may not be entirely pure. The standard advertising model on the web is based on something called *CPM* (clicks per thousand impressions), where the advertiser pays for the number of times their banner is displayed. If a web page sits on a browser screen, without updating, this is counted as just one page impression. Some web site owners, keen to maximise their hits, include a Refresh tag (with an aggressive refresh value of 30 seconds) and the web page will refresh every half-minute. If a user stares at one page for 10 minutes, it would count as 20 page impressions for the purposes of selling banner ads. Good news for the web site owner, not so good for the advertiser.

There is a nasty potential side effect of Refresh commands too. They can cause your computer to re-connect to the internet even when you don't want it to. For example, if you load the Bloomberg home page into your browser, and then disconnect from the net (by double-clicking on the two flashing terminals icon in the bottom right system tray), you might find - depending on your computer set up - that after 5 minutes your computer dials and tries to re-connect to the net, as the browser is trying to re-load the Bloomberg page. This can be a nuisance if you're in front of the computer. And it can be an expensive nuisance if it happens after you've left the computer running unattended for a few hours.

BBC (news): news.bbc.co.uk

Bloomberg: www.bloomberg.com

Internet Explorer shortcuts

Q I've set up my Win98 computer to access certain programs quickly using keyboard shortcuts. Is it possible to access web sites using keyboard shortcuts as well?

A Yes. And it can be a very good idea, as it speeds things up a lot.

As an example, go to the home of **Citywire**. At the very left of the top address bar you'll see the little Internet Explorer icon. Drag this icon with the mouse onto the desktop and release. You should now have an icon on your desktop with the title, *citywire.co.uk - news to make investors money*.

Right-click on this icon, and select `Properties`. Highlight the input box for Shortcut key, and then on the keyboard the three keys, `Ctrl-Alt-C`. This selected combination should now appear in the input box. If it does, click `OK`. Everything should now be set. Anytime you press `Ctrl-Alt-C`, a browser window will open, and the Citywire home page will automatically be loaded into it.

Obviously doing this for just one web site is hardly worth it, but setting up a series of web links could be interesting. For example, the top row of the keyboard (letters Q to P) could be reserved for links to news sites, the second row to bulletin boards, and the third row to market prices.

L Citywire: www.citywire.co.uk

Keyboard shortcuts

Q You mentioned recently some keyboard shortcuts for use on a PC. Where can I find a list of all of these?

A I'm a great fan of keyboard shortcuts, as they can speed up things enormously. For example, `CTRL+W` will close a window, and `Windows key + E` will open Windows Explorer. So much quicker than using the mouse.

One source for information on short cuts is Windows' own Help files: run `Start > Help`, and then search on the Index for *shortcut*.

The definitive reference source can be found at the **Microsoft** web site. This also includes shortcut keys for use in MS Word, Excel and many other programs.

L
```
Microsoft (shortcuts):
microsoft.com/enable/products/keyboard/keyboardsearch.asp
```

Internet Explorer add-ons

Q Are there any finance-specific enhancements that can be made to Internet Explorer?

A The main source of accessories for Internet Explorer is at the **Microsoft** web site. This lists quite a few accessories, such as extra *Explorer Bars* from Alexa or NY Times; although, frankly, I don't find any that exciting. There is one from **Bloomberg** which adds a markets and news ticker to Internet Explorer. It's moderately interesting, but cannot be customised, so won't suit many investors. Personally, I find that most browser extensions can be replicated more easily by opening multiple browser windows.

L Bloomberg: www.bloomberg.com/ie5bar/

Microsoft (IE add-ons): www.microsoft.com/windows/ie/webaccess/

Q Which search engine do you recommend for investors?

A The leading search engine is probably **Google** and that's certainly the one I use most of the time. Many of the other, older search engines have either merged, or are not being updated any longer. The remaining search engines include: **Altavista**, **HotBot** and **Lycos**. **Yahoo**, by the way, is not a search engine as such, but a manually-compiled directory, although it does now have a full search engine attached (courtesy of **Google**).

There are several search engines on the web offering *metasearches*. These take your keyword and automatically submit it to a range of other search engines, and present the results in one integrated report. It sounds like a good idea, and they are popular with many people, but I'm not convinced they are better than competently using just one search engine. After all, the problem with the internet is not that it is difficult to find occurrences of particular keywords, but that you frequently get **too many** irrelevant results. The solution is not *more* search engines, but more sophisticated use of the existing services like **Google**. (i.e. you need to be familiar with the search language syntax.)

However, for genuinely obscure topics, metasearches have their uses. The main ones are at: **Alltheweb**, **Dogpile**, **Vivisimo**, **Metacrawler** and **Copernic**. The last one, Copernic, is not a web site, but an application that you have to download and run on your PC.

Finally, if you want to search on archives of articles the best search engines are **NorthernLight** and the **FT**.

L
Alltheweb: www.alltheweb.com

Altavista: www.altavista.com

Copernic: www.copernic.com

Dogpile: www.dogpile.com

FT (GlobalArchive): globalarchive.ft.com

Google: www.google.com

HotBot: www.hotbot.com

Lycos: www.lycos.com

Metacrawler: www.metacrawler.com

NorthernLight: www.northernlight.com

Vivisimo: www.vivisimo.com

Yahoo: www.yahoo.com

IC article archives

Q I have been looking for a survey of online brokers which I read in *Investors Chronicle* some time ago. I know that it mentioned Charles Schwab and TD Waterhouse among others. I have searched through my own back copies of the magazine, but cannot find the article. Is it on the web?

A On a desk, in a corner of my study, I have a teetering tower of back copies of *Investors Chronicle*. Some day I intend to sort them properly into date order, and file them neatly in boxes. Some day. Until then, like many other IC readers I suspect, I could spend hours looking for half-remembered articles. But there is a better way . . .

The debate on the roles of offline and online media is often carried out in a confrontational manner. In fact, each medium has its strengths and weaknesses. Given the choice, most people prefer to read a long article on paper rather than on a computer screen. But web sites have their own advantages. Information can be **updated** far quicker online, and the information presented in a way that has been customised for the user. Another great advantage of online systems is the ability to **search for keywords** in databases, such as an archive of articles.

The *Investors Chronicle* web site is, in fact, one of the best examples of a searchable archive of articles that I know of. You, for example, are looking for a particular survey on online brokers, and you know that it mentioned Charles Schwab. Simple. You input 'Schwab' to the search box at top right on the home page, and click `Go`. This tells you that there has been 1 article in the last 28 days mentioning Schwab, dated 9th May and entitled 'High-Tech Paradox'.

This may or may not be the article which you are looking for. By default, the simple search covers just the previous 28 days. To search over a longer period, return to the home page, and click `Search Home`, just below the Search box. On this more detailed search page, you have the option of specifying any period over the past five years. If you extend the Schwab search to cover the past 12 months, you get 21 articles instead of 1, and the one by John McLeod on 22nd June 2001 called 'Survey: Online Investing' looks like it is the one you are after. Both Schwab and TD Waterhouse are mentioned.

Search engines like this have many uses. If you were thinking of subscribing to the **Sharescope** program and wanted to see what the IC has said about it in the past, a keyword search on 'Sharescope' would list lots of articles which mention the program. If you wanted to compare Sharescope with **Updata**, a search on 'sharescope updata' would reveal articles talking about both programs.

The parameters for the search engine are very flexible. For example, the search can be restricted to just the article headlines. Inputting, say, 'No free lunch' will list all those columns. While inputting 'No free lunch Weir' will find the *No free lunch* column that discussed the Weir Group (in the 30 March 2001 issue).

Searches can be made by author name as well. I remember that Philip Ryland wrote a good article that included a list of investing maxims some months ago. I input 'Philip Ryland' in the search engine, and find the article in the 12 January 2001 issue. The article can then be read online, or used as an online index for your offline journal towers.

The search engine on the IC web site is actually a customised version of the larger search facility on **FT.com***. This latter search engine is one of the great, and probably greatly underused services on the internet. It offers extremely powerful searching across not only FT and FT-related media, but also across 2,000 other worldwide publications. Streaming real-time prices and interactive charts with a gazillion technical indicators tend to get the most attention; but for me this ability to search for information among millions of articles is where the real magic of the internet lies.

L   FT (GlobalArchive): globalarchive.ft.com

     Investors Chronicle: www.investorschronicle.co.uk

************   * Investors Chronicle is about to be sold by Pearson and at the time of writing it is not clear whether the online relationship with FT.com will remain in place after the sale.   ************

Saving web pages

Q I sometimes read about 'saving web pages'. Please explain how can I do this.

A Saving web pages to your own computer can be a very good idea, as it allows you to **read the pages offline** (after logging off from the internet), and also you can store the information for **later retrieval**.

The procedure is simple. If you are viewing a web page, select `File` from the menu bar of your browser program, and then click `Save As` from the drop down box. At this point a standard file save box will appear. Assign a name to the file, and select the folder where you want it to be stored.

The location where you save the file is important. If you do not specify precisely where you want to store the file on your hard disk, you may not be able to find it later.

If you are saving files (of whatever type) on your computer, it is sensible to create a properly organised directory structure on your hard disk. For example, you might create a new folder called 'Investment' and then several new sub-folders within this: 'Stock Ideas', 'Market Comment', 'Economy' etc. All investment-related files should then subsequently be stored in one of these folders, rather than randomly in the program's default folder.

After a file (e.g. a web page) has been saved on your computer, you will later want to read this page. To do this, open Windows Explorer, find the folder where you stored the file, and then double-click on the file name itself. This will load the stored web page into your browser.

Saving web pages with graphics

Q When I am trying to save web pages to my own computer, I find that only the 'Save As Text' option works. This is annoying when a price chart is in the file as it means I have to re-enter the source page. Is there a way to save web pages with their graphics?

A There is no single answer to this question because the techniques depend so much on the specific browser which you are using. My comments below apply to Internet Explorer, and may – but there is no guarantee – also apply to Netscape and other browsers.

When viewing a web page that you want to save, select `File` from the top menu bar, and then `Save As`. Up pops the standard Windows Save As dialogue box. There are now three parameters that need to be input. **The least important is the file name**. I say this, slightly provocatively, because I still believe that many users prematurely hit the `Save` button, and think that's it. The most important parameter to decide is the file **Location** – *where* the file will be saved on your computer. I have mentioned this many times before, and therefore will not labour the point here.

The third parameter is the box labeled, `Save as type`. There are four options here - assuming that your using IE v5.0 or above. In theory, the first option, `Web page, complete`, will save the file in a format which most closely replicates the web page, including all the charts contained in it. But a problem with this method is that not only will the charts be stored on your computer, but so will all the other unnecessary little logos, icons and general web page design clutter. If you intend to store lots of web pages, all these extra images start to use up memory. It is also fiddly later on if you want to move the stored file to another folder.

An alternative method, which data purists might favour, is to save the file as, `Text file`. This will store all the words, but no images, and all the formatting will be lost. Lack of formatting can be a problem if the page contains tables of data, as the rows and columns will be knocked out of line.

The best compromise is probably to save the web page as, `Web page, HTML only`. To view the file later, you'll need to open a browser, but the overall look of the page will be roughly maintained, and the tables will display properly. There just won't be any images. If there are one or two images that you are keen to have, the best thing is to save them separately: position the mouse pointer over the images in the web page, right-click, and select `Save Picture As`.

Q I saved some web pages on my computer, but cannot find them now. How can I track them down?

A One of the more useful feature of Windows is its `File Search` facility. To access this, run Windows Explorer and then tap the function key `F3` to bring up the search dialogue box. If you think you remember a part of the file name, input the text into the input box labeled *Named*. In the old days, you had to use wild cards, such as '?' and '*' to indicate missing letters, but nowadays Windows automatically assumes them. For example, if the text 'con' is input, it will be interpreted as '*con*', and file names like Marconi or Connaught will be found.

It's important to **narrow the search as much as possible** by telling the program where to look for the files. This can be controlled with the drop-down box labeled `Look in`. If you think you know the rough location of the file specify the folder here; if not, selecting `My computer` will force the computer to search the whole of the computer.

If you don't know a fragment of the file name but you do know one of the words that is contained within the file, it is also possible to search on text within the file itself. To do this, enter the text in the input box labeled `Containing text`. Putting, say, 'Halifax' in here, and selecting `My computer` in the `Location` box, will find all files on your computer containing the word Halifax.

If you're not sure of either the file name or of text within it, you can **search by date**. At the top of the search dialogue box, select the `Date` tab. This allows you to search for files that have been modified or created over a specified date range. Clicking the bottom radio box (`during the previous`) and selecting `1 day` will list all files that have been modified over the previous 24 hours. This type of search can be very useful, and has many others uses. For example, if you think a program has changed some configuration or data files, but you're not sure which ones, this search facility can reveal them.

Copying text from a web page

Q The Sunday Times online had an article 'Don't be tempted by tumbling shares', which also tipped some rising shares, including Spirent, Logica and Aggreko. Is it possible to extract from the above article only the printed portion referring to Logica, for example, for subsequent filing?

A We've covered previously how to save whole web pages to your hard disk by using the `File > Save as` command on your browser's menu bar, but this isn't very efficient if the web page is large, and you are only interested in a small portion of it. In this case, the best thing is to copy and paste the text into another program.

This is done exactly the same way that you would normally copy and paste in any Windows program. First, click and drag the mouse over the relevant text portion to select it (when viewing the web page in the browser), then copy into the clipboard with `Edit > Copy` (although the keyboard shortcut `Ctrl-C` is quicker). Then switch to the other application (e.g. a text editor, or MS Word), and paste the stored text using `Edit > Paste` (or, again, better to use the keyboard shortcut: `Ctrl-V`).

If you paste into Word, you may find that the text is copied along with all of its formatting – which can be annoying if all you want is the plain text. In this case, when pasting select `Edit > Paste Special`, and then choose the `Unformatted text` option. Because of this annoying feature of Word, I prefer storing all my information, retrieved from the net, in simple text files.

Don't forget, saving this data won't be much use unless it is stored in a well-structured directory system. On my hard disk I have a directory called *stocks*, which contains many sub-directories – one for each stock I am following. Such that, in the stocks directory, I may have a directory called VOD (EPIC code for Vodafone) in which I would store all data about that company.

Importing web data into a spreadsheet

Q You mentioned in a previous article that data can be copied from a web page into a spreadsheet. Can you explain in more detail how to do this?

A If a web page contains a large table of text and figures, you may want to import it into a spreadsheet in order to manipulate the data and produce graphs from it. The simplest way to do this is to highlight the data on the web page, copy it, then paste it straight into a new spreadsheet.

Sometimes this routine will work perfectly: the column breaks of the table will be represented in the clipboard (where the data is saved between the Copy and Paste stages) as tabs, and when you paste into the spreadsheet, the spreadsheet will recognise the tabs and automatically parse each column into different cells.

Other times, it won't work well: the columns and rows of the table will be lost in the transfer, and your spreadsheet will look a mess. The cause of this problem is that the gaps which indicate column breaks in the original data are being represented in the clipboard by blank characters. The spreadsheet doesn't interpret the blank characters as cell separators, so you end up with a jumble that bears no resemblance to the web page.

It is not difficult to solve this problem, though. All you need is to do a bit of tidying up of the data in a text editor before pasting it into a spreadsheet. I explain the steps below.

Text editors

First of all, you need a text editor. Windows comes equipped with one called *Notepad*, but your first task after installing Windows should be to replace this silly program with something more powerful. Fortunately, there are lots of free alternatives available from sites such as **Download.com**. My personal favourite is **Editplus**.

The feature you're after in these text editors is the 'search & replace' function. Search and replace enables you to find all the anomalous characters in your text and replace them with characters which Excel will understand. Here's what to do:

1. Copy the data from the web page.

2. Paste it into the text editor.

3. Search on all instances of *two* space characters, and replace these with a temporary character not appearing in the data itself ('\' is usually a good choice).

4. Repeat Step 3 until all double spaces have been replaced by '\'.

5. Search on all instances of two '\'s appearing together and replace with one.

6. Open the text file straight into a spreadsheet program, or copy and paste the data from the text file to a new spreadsheet.

If you follow these steps, the data in the spreadsheet should be separated into different columns. If it isn't, highlight the first column of data, and then from the menu bar select `Data > Text to Columns...`, then click `Delimited` in the first dialogue box and then `Next`, then click `Other` under the Delimiters section, and input the character that you used (i.e. '\'), and then click `Finish`. The data should now be parsed into separate columns.

The procedure may seem rather clumsy and laborious; but with a little practice, tabular data can be imported from any web page in a matter of seconds – without any programming knowledge required. A refinement of the above is obviously to write a small macro in the text editor, or a routine in the spreadsheet itself.

Note: the reason for Step 5 is that sometimes the text which you paste into your text editor will have instances of 3, 4 or 5 blank characters together. It all depends on the code used on the web page. Only by performing Step 5 can you reduce these sequences of blank characters to a single '\' which the spreadsheet will recognise.

```
Download.com: www.download.com

Editplus: www.editplus.com
```

Q Is there an easy way to get share prices from a web page into a spreadsheet?

A It is usually possible to copy and paste data from a web page directly into a spreadsheet. If the data doesn't import neatly into separate columns, try using the `Data -> Text to columns` function (Excel). (See page 32 for more on this.)

However, there's a great program, **MyTrack**, which allows you to create spreadsheets that directly call (real-time and delayed) data into cells of the spreadsheet. This is fantastic, as it allows you to create all sorts of programs, such as stock watches, and portfolio valuations.

As an example, I've set up a simple spreadsheet (`uk_adr_trac.xls`: download from this book's web site) to monitor the prices of UK stocks in London and their related shares (ADRs) trading in the US. The purpose of this spreadsheet is to spot arbitrage opportunities if the prices get out of alignment. If, for example, the US shares trade expensively relative to the London shares, this is highlighted. Without the ability to easily import prices, this would not be the practical tool that it is.

You can, by the way, buy specialised programs that do a similar job, but they come as expensive add-ons to a Reuters price feed. Generally, I am sceptical about using off-the-shelf investment programs, because you end up using the same program as thousands of other investors, and you are restricted to the tools and indicators which have been built into the specific program. By contrast, if you call prices into your own spreadsheet, you can create unique analytical tools, customised exactly the way you want them.

L MyTrack: www.mytrack.com

Excel Web Queries

Q I have a book on Excel97 which explains how to download information from a web site directly into Excel using a Web Query. Is it possible to use the Web Query facility in Excel with the Investors Chronicle site?

A Yes. The basic procedure is to create a query file (a simple text file with an extension `.iqy`), and load this file into the *Queries* folder (usually found in the path something like, `C:\Program Files\Microsoft Office\Queries`). Next, run Excel, from the menu bar select `Data > Get External Data`; Run `Web Query`, and then select the query file you previously created.

Simple. Or not quite so simple perhaps. For a start, I glossed over the process of creating the query file. If you're using Excel 2000 or later, then the menu `Data > Get External Data` includes a `Create Web Query` option to help. On earlier versions, the query file has to be created manually, although this is not difficult to do. As an example I've included a simple query file (`ic_quote.iqy`: download from this book's web site) that will retrieve price quotes from the Investors Chronicle web site.

Further information on this topic can be found at the **Microsoft Office** web site, where you can see a number of examples in action and also download the Microsoft Excel Web Connectivity Kit.

In theory, the idea of loading data from web pages direct into a spreadsheet sounds very appealing. However, in practice, it's a bit more fiddly than it seems. This is partly because the query is not good at selecting precise data from a page (in some cases it just grabs everything). As such, to get the most of this feature you probably need programming skills (for example in Visual Basic) to refine the process.

L Investors Chronicle: www.investorschronicle.co.uk

Microsoft Office:
officeupdate.microsoft.com/excel/webquery/samples.htm

Printing charts

Q I would like to be able to print some of the share charts that I come across on the web, but is it possible to do this without getting all the rest of the surrounding web page printing out as well?

A Yes. To illustrate this we'll look at the chart service on Ample which is one of the best on the web. From its `Shares` page, input 'ARM' in the `Quote search` box, and then click on `ARM Holdings PLC,` and finally click `chart`.

Ample's charts are highly configurable, offering a good selection of technical analysis indicators, time periods and ranges, and graph types (i.e. line, bar or candlestick). In this particular case we'll make just one change, which is to click the bottom `Gridlines` box (and then click `Plot`) to make the chart a bit easier to read. Conveniently (or not, for the purposes of this explanation) these fully-featured Ample charts also offer an option - `Printable Version` - which we'll ignore for now to demonstrate what you would have to do on other web pages if they didn't offer this option.

Assuming that you are using Windows, right-clicking anywhere on the graph image itself should bring up a small context-sensitive menu by the mouse pointer, within which there should be an option, `Copy`. Select this, and the image will be copied to the clipboard, and can then be pasted into (almost) any Windows program. For example, open MS Word, press `Ctrl-V` (or select `Edit > Paste` from the menu bar) and the chart should be pasted into a new document, and from there it can be printed.

Using a graphics program

If you want to create a portfolio of charts for future reference, you could simply paste them into Word documents and store them in a folder on your hard disc. The trouble is that Word saves images in Windows *BMP* format which produces good quality images but churns out large, memory-hungry, file sizes. Since you don't *need* particularly high-quality for basic stock charts, it can be better to paste charts into a proper graphics program instead of Word. The one I use is called **Paint Shop Pro**.

The two popular formats for saving web images are *JPG* and *GIF*. JPG is good for colourful images, including those that have been scanned from photographs, while GIFs are good for line drawings and images with expanses of the same colour - as is the case for charts. Charts saved as GIFs take up much less hard disk space than charts saved as Word documents. In addition, a graphics program can be used to tweak the graphic (e.g. removing a background colour or adding comments).

L Ample: www.iii.co.uk

Paint Shop Pro: www.jasc.com

Newsgroups

Q All the financial bulletin boards I have come across are web-based. Are any available in newsgroup form which, as I understand it, would allow me to read and write messages offline.

A In the early days of the internet, newsgroups were one of its most important features, but recently their role has been usurped by bulletin boards on web sites. Neverthless, they still have a couple of advantages over bulletin boards:

• newsgroup messages can be read and replied to offline, whereas web-based bulletin board messages have to be scanned and read online.

• messages can be filtered with pre-set criteria, and stored locally on your own computer.

The most common way is to use a browser such as Netscape, which connects direct to a news server and displays all the groups. You choose to 'subscribe' to the groups that interest you, and periodically go online to download messages which have been posted to that group. After downloading them, you can disconnect, read and reply to the messages offline when it suits you, and at some point go back online and upload them. As an alternative to Netscape, you can use a dedicated program, called a news reader, to access groups - one of the more popular such programs is **Forte's Free Agent**.

It's also possible to view the newsgroups via the web, although this negates the 'can-be-read-and-replied-to-offline' benefit. The definitive newsgroup service is **Google** which archives all newsgroup postings on a searchable database. To get an idea of what types of financial newsgroups are available, go to **Google Groups**, click `misc` and then `misc.invest`, About 20 newsgroups will be displayed, with names like: misc.invest.futures, misc.invest.stocks, misc.invest.technical. All of these, admittedly, are US-oriented, although newsgroups on topics such as options, futures and technical analysis should have a broad international relevance. One problem with the newsgroups is that they tend to be unmonitored, and therefore do attract an annoyingly high proportion of spam and off-topic posts.

There are a couple of newsgroups focused on UK finance – to find these return to the search box at Google Groups and input 'uk.finance'. Further information about newsgroups can be found at **Learn The Net**.

L
Ample: www.iii.co.uk

Free Agent: www.forteinc.com

Google (newsgroups): groups.google.com

Learn The Net: www.learnthenet.com/english/section/newsgroup.html

Motley Fool www.fool.co.uk

Scams

Q In the wake of the PairGain scam [in which a fake Bloomberg news report was posted on the web], how is it possible to tell if information on the net is genuine or not?

A There is no simple answer to this question, but there are a few rules of thumb you can follow.

Firstly, it is a good idea to be aware of the URL (the web address, which is usually indicated in the location box near the top of the browser) of pages you are looking at. For example, if you are looking at a web page that purports to be from Bloomberg, but the URL starts with something like, www.geocities.com/ - instead of www.bloomberg.com - that's a warning sign.

Secondly, if you come across a web site of unknown provenance that looks interesting you can always check who the registered owners are. There are lots of web sites offering this domain name look-up service, one of the best being **SamSpade**.

If you're downright suspicious, have a look at **The Stock Detective** which highlights many of the current online investing scams. It also includes stocks currently being puffed, and a list of web sites where stock tips are likely to be the result of paid promotion rather than objective analysis.

Slightly less fun, but still useful, are the web sites of the financial regulators: SEC (US) and the FSA (UK), both of which maintain databases of known scams and records of enforcement actions taken.

L FSA (UK): www.fsa.gov.uk

SamSpade: samspade.org/t/

SEC (US): www.sec.gov

The Stock Detective: www.thestockdetective.com

Q I am constantly targeted with web-based services offering me free portfolio management tools, financial news services, prices and statistics, and so on. The services are described as 'free' but require registration. What's the catch?

A To understand what the 'catch' is, it helps to appreciate the shifting sands on which many web sites are built. Back in 1998 the consensus was that if you had a site with lots of users, the money would follow. Attracting users was top priority, and never mind the immediate cash flow. Of course, visitors with names and addresses are more valuable than anonymous users, so sites introduced obligatory registration for some of their pages. The general idea – in retrospect, *business plan* seems too scientific a term – was: build a large database of registered users, and get bought out by a media or financial services company.

The plan worked for some sites. When Interactive Investor floated in February 2000, each registered user was valued at £1,000, and its owners eventually sold the business on to Ample, albeit at a much reduced valuation. For other sites, the plan was completely undone by the dot com crash. In November 2000, just 10 months after the iii flotation, themutual.net bought the entire client database of the defunct TheStreet.co.uk for around £2 per user. Replacing individual user worth of £1,000 with £2 in the business model spreadsheets must have been a pretty painful process for many web sites.

The search for revenue by surviving web sites continues, and one lucrative revenue stream is to rent out their user names to other companies. This is perfectly legitimate, provided data protection guidelines are followed. Not all sites do it, and if you want to know whether a site you are using is likely to rent your name on, read its Privacy Policy. Most sites have them and, theoretically, they tell you how the web site handles client information.

In practice, don't place too much faith in data protection legislation or in privacy policies. The smart approach is to **be very reticent about divulging personal information over the net**. If you charge around merrily signing up for free portfolios, real-time prices, alerts and all the other paraphernalia of the modern wired investor, expect your name and address to end up on a database being traded around the world and, a short time later, your email inbox to fill up with messages written in upper case and using lots of exclamation marks.

I'd also recommend that you set up an 'anonymous' email address with **Hotmail**, **Yahoo** or **Bigfoot**. They give you an address like smith0123@hotmail.com which you can then use for all free sites requiring registration, reserving your proper email address (usually assigned to you by your ISP) for friends and business contacts. Online banks and brokers will naturally require your true contact details and these will have to be given (unless you are a very conscientious tax evader). If, at a later stage, you find your anonymous email address is receiving too much spam, simply stop using it, and create a new one.

L Bigfoot: www.bigfoot.com
Hotmail: www.hotmail.com
Yahoo: www.yahoo.com

Q Which are the best programs that can be downloaded free from the web?

A The 'serious' investment programs like **MetaStock, TradeStation, Updata** and **Sharescope** require you to install software on your hard disc, and download data updates over the internet. They are good, but they aren't free. But there are lots of programs that you can download from the web onto your computer which are free. Below is my Top 10. Note that many of them are oriented towards the US market.

myTrack (www.mytrack.com). This is one of my favourites. US and UK stock portfolios can be created, with prices updated automatically via a streaming data feed, which can also be called from within an Excel spreadsheet. (This program is also available from www.myBroker.co.uk in the UK.)

MedVed QuoteTracker (www.quotetracker.com). There are literally hundreds of stock quote programs available that link automatically to quote servers such as Yahoo Finance. But the best is probably QuoteTracker. It tracks portfolios of international stocks, including use of the real-time quote servers from Datek in the US and ADVFN, E*Trade UK and Ample in the UK. (Note: to use these quote servers, you must already have an account with them.)

Personal Stock Monitor (www.dtlink.com). Another quote program, which allows multiple portfolios of stocks to be tracked from 15 markets worldwide, including the UK.

WinStock (www.winstocksw.com). Another stock quote program similar to the above, with functionality for tracking multiple portfolios of stocks, plus internet links to charts, news alerts, email alerts and data export.

CyberTrader (www.cybertrader.com). This is a brilliant program that simulates real time day trading by downloading the previous tick-by-tick stock prices.

SpeedResearch (www.speedresearch.com). Fundamentally, this is just an internet links program - but a links program on steroids. It's constructed very cleverly: down two thin columns, either side of the main browser window, are hundreds of direct links to web pages with stock data. Out of the box, these are mainly to US web sites, but the program can be configured for UK web sites as well.

Loan*Calculator! Plus (www.pine-grove.com). Another US program, with a variety of loan calculations, but if you mentally replace the $ signs with £ ones, many of the functions are equally applicable on this side of the pond.

Snowgold Option Calculator (www.snowgold.com). An options calculator which supports European and American style options, and options on futures.

Option ++ Internet (www.aadsoft.com). A more advanced options calculator than the above, with pricing matrix and data links to the internet.

Talking Stocks (www.4developers.com). A ludicrous program - but also tremendous fun. A stock ticker program that reads aloud the latest prices and alerts. No more squinting at dingy monitors.

Q We hear an awful lot about the advantages of online investing, like cheap commissions, but what are the disadvantages?

A The internet is changing the landscape of the investing world, and the individual investor is definitely one of its main beneficiaries. To use an overworked phrase, *we are being empowered*, and sloping, or bumpy, playing fields are becoming flat. However, this progress comes at a cost. With empowerment comes *responsibility*. Responsibility for your own financial destiny, and responsibility for protecting your interests. You can no longer rely on the government to act as your safety-net. BCCI, Barings and Equitable Life should have made that clear.

Everything you do as an online investor should be carefully subjected to risk analysis. For example, if you have one broker, what happens if that broker's computers die one day, or its telephone system collapses? It would seem, at the very least, sensible to consider having **accounts with two different brokers**. Similarly, ISPs. If the market is melting down, and all your stock details are online with your broker, you don't want to hear an engaged tone when trying to log onto the internet, or suffer download speeds of 1bps when your ISP gets swamped with new subscribers. **Use more than one ISP.**

Whether you like it or not, more and more of your life is going to be managed on computers: online broking, online banking, online mortgages etc. If records of all your financial activities are on your computer, what would the impact be if one morning your computer wanted a lie-in, and refused to wake up? Your portfolio of stocks might be on there, but also all the contact details for your online broker, your online banker etc. **First three laws of computing – back-up, back-up, back-up**. But is that enough? It's all very well having a dead computer, and waving some back-up disks in the air – what if the market is melting down at that very moment? Again, some forethought might suggest that it's worth having two computers, each holding the same data and backing each other up.

Another danger of online trading is the **growth industry of stock scams**. These are becoming increasingly sophisticated – a recent Mafia-run scam in New York involved the planning of a full-scale IPO. At a more mundane level, false web sites can be created and stories planted on bulletin boards to hoodwink unsuspecting investors.

If you become more aware of risk, and learn how to manage it, you will find that it helps you to become a better online investor. In the short-term, however, there is likely to be a J-curve effect, with a fall-off in investing efficiency. One of the main reasons for this is that the novelty of online trading may encourage you to over-trade. If you wake up every morning thinking, *what shall I buy today?*, you're still at the bottom of the J!

2 Investing Basics

- Top 10 finance web sites
- Getting email alerts on favourite stocks
- FTSE indices
- Using stock screeners
- AIM and OFEX companies
- Analysing sector performance
- Portfolio management on the web
- Number-crunching with online calculators
- Monitoring share tips
- Bulletin boards
- New issues
- Finding out about funds
- Tax

Q Which are the best investment web sites in the UK?

A Below is a list of the Top Ten investment web sites in the UK. Completely subjective, of course, not to say a little silly, as all investors are different. The most useful web sites for a growth investor would be unlikely to be interesting to a day trader. However, Top Tens are compelling and controversial, so here's mine, in alphabetical order, not order of preference:

ADVFN (www.advfn.com). The most comprehensive market data site in the UK, with the most active bulletin boards.

Ample (www.iii.co.uk). Not outstanding in any one area, strong in all of them, providing a sensibly designed package with good portfolios.

Bloomberg UK (www.bloomberg.com/uk/). Bloomberg's one-page company snapshots provide one of the best fundamental and technical summaries with latest company news; the charts are good; and for anyone without satellite, the streaming video Bloomberg TV is excellent.

Citywire (www.citywire.co.uk). Foremost site for up-to-the minute UK company news. Also good on funds and fund managers.

DigitalLook (www.digitallook.com). The only web site providing customised monitoring of bulletin boards and news services for company information, and delivering it via the web, email, PDAs and WAP.

FT Investor (www.ft.com/investor). Sister site to FT.com and CBS MarketWatch. Good commentary and excellent charts.

hemscott.NET (www.hemscott.net). In the throes of developing into a more general investment and business portal site, it still remains the premier source for company fundamental data.

Motley Fool (www.fool.co.uk). By far the best site for beginner investors, although the rather esoteric design results in a stream of consciousness approach to education.

OnVista (www.onvista.co.uk). One of the most advanced analytical sites in the UK, especially strong in risk analysis.

Yahoo Finance (finance.yahoo.co.uk). No-nonsense, simple design, with masses of links to news and good international coverage.

EPIC codes

Q There seem to be hundreds of obscure abbreviations used in the stock market. I keep on seeing references to Epic codes - what are they, and where do I find them?

A I seem to answer questions on EPIC codes every month, but looking back I see that it was some time ago that I last covered the topic. OK, here is the final, and (hopefully) definitive, EPIC explanation.

Some time ago the London Stock Exchange devised a system of code names for listed companies. For example, the code for Marks & Spencer is MKS. Whenever referring to the stock (especially online), it is far better to use the short code than the longer, frequently ambiguous, company name. MKS is better than wondering whether one should use 'Marks & Spencer', 'Marks and Spencer' or 'Marks & Spencer plc'. These codes were called EPIC codes, after the name of the Stock Exchange's central computer prior to 1996. Codes are standardised now as 3 characters, with a fourth character indicating a secondary stock (e.g. NMSW, for New Media Spark *warrants*), but there are still some securities (e.g. Boots, Barclays) that have 4 characters from an earlier era.

When investors dealt only with live stockbrokers, they didn't have to worry about all this EPIC code stuff. They called their broker, instructed him to buy shares in, say, Unilever, and it was the broker's job to know that the company's code was *ULVR*. But now, as part of the price for using cheaper online broking services, you have to do more yourself – including knowing what EPIC codes are. Nearly every financial web site I can think of requires knowledge of the EPIC code to find information on a specific company. But in almost every case, there will also be a reference guide for the codes (called something like *Symbol Lookup*). My favourite quick reference to find EPICs is at **Yahoo Finance**, but, as I said, every web site will have a similar service.

The definitive reference source for EPICs is the Stock Exchange's RNS site. In passing, I would recommend keeping an eye on this site. The Exchange has lost its monopoly on company news distribution, and therefore, exposed to the cold wind of competition, will have to develop this site into a genuinely useful resource.

Ironically, you will notice that there is no actual mention of EPIC codes on the Exchange's site. That's because after the introduction of the Sequence trading platform, EPIC codes were renamed *Tradable Instrument Display Mnemonics (TIDMs)*, or *Mnemonics* for short. So, strictly, we should be calling them TIDMs or Mnemonics, but nearly all web sites still refer to them as EPIC codes, and it is sublime optimism on the part of the Exchange to expect that to change anytime soon.

L London Stock Exchange (RNS): www.londonstockexchange.com/rns/

Yahoo Finance: finance.yahoo.co.uk

SEDOL codes

Q I am creating my own database system to monitor stock prices. I need a unique code to represent each stock and am having problems with EPIC codes because they do not appear to be very standardised. Someone suggested I use SEDOL codes instead. Any idea what these are, and where I can find them?

A EPIC codes are the London Stock Exchange's three and four letter symbols for listed securities. Many investors will be familiar with them, as they are used on most web sites. However, as I've mentioned before, these codes have been re-named TIDM codes by the Stock Exchange. In addition to TIDMs there are a few other securities codes used as well. A good reference source for all these codes can be found at the **Corporate Information** web site.

If you plan to include international securities in your database, the best code system would be **ISIN** (International Securities Identification Number). For the UK only, **SEDOL** (Stock Exchange Daily Official List) codes may be preferable to EPIC codes, as the former consist of a standard seven digit number. A good source for SEDOL numbers is the FTSE web site, where a CSV file matching TIDM and SEDOL codes can be downloaded.

L Corporate Information:
www.corporateinformation.com/definitions.html

FTSE: www.ftse.com/mn_list.html

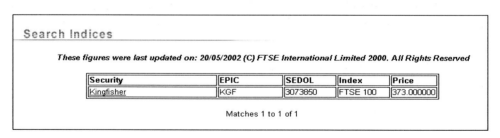

Search Indices

These figures were last updated on: 20/05/2002 (C) FTSE International Limited 2000. All Rights Reserved

Security	EPIC	SEDOL	Index	Price
Kingfisher	KGF	3073850	FTSE 100	373.000000

Matches 1 to 1 of 1

Security codes and bond quotes

Q I use an online portfolio service and would like to include some bonds. Could you explain the difference between ISIN, EPIC & SEDOL and how to find them out for a particular online portfolio service?

A I recently covered the topic of securities codes (e.g. ISIN, EPIC and SEDOL). To recap briefly -

ISIN numbers are 12 digit alphanumeric identifiers assigned by the International Standards Organisation (ISO) in order to provide standardisation of international securities.

SEDOL numbers (Stock Exchange Daily Official List Number) are seven digit security identifiers assigned by the London Stock Exchange.

And then there are **EPIC** codes (now called **TIDMs**), which are three to four-character symbols assigned by the London Stock Exchange.

Services such **Yahoo**, **ThomsonFN** and **Bondscape** include bonds in their search engines. For example, a search on 'Vodafone' at ThomsonFN can be restricted to just fixed income securities - in which case, Vodafone bonds are found, among others, listed on the Stuttgart and Zurich exchanges. For bonds, ThomsonFN also provides details on their maturity date, coupon, yield to maturity, Macauley Duration and convexity.

But the major problem with bonds is that many are traded OTC (over the counter), and are not listed on any exchange. The ramification of this is that there is no centralised trading, and no price discovery systems to feed prices to web sites. Information on these bonds remains the preserve of proprietary information providers such as Reuters and Bloomberg. This is one of the reasons why there is so little information to be found about bonds on the net.

L Bondscape: www.bondscape.net

ThomsonFN: global.thomsonfn.co.uk

Yahoo Finance: finance.yahoo.com

Information on company share issues

Q Sometimes I am looking for the code of a company to input to a web site to get a chart or share price, but I find lots of different codes for just the one company. Which one should I use, and is there some central web site that lists all the securities associated with one company?

A Large companies often issue many different types of securities, and I agree that it can be confusing. The normal issue, called an **ordinary share,** is the share usually listed on the London Stock Exchange (for UK companies) and this is what is most commonly traded by investors.

However, a company might issue other securities in addition to its ordinary shares, including **bonds, convertible bonds or warrants**. The reason for this multiplicity of securities is that a company which needs to raise external capital will always try to do so at the cheapest price. Sometimes, equities will be its best bet; at other times, the market's appetite for new equity issues may be subdued, and it will have to resort to the debt (bond) markets, or a hybrid of equity and debt. It all depends on prevailing factors such as the current share price, interest rates, the company's financing timescale, and the state of the markets generally.

In addition to different types of shares, companies may also elect to **issue shares in different countries**. In general, most companies have a continuing need to raise money from investors on the cheapest possible terms. They will be advised on their financing options by their bankers, who make money by arranging these financings, and make more money the more complex the deal is. Put all this together and the result is a merry potpourri of different shares trading all over the place. In principle, this activity reduces the cost of capital for companies. In practice, investment bankers get big fees, and the markets get so complicated for investors that they need investment advisers to help them.

Unfortunately, there is no one central reference source for all issues associated with a particular company. As an example, look at the **FT.com** web site. On the home page, if you input 'Vodafone' to the `Search & quotes` box, you get a list of 13 shares all associated with the company. These are listed on Dutch, German, UK and US exchanges. You're unlikely to be interested in, say, the shares listed on the German exchanges - these shares were probably placed with a few German institutions, and then listed on local exchanges for the convenience of those investors, but trading volume will be low or non-existent. The share you'd expect to trade would be the one listed on the London Stock Exchange (with EPIC code: VOD), or possibly the Vodafone ADR trading on the NYSE (New York Stock Exchange), also with the symbol VOD.

Now go to **Yahoo Finance**. Click on `Symbol Lookup` at the top, and input 'Vodafone' again, and you will get a list of about 20 issues. This time, the first listed issue is the ordinary share that trades on the LSE.

Note, in passing, that the symbol on **Yahoo** is VOD.L, whereas at **FT.com** it was VOD – they don't make it easy for us do they! The official EPIC code for Vodafone shares trading on the LSE is VOD, however, Yahoo (and many other web sites) uses its own system for referencing shares. In this case, Yahoo adds '.L' to the EPIC code, to indicate that it is traded in London. While the suffix '.L' is the most common form of exchange identifier, other methods are used by some information providers. For example, **myTrack** would use the form VOD-L.

Returning to the Yahoo page, at the top you are given the choice of searching on stocks (default) or bonds. If you choose the latter, you find a further 11 (bond) issues.

We're not finished with **Yahoo** yet. Go to the **Yahoo US** site, again click on `Symbol Lookup` and input 'Vodafone'. Change the geographical parameter from the default (US & Canada) to `World Markets`. This time you get 80 issues listed!

Another source to check for Vodafone-related issues is **Wright Investors' Service**. Finally, a search on Vodafone at **Reuters** produces 30 issues.

For the vast majority of investors the above is (hopefully) interesting, but academic. They will be interested solely in the most active Vodafone share issue, the one listed on the London Stock Exchange. However, for the dedicated arbitrageur, the proliferation of Vodafone issues worldwide suggests opportunity, and will invite further research.

```
FT.com: www.ft.com

Reuters: www.reuters.com

Wright Investors' Service: profiles.wisi.com

Yahoo Finance (UK): uk.finance.yahoo.com

Yahoo Finance (US): finance.yahoo.com
```

FTSE Actuaries Share Indices

Q Do you know of an online source for the FT Actuaries Industry Sector indices?

A FTSE is a provider of indices around the world and operates as a separate company from its co-owners, the Financial Times and the London Stock Exchange. Its web site gives information and free data on many indices it compiles, including descriptions of calculation methods and latest values.

One series of indices that FTSE compiles is the *FTSE Actuaries Share Indices* (from the FTSE home page: `Index Values > FTSE UK Indices`). The table presents all the major and sector index values, with further information on:

- Number of Constituents
- Dividend Yield
- PE Ratio
- XD Adjustment YTD
- XD Adjustment Today
- Total Return Figure
- Percentage Change on day

The whole table is rather large, but fortunately can be copied and pasted from the browser directly into a spreadsheet – where all the values are parsed neatly into discrete cells.

L `FTSE International: www.ftse.com`

FTSE 100 constituents' weightings

Q Is there a web site that lists the stocks, and their weightings, in the FTSE 100 Index?

A A quick reference for this can be found at the **OnVista** site. The definitive reference however is **FTSE International**. The FTSE web site is a little quirky, but the information is there if you look hard enough.

From the left-hand margin of the home page, click `FTSE UK Indices`, then click `Constituent Search` at the bottom left of the next page. That gives you a drop-down list of the FTSE 100, FTSE 250, FTSE 350, Small Cap, Fledgling, All-Share, Fledgling and AIM indices. The default selection is FTSE 100. Select `Normal text` in the drop-down box underneath, click `Send to FTSE` (isn't that so 1995!), and you'll get a table with all the FTSE 100 constituents and their respective SEDOL, EPIC, sector, current price, and per cent weighting in the index.

The data in these tables is updated daily, which is often enough for most uses. If you want more frequent updating, you could create a spreadsheet with the 100 stocks, manually input the number of shares in issue for each stock, and then use a program like **myTrack** to automatically call the current share prices. This would get close to a real-time weighting table, although I can't see much point in it. However, the idea of real-time adjustment of indices is rather fun, with stocks like Bookham Technology bouncing in and out several times in an afternoon. Imagine managing an index fund with real-time index adjustments!

One problem with the weighting table on the FTSE web page is that you can't manipulate it. But you can get round this by importing the data into a spreadsheet and playing with it offline. Click `Back` on the browser to return to the page titled, `Search Indices`. This time, instead of selecting, `Normal text`, select `Comma delimited text`. Highlight all the data (by clicking and dragging the mouse), copy the data in the clipboard, switch to a spreadsheet, and paste the data into that. (In this case, because the source data has been bizarrely centered on the web page, you might have to paste it into a text editor first, and then re-copy-and-paste the data from there into the spreadsheet). All the pasted data should go into a single column of cells. To parse the data into individual cells (in Excel), highlight the whole column, select `Data > Text to columns…`, select the `Delimited` radio button, `Next`, select the `Comma` checkbox and `Finish`. The result should be the table in six columns reproduced in your spreadsheet.

This spreadsheet could be used in many ways. For example, if you manage your own funds, and you don't like the fact that the FTSE 100 Index is so heavily weighted towards a very few large stocks, you could **create your own amended FTSE 100 Index** (e.g. every stock weighted 1%). Alternatively, you could create a simple index tracking fund (with just a key 10 stocks), possibly omitting those stocks you don't like on a fundamental basis.

L FTSE International: www.ftse.com

myTrack: www.mytrack.com

OnVista site: www.onvista.co.uk

FTSE 100 quarterly indices review

Q When are the next changes to the FTSE 100 Index expected? Is it possible to forecast which stocks will be added and dropped?

A Every quarter **FTSE** reviews the constituents of the FTSE 100 Index, and ejects stocks that no longer satisfy the membership criteria – usually because a company's share price (and thereby its market capitalisation) has fallen. Other stocks may disappear from the index following merger or acquisition activity. New stocks are then selected for addition to the index as replacements. Announcements (including timetables for Index changes), and explanations of the whole process, can be found at the **FTSE** web site.

The big question – well, big if you're into this type of thing, value investors should skip it – is which stocks will be dropped from the Index, and which ones added at the next review? After the FTSE web site, the best source of information on this is the research section of **GNI** which contains a wealth of useful research. Of importance here is the daily report ranking the top 150 companies by market capitalisation, with current FTSE 100 constituents flagged in the table. From this report, you can quickly see which FTSE 100 stocks are most at risk of being ejected from the Index, and which are likely to take their place.

The usual interpretation of these Index reviews is that the prices of stocks coming into the Index will rise (as index funds re-balance their portfolios to achieve the required weightings in the new stocks); and conversely prices will fall for those stocks leaving the Index.

Is this true in practice?

A way to test this is to create a portfolio of the stocks added to the Index at the last review. A good web-based portfolio to use is at **FT Investor**, as its *Chart Analyser* feature allows the performance of stocks to be plotted simultaneously against the FTSE 100 Index. You can do the same analysis for the stocks that were ejected from the Index.

A possible trading strategy suggested by these patterns would be to open a position a couple of weeks before the Index review, going long on the admission candidates and short on the ejection candidates (CFDs would probably be the best vehicle for this). And then at the end of trading on the day before the review announcement, to reverse the positions (short on the admissions and long on the ejections), with a view to closing all the positions a few days afterwards.

L FT Investor: www.ft.com/investor

FTSE International: www.ftse.com

GNI: www.gni.co.uk

Q Is information on AIM companies available on the web? I'm looking for details of recent listings on AIM. Names of companies, amount raised, and advisers, that type of information. Is there anywhere I can find this on the web?

A Most of the sites that carry data on London Stock Exchange stocks also include AIM companies as well. So, sites such as **hemscott.NET**, **Reuters** and **Yahoo Finance** all carry information on AIM stocks, along with the main board stocks.

Of course the **LSE** web site itself also carries AIM data. The LSE belongs to the, unfortunately not so exclusive, Obscurantist School of Web Design, meaning that if you spend long enough poking around, some nuggets may be accidentally unearthed.

One such nugget is the `Statistics` page, which offers information on the Primary and Secondary markets, including AIM. Clicking on the AIM link (left margin) displays a list of monthly *Factsheets* from December 1998. Ignoring the PDF file format, these factsheets can be downloaded as Excel spreadsheets. For example, position the pointer over the April 2000 link, and right-click on the mouse. In Internet Explorer a little menu will pop up with the option `Save Target As…`, select that, and a standard Windows `Save File` dialogue box appears. Accept the default file name (something like `AIM0004.xls`), and then select your usual temporary folder in the 'Save in' box.

[You do have a special folder for storing temporary files that you download from the internet don't you? If you haven't, don't take another breath until you've created one. Otherwise you will deserve no sympathy if you lose files. *I saved the file, I'm sure, but now I can't find it* – is just sooo last century.]

Back to the AIM factsheets; while you're at it, you might as well download the last few months for comparison. What sort of information is included in these spreadsheets? Well, it turns out to be quite a treasure trove of interesting figures. First off, on Page 1 of the spreadsheet, there's a summary of the overall market. For example, from the April 2002 Factsheet, we learn that there are 644 companies listed on AIM, with a total market capitalisation of £11 billion. Further, in April 2002 itself, £100m of new capital was raised through AIM listings and there were approximately 2,200 trades every day. Below the general figures, are details on new listings on AIM. In April, there were 14 admissions - the smallest raising £1m for Leisure Ventures, and the largest raising £36m for Peter Hambro Mining. This page also includes details on the financial advisers for each issue.

For investors so inclined, there's huge scope for interesting analysis of these figures – made easier by the fact that everything is in a spreadsheet to start with. One example might be to **monitor the effectiveness of the financial advisers** by tracking the subsequent performance of their sponsored issues. The success of new issues can depend greatly on the skill of the advisers in being able to place the shares initially with reliable investors who will hold the shares for a decent period, and not 'flip' them. And also, after the IPO, being able to support the share price through sales efforts and provision of research reports (thereby encouraging investors to follow the stock).

The second page of the spreadsheet covers further issues on AIM – typically the exercise of options or warrants for shares on existing AIM-listed companies. The next page details cancellations of listing; usually these occur where the company is graduating to the big boys club (a full LSE listing), the company is being taken over (e.g. cash shells being bought as an easy route to an AIM listing), or the company gets fed up with tedious investors and withdraws to the quieter world of the private company.

We now come on to the trading page, where (by using the `Data > Sort` function of Excel) you will find that the most actively traded stocks in April were: Chorion, Brancote Holdings, Sibir Energy, Oystertec, Pan Andean Resources and Surgical Innovations Group – together accounting for 16% of all AIM trades that month. At the other end of the spectrum, quite a few AIM stocks traded just once, or not at all, during the month. These figures reflect the *liquidity* of a stock, and an investor would be wise to **pay very close attention to these turnover numbers** before committing significant sums to any stock.

The same page also lists the much-loved market makers associated with each individual stock. So, if your favourite stock is marked down 20% after positive results have been announced, and you want to know who to blame, this is where to look. Again, the list is significant for liquidity reasons – **the more market makers associated with a stock the better**; and caution is required if there are only one or two MMs for a stock.

The next page, titled `Notes`, is not interesting, besides carrying an index of market makers' full names and codes. Finally, the page, `Sector`, breaks down the AIM market by industry classification. As the old economy transmogrifies into the new, these old classifications become less and less useful; but it is interesting to note that the great majority of AIM stocks are in just three sectors: Cyclical Services, Financials and Information Technology.

hemscott.NET: www.hemscott.net

London Stock Exchange: www.londonstockexchange.com

Reuters: www.reuters.co.uk

Yahoo Finance: finance.yahoo.co.uk

FTSE SmallCap and techMARK

Q Is there anywhere on the internet where I can find the entire list of companies in the FTSE SmallCap Index?

A The constituents for all the FTSE family of indices can be found at the **FTSE International** web site. Click `FTSE UK Indices` in the left-hand menu, then `Constituent search` at bottom left of the next page, then select `FTSE SmallCap` from the drop-down box. From there, you can downloaded the data direct to a spreadsheet.

The FTSE SmallCap Index is not covered by many other web sites, the majority of which restrict themselves to the FTSE 100, FTSE 250 and techMARK. Fortunately quotes and charts for the FTSE SmallCap index can be found at **Sharepages** and **Yahoo Finance**.

What about sites reporting on techMARK companies?

The best news sites for technology companies are: **AFX Press**, **Citywire**, **Bloomberg**, **Equity Investigator**, **Multex Investor**, **Sharecast** and finally, **The Register** is amusing for industry tittle-tattle.

L
```
AFX Press: www.afxpress.com

Bloomberg: www.bloomberg.co.uk/bbn/uk_technology.html

Citywire: www.citywire.co.uk/previewtechnews/

Equity Investigator: www.equityinvestigator.com

FTSE International: www.ftse.com

Multex Investor: www.multexinvestor.co.uk

Sharecast: www.sharecast.co.uk

Sharepages: www.sharepages.com

The Register: www.theregister.co.uk

Yahoo Finance: finance.yahoo.co.uk
```

OFEX

Q Do you know of an internet portfolio service which provides share prices of OFEX Companies? And is it possible to place orders online for OFEX companies?

A Unfortunately, OFEX companies are not covered by most of the portfolio services on the web. This might be because OFEX is not an exchange as such, but a dealing facility organised by **J P Jenkins Limited**. This firm is the principal market maker in all OFEX stocks and has an interest in keeping tight control over the dissemination of prices.

The good news is that the OFEX web site is extremely good. It provides prices on all OFEX companies, updated every five minutes, and a portfolio facility for users is due soon.

As far as online dealing is concerned, no broker offers a service for OFEX companies at the moment, but many accept orders by telephone. If you are interested in OFEX companies, **EO.net** provides information on upcoming IPOs, and **Durlacher** has the occasional research report. Another good site is **unquoted.co.uk** which carries news and research.

L Durlacher: www.durlacher.co.uk

EO.net: www.eo.net

OFEX : www.ofex.co.uk

unquoted.co.uk: www.unquoted.co.uk

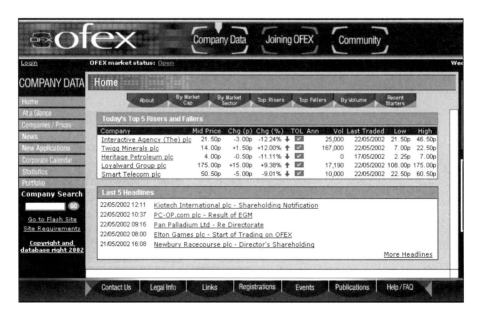

Q Can you recommend a web site that will enable me to enter values for a range of criteria, such as market capitalisation, PER and PEG etc., and then search for stocks which satisfy the criteria?

A The type of program you're looking for is called a *stock screener*. Its function is to filter all companies in a market on specified criteria, and it should be a fundamental tool for all investors. You've read the books, you now know that companies with a low PEG are good, what next? Crank up a stock screener to find the companies that match your criteria.

The best stock screener for UK stocks is at **ADVFN**, in the `Advanced Search` part of the `Fundamentals` section. This allows filters to be set for 37 criteria including turnover, PE Ratio, PEG factor and dividend cover. At the time of writing, searching with criteria of a PEG less than 1, market cap greater than £5bn and dividend cover greater than 4 yields four companies: Amvescap, Cable & Wireless, Tyco and WPP. Another good online stock screener is on the **iTruffle** site, although this has a more limited range of search criteria.

Off the web, the best program is probably **Sharescope**, which is not a web service but a free-standing portfolio program (to which data can be updated daily over the internet). A recent version of Sharescope introduced a new *data mining* module, which is very powerful. Complex filters can be built to filter the whole market on a range of specified criteria.

If you want to see how sophisticated stock screening programs can get, look at the US **MarketGuide**. This employs its own macro language for creating minutely detailed filters.

All the above resources allow you to filter a universe of stocks with a customised set of search criteria. Other web sites offer less sophisticated stock screeners, allowing you to generate lists based on pre-configured criteria. On **DigitalLook**, for instance, pre-configured criteria exist to list, among others, stocks with the highest dividend yield or lowest PEG. Similar pre-configured screens exist on **FT Investor**, **OnVista** and **Yahoo Finance**.

L
```
ADVFN (stock screenr): www.advfn.com/cmn/fun/adv_search.php3

DigitalLook site: www.digitallook.com

FT Investor: www.ft.com/investor

iTruffle site: www.itruffle.com

MarketGuide: www.marketguide.com

MSN UK: uk.moneycentral.msn.com/investor/finder/custstoc.asp

OnVista: www.onvista.co.uk

Sharescope: www.sharescope.com

Yahoo Finance: uk.biz.yahoo.com/screen/i_ftse100.html
```

Sector performance

Q Are there any sites where I can track real-time or near real-time FTSE activity by sector? For example where could I go if I wanted to find out which sector is currently having the most impact on FTSE 100 movement?

A **Ample** has a sector page which ranks sector movements by percentage change, making it easy to identify the significant sectors of the day. **ADVFN** has a similar table and you can choose to rank the list by either percentage or absolute movement. But the best sector table is the one on **Comdirect**:

- it allows you to sort the list by different columns

- the direction of the last tick movement is indicated

- percentage changes over the 1-day, 1-month and 3-month are calculated and illustrated with a small histogram.

Note that all the above sector indices are calculated on the FTSE 350 Index constituents, and so will not necessarily match perfectly the FTSE 100 Index. For example, with the evolution of the economy, some sectors may no longer be represented within the narrow FTSE 100. In fact, the profile of the FTSE 100 is now so skewed that it's probably easier to analyse the individual influence of stocks on it, rather than sectors. Just three stocks (Vodafone, Glaxo Wellcome and HSBC) have a weighting of over 25% in the index, and the top 10 stocks have a weighting of around 50%. If you want to analyse influences on the Index, the simplest thing to do might be to just create an online portfolio of those 10 stocks, and watch that.

L ADVFN (sector performance): www.advfn.com/cmn/tl/sectors.php3

Ample (sector performance): www.iii.co.uk/ukequity/?type=sectors

Comdirect: focus.comdirect.co.uk

Top performing FTSE stocks

Q How do I find out which 10 stocks in the FTSE 100 and FTSE 250 grew their share price the most over the last 12 months?

A **Moneyextra** lists best and worst performers over 1, 3 and 5 years, for the FTSE All Share, or any sub-sector. In the `Fast Find` drop-down box near the top of the home page, select `Investment Centre home`. From there, select `Stockmarkets` in the left-hand margin, and you'll see that it offers you a whole menu of useful links, including `Biggest Risers`, `Biggest Fallers`, `FTSE 100`, `FTSE 250`, `Most Active Stocks`, and much more.

Also worth a look is **OnVista**, which ranks stocks by performance over 1 day, 1 week, 1 month and 1 year.

L Moneyextra (stock performance):
www.moneyextra.com/powersearch/?fundid=EL

OnVista (stock performance): stocks.onvista.co.uk/top_flop.html

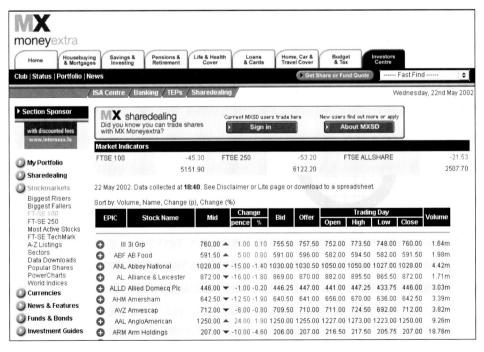

Stock portfolios

Q Are there any simple services on the web that will allow me to keep track of my small share portfolio. And I mean simple!

A Simple share portfolio management is one of the areas that the net excels in. If you're thinking of dipping your toes into the cyber investment world, they are a good place to start.

Some of the simplest portfolios are to be found at the **Motley Fool** and **Yahoo Finance** web sites – both of which are perfectly satisfactory. But the best portfolios for the UK market are at **FT Investor** and **Ample**: They offer a high degree of customisation for the portfolio display, and multiple portfolios can be tracked.

Some online portfolio services use 'cookies', which recognise your computer automatically and display your portfolio immediately. This is a neat feature, but can be a nuisance if you access the internet from different computers; because of this I tend to prefer the services which require a manual log-on such as Ample.

A secondary use of online portfolios, apart from tracking the progress of your *real* portfolio, is that they allow you to set up dummy portfolios to test out a theory you have. For instance, you might have read a book about a particular method for identifying undervalued stocks, or for trading acccording to some technical indicator. Rather than testing these theories with real money, you can set up dummy portfolios, trade them as if they were real, and see what results they produce.

L Ample: www.iii.co.uk

FT Investor: www.ft.com/investor

Motley Fool: www.fool.co.uk

Yahoo Finance: uk.my.yahoo.com

Benchmarking portfolio performance

Q I run an investment club with a portfolio of eleven shares. Can you recommend a web site that will display the whole portfolio on a graph and enable me to compare its performance against the FTSE?

A There are quite a few good portfolio programs on the web. Those at: **ADVFN**, **Ample** and **FT Investor**, are all useful. FT Investor displays charts of individual portfolio constituents against various indices, such as the FTSE 100, but none of the three measures an entire portfolio performance against an index. About the only web site that *does* is **hemscott.NET**, where portfolio performance can be measured against a range of indices.

Although it's natural to want to compare the performance of a portfolio against a benchmark like the FTSE 100 Index, it's not quite as easy as you'd think. Account must obviously be taken of all cash flows in and out of the portfolio, including dividend payments. As such it may be better to keep track of this in an Excel spreadsheet (and simply import the FTSE 100 data); or to use a dedicated portfolio program such as **Sharescope** or **Fairshares** (now owned by **Updata**).

L ADVFN: www.advfn.com

Ample: www.iii.co.uk

Fairshares: www.updata.co.uk

FT Investor: www.ft.com/investor

hemscott.NET: www.hemscott.net

Sharescope: www.sharescope.co.uk

Downloading portfolio data to a spreadsheet

Q I use a portfolio service on the web, but I also like to keep a record of my holdings in a spreadsheet. Up to now I've had to input the prices into a spreadsheet manually. Is there a way of doing this automatically?

A There are quite a few online portfolio services now available, but not all of them have the ability to download portfolio prices to a spreadsheet. The ones that do are: **Moneyextra**, **Motley Fool** and **Yahoo Finance**.

The best is Motley Fool, where you can download your portfolio as a CSV file – a format recognised by most spreadsheets. The process is quite simple: select the `download portfolio info` option; then (on Windows) a box will appear asking whether you want to `Open the file from the current location` or `Save the file to disk`; choose the latter; a standard Windows file save box will appear, input a file name and where you want to save the file. After saving the file, you can log off from the internet, open Windows Explorer, find the file you saved (unless you changed the default, it will be called something like `myport.csv`) and double-click on the file. If Windows is configured correctly on your computer, Excel should open and load the portfolio file directly into a spreadsheet.

L Moneyextra: www.moneyextra.com

Motley Fool: www.fool.co.uk

Yahoo Finance: uk.finance.yahoo.com

Email alerts on portfolio stocks

Q Are there any online portfolio services that offer email alerts?

A Email alerts are a great idea. Briefly, they allow you to set up target prices for specific stocks, such that when a stock price hits the target, an email is sent to you automatically alerting you to the fact.

For example, if you're holding a stock with a current price of 114p, you might want to be informed if the price falls below 100p. Assuming you don't want to watch a computer screen all day, the best way to stay in the loop is to set up an automatic email alert. It's like a crude stop loss system.

The best portfolio services with email alerts are **Ample**, **Moneyextra** and **ADVFN**. ADVFN's is the most flexible, allowing you to set an alert according to the value of the bid, offer, mid or closing price, or according to the price change or volume traded. Furthermore, you can have the alert sent to a mobile phone. Ample and **hemscott.NET** offer alerts on the release of an RNS story related to a stock.

L ADVFN: www.advfn.com

Ample: www.iii.co.uk

hemscott.NET: www.hemscott.net

Moneyextra: www.moneyextra.com

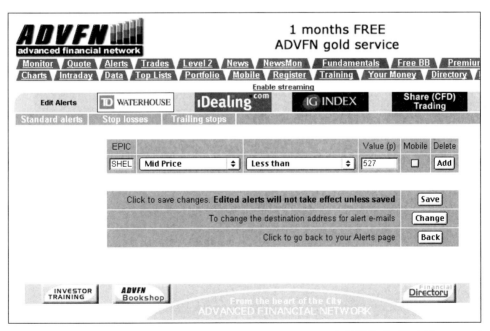

News on portfolio stocks

Q Is there an online service where you can input a portfolio of stocks, and pick up price and RNS information for all of them without having to interrogate each individual stock?

A There are a few services on the web that do this, for example, take a look at ADVFN. Portfolios of stocks can be created, in their *Monitor* section. Click on any of the stocks in your portfolio and a summary page is displayed with a list of the most recent RNS and AFX news stories.

A similar service exists on **Ample**. Create a portfolio of stocks, and a list of recent RNS and AFX news stories for each component stock can be viewed.

If you want something different from the standard AFX/RNS news feeds, other sites are: **Bloomberg**, **FT Investor**, **Comdirect** and **Citywire**. For all of the above you do have to focus on one stock at a time, which isn't quite what you want. An alternative may be to use the email service of **DigitalLook**, which aggregates news information on portfolios of stocks and emails it to the users.

L ADVFN: www.advfn.com

Ample: www.iii.co.uk

Bloomberg: www.bloomberg.com/uk

Citywire: www.citywire.co.uk

Comdirect: www.comdirect.co.uk

DigitalLook: www.digitallook.com

FT Investor: www.ft.com/investor

PEG Ratio

Q I have heard mention of something called a PEG ratio – what is it, and could I have found out the definition, and those of other ratios, on the internet?

A The PEG is an accounting ratio popularised by Jim Slater in his book, *The Zulu Principle*, and favoured as a share selection tool by sites such as the Motley Fool. Briefly, the PEG of a company is calculated by dividing its prospective PE ratio by the estimated future growth rate in its earnings per share. So to calculate a PEG, you first need to calculate its PE ratio.

PE = current share price divided by earnings per share (eps)

A company with a share price of 100p and eps of 5p has a PE ratio of 20 (100/5)

By itself the PE ratio is a useful ratio because it shows how many times the current earnings the shares cost - in a sense, how many years you would have to wait to get your money back if the company paid out all its earnings to shareholders. But the limitation of the PE ratio is that it looks at historical information and does not relate the price of the shares to its future performance. The PEG ratio builds in that extra layer of sophistication.

Using the example of the same company, imagine that the consensus brokers' forecast for its future earnings growth rate is 15%. For this company, the PEG would be 20 (the PE) divided by 15 (the estimated earnings growth rate) = 1.33 According to Jim Slater, a share with a PEG of 1 or lower is attractive, though other criteria have to be satisfied too.

Could you have found this definition on the web? Yes, by looking at one of the main financial glossaries like the one at **finance-glossary.com** or **Investorwords**. If you want more than just a definition, check out the Motley Fool site, which has more information than you can shake a jester's stick at, including an interactive *PEGulator* (American, but works perfectly well for UK companies). For PEG data on UK stocks, go to **DigitalLook** or **Yahoo Finance**.

DigitalLook: www.digitallook.com

Finance Glossary: www.finance-glossary.com

Investorwords: www.investorwords.com

Motley Fool (PEGulator): www.fool.com/pegulator/pegulator.htm

Yahoo Finance: uk.finance.yahoo.com

Q Is there a single web page that will give me an instant snapshot of what is happening in the markets at-a-glance?

A Different websites have different qualities and, if I was ungracious, my reply would be to bookmark the best pages of the best sites, and refer to them when you want an overview. But your question is whether there is a *single* web page that summarises the market. For good measure, we'll add two further requirements: it has to be a page that contains all the information within one screen shot (i.e. no scrolling), and the URL has to be short and easy to remember, preferably the site's home page. Right: let's review the contenders.

The two general finance sites, **Ample** and **Moneyextra** do not score particularly highly. To be fair, they don't style themselves as narrowly focused market-oriented sites, but as broader personal finance sites. In the latter's case, if you type www.moneyextra.com/stocks/ you will get straight to their stockmarket page, but it still fails the 'useful data on first screen' test. Another also-ran is **Motley Fool**, but given the Fool creed of long-term investing its editors would probably be worried if they fared any different (who cares if the FTSE 100 is down 300 points, our medium-term, 30-year view, is positive!).

Yahoo Finance manages a bit better with a box of the major indices, and one of the best summaries of latest news headlines. If you're interested in the wider scene, then **Bloomberg** has a good list of global equity indices, interest rates and currencies.

Moving on, the competition hots up when we look at the Market Data page of the **BBC**, which has an intraday chart of the FTSE 100, top three stock increase/decreases, and data on currencies, gilts and commodities. But, unfortunately, it also has a very long and completely unmemorable URL - where it comes a cropper.

The **Sharepages** home page displays intraday charts for the FTSE 100 and techMARK indices, and data on other indices, including international, and lists headlines for the latest AFX and RNS news. A slightly longer URL, www.sharepages.com/MA_SE.smart, displays a table of sector performance for the day.

The online broker, **comdirect**, has a market overview page which is a model of its kind. Intraday and longer term charts are displayed for the FTSE indices, Dow Jones and Euro/Dollar/Pound currencies. In addition, performance tables for index constituent stocks are available for FTSE 100, FTSE 250, Small Cap, Fledging, Aim and techMARK, with performance represented by proportionally sized, coloured bars for quick scanning. Its information on other markets is also first-rate. If it weren't for the length of the market overview URL (focus.comdirect.co.uk/en/quick/) it would be pushing for number one spot.

Another strong contender is **FT Investor**. Its home page displays European indices, an intraday FTSE 100 chart and the latest news stories. If you drill down from the home page to www.ft.com/investor/tools/, you get a better page with more detailed equity index data as well as currency, futures and bond prices.

The link `Europe` from this page is better still, but only directly accessible if you are a speed-typing Memory Fiend.

That leaves our winner in the 'Market-at-a-Glance' competition - **ADVFN**, which satisfies every criteria. The URL is short, and all the data is displayed on one screen. The data includes: latest index values and intraday charts; the important advance/decline ratio (surprisingly rarely available on UK web sites); stock gainers, losers and volume leaders; and latest AFX news headlines. So, next time you're passing a computer and wonder what's happening in the market...type `www.advfn.com` to find out.

ADVFN: www.advfn.com

Ample: www.iii.co.uk

BBC (market data): news.bbc.co.uk/hi/english/business/market_data/

Bloomberg: www.bloomberg.co.uk

comdirect: www.comdirect.co.uk

FT Investor: www.ft.com/investor

Moneyextra: www.moneyextra.com

Motley Fool: www.fool.co.uk

Sharepages: www.sharepages.com

Yahoo Finance: finance.yahoo.co.uk

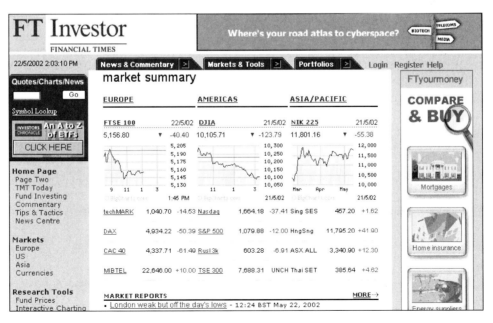

Q Is there somewhere on the web which gives a list of shares currently being tipped, and which also tells you how shares tipped in the past have subsequently performed?

A There are several services that monitor the daily news stories and tips in newspapers and other media. They can be very useful too, allowing you to receive a wide range of news sources without having to buy all the newspapers, and saving you the trouble of having to locate the tips within the articles.

The earliest service off the mark each day is probably the one from AFX. Its news feed is syndicated to lots of financial web sites, including **ADVFN** and **Ample**. Each day, at around 07h30, they will post a story with a title like, *AFX UK at a glance share guide* which contains a round-up of newspaper stories and tips.

Other good round-ups of the newspapers can be found at **Citywire**, **FT Investor** and **ShareCrazy**. The **Telegraph** money site also gives a round-up of the Sunday newspapers.

A digest of newspaper tips (*Tip Tracker*) is maintained by **hemscott.NET**. One of the best services is that from **DigitalLook**, which not only records the tips but also monitors their performance over the following few days.

L
ADVFN: www.advfn.com

Ample: www.iii.co.uk

Citywire: www.citywire.co.uk

DigitalLook: www.digitallook.com

FT Investor: www.ft.com/investor

hemscott.NET: www.hemscott.net

ShareCrazy: www.sharecrazy.com

Telegraph (money): money.telegraph.co.uk

News by email

Q Which email news bulletins do you recommend?

A I'm a big fan of email bulletins, if only as an alternative to browsing web pages. Web site design is improving, but sometimes it feels like the pages are designed by computer experts ignorant of business, controlled by business managers ignorant of computers, and financed by gamblers ignorant of both computers *and* business. As an alternative to hacking around dismal web sites, email reports are pure joy. They also benefit from being readable offline, and from being presented in a standard text format.

Fortunately, there are plenty of good email services around. Top of the list are: **DigitalLook**, which monitors news and bulletin board chat, and the news summary from **FT.com**. The latter is useful for monitoring stories in specific industries, and far easier than trawling the FT's vast web site for the same information. Other useful news services are those from **FT Investor**, **ADVFN** and **Investors Chronicle**. Less directly market-related are those from **Ample**, **hemscott.NET** and **CityComment**. General world news bulletins are available from **Bloomberg** and the **Economist**, the latter providing a weekly round-up.

As you can imagine, there's no shortage of similar services in the US. My favourites are **Marketwatch**, **Silicon Investor**, **CNET**, and **Real Money** but I also rate Reuters' **Moneynet**, and **Lycos Finance**. One interesting variant of the standard service is **The Fetcher**. Input a series of web addresses, and it will email you the web pages at intervals which you specify. This can be a great time-saver, and is useful when travelling.

L
ADVFN: www.advfn.com
Ample: www.iii.co.uk
Bloomberg: www.bloomberg.co.uk
CityComment: www.citycomment.co.uk
CNET: www.news.com
DigitalLook: www.digitallook.com
Economist: www.economist.com
FT.com: www.ft.com
FT Investor: www.ft.com/investor
hemscott.NET: www.hemscott.net
Investors Chronicle: www.investorschronicle.co.uk
Lycos Finance: www.finance.lycos.com/
Marketwatch: cbs.marketwatch.com
Real Money: www.realmoney.com
Reuters' Moneynet: www.moneynet.com
Silicon Investor: www.siliconinvestor.com
The Fetcher: www.thefetcher.com

Q For someone new to the internet, could you tell me which are the best online bulletin boards to look at?

A This can be a moving target, as web-based bulletin boards (BBs) tend to rise and fall with the seasons. One of the longest established boards on **Moneyextra** has recently been suspended; **MoneyWhispers** seemed to be going well but closed down at the end of 2001, and the **E*Trade** BB – a trailblazer in its day - is now moribund.

The more established BBs tend to develop their own character, and it's good to be aware of the style of discussion before plunging in. On **Ample**, for instance, discussions tend to be structured around specific companies. (Example post: *'Marconi - 40p the make or break?'*). Another BB, also oriented towards specific companies, but possibly more suitable for novice investors, is the one on **Motley Fool** (Example post: *'Why do stocks move?'*).

For BBs with a trading slant to them, look at **ADVFN**, which has both a free BB and a premium one reserved for subscribers (Example post: *'Rocket rage are on the pad!!!'*), and **hemscott.NET** (Example post: *'Parthus looking strong with MM buys at offer'*), although many find the latter too chaotic. Hardcore trading BBs, focused on technical analysis can be found at **IRD** and **Trade2Win**.

For more detailed discussions on technical topics such as options and day trading, it might be worth looking at BBs in the US such as: **Raging Bull**, **Silicon Investor**, and **Yahoo Finance**.

L
ADVFN: www.advfn.com

Ample: www.iii.co.uk

hemscott.NET: www.hemscott.net

IRD: www.ird.com

Motley Fool: www.fool.co.uk

Raging Bull: www.ragingbull.com

Silicon Investor: www.siliconinvestor.com

Trade2Win: www.Trade2Win.co.uk

Yahoo Finance:
messages.yahoo.com/yahoo/Business___Finance/index.html

Beta values

Q Do you know of any web sites that give the beta values of shares?

A For readers who don't know, the *beta* value of a stock is a measure of its volatility relative to the general market. A beta of over 1 indicates that, historically, a stock has moved up and down more than the general market has moved. A beta below 1 indicates that a stock has low volatility relative to the market.

Traditionally, low beta stocks are found in sectors such as utilities, and high betas found in sectors like technology. Stocks with low betas are sometimes referred to as *defensive stocks*, on the grounds that if the market falls, the stocks will decrease less than the market. Having said that, in recent years many stocks and sectors have exhibited abnormal behaviour.

The best online source for this data is **OnVista**. Looking at its Snapshot page for, say, ARM Holdings [ARM], the technical ratios include Beta, Correlation and Volatility values. The correlation is a number between -1 and 1 which measures the degree to which two variables are related. The figure can be used as a confidence filter for the beta value. If a stock has a high correlation coefficient (near 1), you can be more confident that its relative volatility in practice will be close to that forecast theoretically by the beta value. If the correlation is low, you should have less confidence in the predictive power of the beta.

In the case of ARM, OnVista calculates a 30-day beta of 3.62, meaning that the stock is roughly three and a half times more volatile than the whole market. For comparison, if you look at the Snapshot page for Centrica [CAN], you will see that the 30-day beta is 0.21, indicating that the stock is one fifth as volatile as the market. Although, note that it has a very low correlation coefficient.

L OnVista: www.onvista.co.uk

Q I've just found an old share certificate in ARM Holdings. Is there somewhere online which will tell me if a company has had a share split in the last couple of years?

A Yes. The quickest source to check is the web site of the company itself. In this case, ARM Holdings has a good web site at `www.arm.com`, where, in the `Investor Relations` section there's a historic news archive. If you look at this, you will find the news headline, *ARM Holdings plc Sub-Division* for 18 April 2000, which gives details of the five-for-one bonus issue, effective the following day.

However, not all corporate web sites are as helpful as ARM's. If you hit a duffer, the quickest solution may be just to telephone the company and ask them directly, or ask for contact details of their share registrar.

Online, a quick way to check if a company has had a split is to look at its stock chart on **ADVFN**, **Comdirect** or **nothing-ventured.com**. On these web sites, splits are indicated on the charts themselves with a little icon. And, on the ADVFN charts at least, a chart legend gives details of the size of the split.

If you know the approximate date of a share split, but are looking for more details, you can get them in the archive of the Regulatory News Service (RNS). All companies have to inform the London Stock Exchange if there is a bonus issue of their shares, and the Exchange will disseminate this information via the RNS. The Exchange's own web site has an RNS archive, and you can search on announcements up to six months old for free, but if you want to search further back than that you have to pay £60 for the 'RNS Insight' service. An alternative source is **UK-Wire**.

L ADVFN: www.advfn.com

Comdirect: www.comdirect.co.uk

London Stock Exchange: www.londonstockexchange.com

nothing-ventured.com: www.nothing-ventured.com

UK-Wire: www.uk-wire.com

Upcoming share splits

Q Where can I find information on the internet about up and coming share splits?

A This is a common question, and there is no satisfactory answer, particularly if you want the information free of charge.

Offline, you can find what you want in **Investors Chronicle** magazine, in the *Adjustment Factors* section of *Take-overs, Fund-raising & New Issues*. The data is also available online at the Investors Chronicle web site but you have to be a subscriber to get it.

Beyond this, there is no easy online source for this data as far as I know. The best I can think of is to go to the RNS news services on **ADVFN** or **UK-Wire** and use their search facilities to search on headlines containing the word *issue*. This will bring up a list of all official announcements of new issues of shares, including rights issues, placings, and allotments following exercise of warrants, convertible bonds or staff options. However, to get bonus issues it's necessary to search on Corporate Actions. Unfortunately there's no guarantee that the resulting list will be exclusive or comprehensive.

L ADVFN: www.advfn.com

Investors Chronicle: www.investorschronicle.co.uk

UK-Wire: www.uk-wire.co.uk

New issue prospectuses

Q Is there a web site that has a library of prospectuses for past issues? I know of several which offer them for current offers but I am looking for prospectuses on issues which are a year or more old - to compare with subsequent results.

A The first place to look is the web site of the **London Stock Exchange**. This carries an archive of details on new issues back to May 2000.

For example, if you look at the record for Orchestream Holdings [OCH] you will find that the expected offer price was 185p, (from a range 150-190), the expected size of offer was £77m giving a market cap (post issue) of £214m. Further news of the issue can be tracked down at the RNS archive of **UK-Wire** – which can be useful for confirmation of what actually happened. In the case of Orchestream it tells you that just following the issue, an Over-Allotment Option was exercised to issue 6m additional shares to institutions.

Some interesting research on new issues, that I've never seen, would be to rank the aggregate performance of new issues according to the financial sponsor. For example, which of Beeson Gregory or Close Brothers is better at selecting initial prospects and subsequently supporting the post IPO shares in the market? Rankings of financial advisers by total client numbers and profit can be found at **hemscott.NET**, but not, unfortunately, new issue performance.

L hemscott.NET: www.hemscott.net

London Stock Exchange: www.londonstockexchange.com/newissues/

UK-Wire: www.uk-wire.co.uk

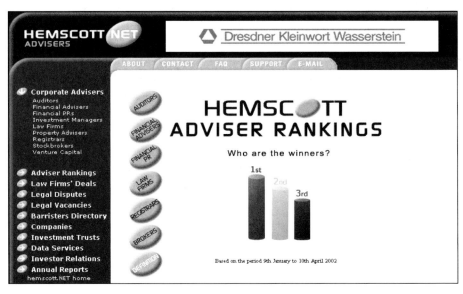

Money flow in the UK

Q Some US web sites carry information on money flow. Is similar information available for the UK market?

A The term *money flow* can mean a number of things.

In a previous article, I listed sources of information on US mutual fund stock sales and purchases, and perhaps it's the equivalent UK information that you want. Why might you want to know about sales and purchases by funds? Well, despite the huge growth of individual investor activity in the stock market, it is still small compared to that of institutional investors. These larger investors, many of which are funds, have a greater influence on stock prices, and so following their buying and selling activity can be useful. Unfortunately, there's no obvious source of this information for the UK market. **Sharepages** monitors large trades throughout the day, and, by implication, the proportion of buying and selling trades attributable to institutions.

Another interpretation of money flow is tracking the number of trades that are considered *buys* against those considered *sells*. Briefly, trades that take place near the prevailing offer price are deemed buy trades, and those near the bid price are deemed sell trades. A good source for this data is **ADVFN**, which calculates the cumulative total trades attributable to buys and sells for each stock throughout the day.

A new service from **Bloomberg** extends this idea to plot the cumulative buy and sell trades over time. In principle, Bloomberg's definition of buy and sell trades is similar to ADVFN's, but it plots the net daily activity over the past few months, to give an indication of whether money is flowing in or out over time. As you'd expect, when a stock price is rising, money can be seen (in this analysis) to be flowing *into* the stock, and vice versa when a stock price is falling. But occasionally there are interesting cases when the movement of the share price and money flow diverge. For example, a stock price may be falling, but money can be seen to be flowing into the stock. According to the Bloomberg analysis, such a case can be regarded as giving a buy signal for the stock. And a sell signal is indicated when a stock price is rising, but the money flow line is falling.

Every day the Bloomberg web site lists two stocks that are recommended a buy or a sell according to diverging signals from analysis of the share price and money flow. Bloomberg also lists, very sportingly, the track record of its recommendations since starting in July 2001. I'm afraid that sceptics will feel vindicated by the track record, which barely outperforms the FTSE 100. Perhaps the behaviour of the market recently has not been in its favour. However, there's no reason to immediately reject the system on this evidence alone, as it may just be that some further filters are required to set it on the road to success.

L ADVFN: www.advfn.com

Bloomberg (money flow): www.bloomberg.com/uk/tv/moneyflow/

Sharepages: www.sharepages.com

Investment trusts

If I want to see up-to-date information on investment trusts, which are the best web sites to look at?

Investment trusts are the Cinderella of the investing world. Unlike unit trusts they are not allowed to market themselves directly, and IFAs earn no commission by selling them, so editors of financial magaines and newspapers, one eye on advertising revenues, are inclined to ignore them. It's a shame because investment trusts (ITs) have a number of useful features, and some significant benefits over unit trusts.

In an effort to raise the profile of ITs among investors, the **AITC** (Association of Investment Trust Companies) launched a £17m marketing campaign in 1999/2000, and its web site is the first place to go for information. It includes essential facts and figures such as the market capitalisation of investment trust industry, the total number of investment trust companies; the average discount on ITs, hurdle rates, and so on. It also provides educational factsheets, a glossary of terms, and a directory of the management groups with contact details.

You might think that an obvious source of information on ITs would be the web sites of trust managers. Some of them have good sites, and they can be useful in providing background information on the trust, but generally speaking they offer little that you cannot get on the big personal finance web sites and - here's the key point - on the personal finance sites, the data is presented in a way that allows comparison.

So, moving to those personal finance sites, which are the ones to look at? **Ample** and **Moneyextra** both put in solid performances, with search functions and performance rankings. On Moneyextra, for instance, you can search for the best and worst performing trusts over a period of 1, 3 or 5 years. You can also narrow your search according to type of trust - for instance where it invests geographically, what its objectives are (income or growth), and what its structure is (split capital, split income, zero etc).

Similar information can be found on the Ample website. From the home page, select `Investments` in the top menu bar, then `Investment Trusts` in the left-hand menu. Here you get a leader board, a search function, a facility which enables you to request brochures from ITs, and news items. Click on the name of any individual IT, and you get its performance table, a chart, a discussion board, and information on the manager of the fund. From the performance chart of any one fund, you can click a button which allows you to instantly compare its performance with another fund in the same sector by overlaying their charts on top of each other. This sort of instant visual comparison is very useful.

Micropal, which is owned by Standard & Poors, is another key player. Its web site covers a very wide range of international funds, including UK investment trusts, and its performance tables can be downloaded directly to an Excel spreadsheet. There is a second web site, called Micropal Analysis, which provides more serious statistics on performance. Besides analysis of the cumulative performance and its consistency, there is quantitative analysis of each trust's volatility and beta relative to its market sector.

The leading funds site in the UK, however, is probably **TrustNet**. As its name implies, it is dedicated to collective funds, and covers the full panoply of unit trusts, OEICS, investment trusts and exchange traded funds (ETFs) in depth. From its home page, click on the `Investment Trusts` link and you get an at-a-glance snapshot of what is going on in ITs: the best performing trusts over the last 5 years, most popular funds, most popular groups, A-Z directories, fund news, and so on. Click on a link to any one trust, and you get detailed performance figures, plus charts comparing its performance with its benchmark index, and comparing its price with its Net Asset Value (NAV). A separate chart shows its historical discount/premium. You can also check what its largest holdings are, and whether there is a regional or sector weighting. All very useful.

One of the advantages of investment trusts over unit trusts is that as they trade on the exchange just like any other stock, and so many of the online analysis tools for stocks can also be applied to ITs. For example, for some more sophisticated analysis, RiskGrades data on ITs can be found on **DigitalLook**.

AITC: www.aitc.co.uk

Ample: www.iii.co.uk

DigitalLook: www.digitallook.com

Micropal: www.funds-sp.com

Moneyextra (ITs): www.moneyextra.com/funds/invtrusts/itlist.htm

TrustNet: www.trustnet.com/it

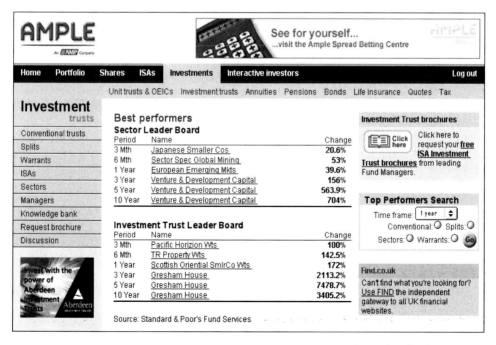

Historic fund prices

Q I have a spreadsheet which I use to calculate and compare the performance of funds, investment trusts and indices. Getting prices for investment trusts is easy, but for unit trusts I have to rely on old newspapers. Is there anywhere on the internet where I can download historic OEIC or unit trust prices?

A The short answer is no. As you say, prices for investment trusts are no problem as they are just like any ordinary share, and it's easy to create graphs by, for instance, using the charting module at **FT Investor**. But unit trust prices are more awkward - for a number of reasons.

Stocks tend to be traded on a central exchange (e.g. the London Stock Exchange) which records and disseminates prices. By contrast, funds have traditionally been bought and sold directly from the fund manager – though this is beginning to change. Also, funds are priced according to their NAV (net asset value), which is rather different from a stock price. The return to an investor is partly the capital appreciation of the NAV but also the income. Therefore a fund's performance can not be judged solely by the historic fluctuation of its NAV. Rather, a *total return* must be calculated which takes into account both NAV and yield.

Until recently, the two principal sources for online information on funds were **Ample**, and **TrustNet**. But a new entrant has arrived, which promises to shake up not only the online information available, but also the funds industry itself. The new service is **Morningstar**, a powerhouse of funds information established in the US some 17 years ago.

The Morningstar site provides a wealth of information on funds including performance data, customisable charts (different time periods, benchmarks, and currency), fund manager data, and a proprietary *style box*. The style box is used to classify each fund by two dimensions: size of company held (small to large), and investment style (value, growth, or a mixture of the two). Morningstar claims that using this proprietary system it is able to compare the performance of similar funds more accurately.

The real star feature of Morningstar though is its *holdings data*. Previously, the only way to tell exactly what stocks a fund owned was to wait for its 6-monthly report. In the periods between publication, you had no way of knowing what the fund manager was doing. It is this specific lack of knowledge that Morningstar has addressed. By getting the data direct from the funds, it is able to maintain a up-to-date database of current holdings.

The site itself provides as much information on funds as you are likely to want. There are total return figures, risk profiles, Morningstar's own proprietary fund rating and a portfolio facility. This last feature can be used to find discrete historic prices. By creating a portfolio and adding a new fund, the price can be found for any transaction date you input.

L
Ample: www.iii.co.uk
FT Investor: www.ft.com/investor
Morningstar: www.morningstar.co.uk
TrustNet: www.trustnet.com

Monitoring fund prices

Q I have several multi-ISA's. My problem is that I cannot find a way of downloading closing prices on a daily basis into Money2001. Any help you could offer - apart from suggesting that I ring the telephone quotation line each day, would be greatly appreciated.

A The best solution is probably to use the portfolio facility from **Morningstar**. This allows you to monitor funds and ISA funds that you own, or just track funds that you're interested in. The portfolio has a **portfolio alert** facility, which emails you the current price of funds and value of your portfolio every day. The email itself cannot be imported direct into a portfolio program (such as Money2001), but if the portfolio is small, then copying and pasting the values should be fairly quick. If you can do basic programming, a little VB or Perl script could automate this. However, if enough people request this facility directly, Morningstar might be persuaded to introduce a download facility in CSV format.

An additional feature of the funds portfolio is the *Portfolio X-Ray*. This is a very clever idea that analyses the diversification (by asset class, geography and sector) of all your fund holdings together. The point of this analysis is to test whether you are getting the diversification that you think you are getting by investing in a number of different funds. It's quite possible that you are not, and the Portfolio X-Ray will do the cross-checking for you.

L Morningstar: www.morningstar.co.uk

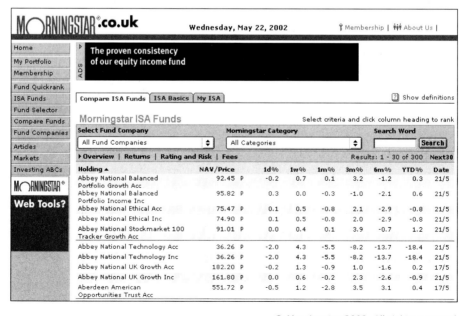

Investment funds and company size

Q Are most investment funds restricted to only investing in FTSE 100 companies, or can they go into FT 250 or even FT 350 stocks?

A There are many funds that *are* restricted to large cap, FTSE 100 type companies, but there are also many that are free to invest in whatever size company and sector the fund manager chooses. A good source for information on this is the Morningstar's UK web site.

On its `Fund Selector` page, for instance, there is a set of criteria for choosing funds. Looking at the `Morningstar Category` near the top, there are three choices which are relevant to the question you asked:

> First, **UK Equity Large Cap** where *large cap* is defined as companies that are in the top 5% of the market by size. At the moment this includes 83 stocks and comprises 79% of the total UK market capitalisation.

> The second, **UK Equity Mid Cap**, is the next 15% by number, or 250 stocks comprising 16% of the total UK market capitalisation.

> And thirdly, there is the **UK Equity Small Cap**, which incorporates all the rest - some 1,334 stocks.

Morningstar then defines *Large funds* as those that invest 55% or more in large cap stocks. *Small funds* invest 55% in small cap stock. And *Medium* incorporates all the rest. According to Morningstar, there are some 106 funds that invest in small cap stocks.

L Morningstar: www.morningstar.co.uk

Fund manager performance

Q Is there any way of tracking the performance of individual fund managers?

A Ever fund advertisement you read includes the FSA-sanctioned warning that past performance is not a reliable guide to future performance, and then in the same breath goes on to boast about how fabulously the fund has done in the past X years, coming in the top quartile of this or that carefully-selected performance table in this or that carefully-selected timescale. What is the investor to make of such a contradictory message?

• The obvious first principle is that you should not regard past performance as any *guarantee* of future performance. Those sorts of guarantees do not exist.

• Your second line of reasoning might be that you are entitled to treat past performance as *some* indication of likely future performance, even if not a very strong one, on the basis that a track record of success is slightly better than a track record of failure.

• And then there is a third line of reasoning which is that information about a fund's historic performance is only really useful if you also know who has been managing it in the time period concerned. In other words, focus on the individual, not the fund.

In crude terms, the performance of a fund has to be strongly influenced by its fund manager, in the same way that the performance of a football team has to be influenced by its strikers' ability to put the ball in the back of the net. And just as there are some football teams which rely heavily on star players and others which play an 11-man game, so there are some funds which allow their star fund managers to operate with a lot of autonomy, and others which take a team approach.

It's reasonable to suppose that funds which are managed by 'stars' are more at risk of underperformance if the star walks than funds which are 'corporate'. Ordinary fund performance tables, which don't tell you which managers have been, and are currently, at the helm, present an incomplete picture. For them, the Optimists UK Growth Fund is presumed to be the same as the fund of the same name five years ago, even if its star fund manager packed his bags last week.

To address this issue **Citywire** launched *Funds Insider*, which tracks the performance records of individual fund managers - regardless of which funds they have managed in the past. Different time periods and sectors can be searched.

For example, the best performing manager over the three years in UK stocks has been Nigel Thomas (recently departed from ABN Amro) with an impressive average monthly return of 2.7%. Although this is beaten by Derek Bartlett (manager of CF Bio Tech), who has chalked up a 3.9% average monthly return.

L Citywire: www.citywire.co.uk

Fund manager holdings

Q Is there a web site that will give me the details of fund managers' holdings in particular companies?

A The closest free web service is **Morningstar**. For each fund, it breaks down the portfolio by asset class, region and sector, as well as listing the top ten holdings.

For example, in the case of the Artemis UK Smaller Companies Fund, the top three holdings are: Premier Oil, European Motor Holdings and City Centre Restaurants.

A more detailed service is available from **Citywatch** but this is subscription-based. i.e. not free.

The other source of information on fund holdings is the web site of the fund company itself. For example, if you look at the **Gartmore** web site, you can see that the top three holdings of the Gartmore UK Focus Fund are: Vodafone, BP and GlaxoSmithKline.

L Citywatch: www.citywatch.co.uk

Gartmore: www.gartmore.co.uk

Morningstar: www.morningstar.co.uk

Capital gains tax - online resources

Q Are there any good sites that help with CGT calculations, especially indexation and tapering?

A The best reference site for CGT is the **Inland Revenue** site, which is very well presented. A good introductory guide can be found at the site, as well as detailed information covering the 1998 CGT reform, and guidelines on the calculation of CGT.

Beyond that, there is a wealth of tax information on the web, but of varying quality. A good introduction to tax and CGT exists at **FTYourMoney**, and the personal finance sites, **Ample**, **Moneyextra** and **This Is Money** acquit themselves well.

The best general site is probably **Yahoo Finance**, which also has a CGT guide. For more detailed information, consider **AccountingWeb**, which is targeted at professional accountants, but still has useful articles and links for non-accountants.

Remember that it's important to make sure that the tax information you read is up to date. In the brief research for this article, 50% of the web sites had not been updated for the latest Budget changes.

Finally, a good tax web site is **Digita**, makers of several tax software programs. The site has a good collection of guides, articles and calculators, including a Celebrity Tax Meter. According to this last calculator, Bernie Ecclestone, the boss of Formula One, paid £246 million in tax in 2000/2001, which is a daily tax rate of £676,000.

L
AccountingWeb: www.accountingweb.co.uk/tax/

Ample (tax): www.iii.co.uk/tax/

Digita: www.digita.com

FTYourMoney: www.ftyourmoney.com

Inland Revenue: www.inlandrevenue.gov.uk

Inland Revenue (CGT introductory guide):
www.inlandrevenue.gov.uk/leaflets/c4.htm

Inland Revenue (CGT 1998 reform):
www.inlandrevenue.gov.uk/cgtreform/

Inland Revenue (CGT calculation):
www.inlandrevenue.gov.uk/pdfs/cgt1_9.htm

Moneyextra (tax): www.moneyextra.com/tax/

This Is Money: www.thisismoney.com/undated/tx3146.html

Yahoo Finance (tax): uk.biz.yahoo.com/tax/home.html

Yahoo Finance (CGT guide): uk.biz.yahoo.com/tax/taxguide/cgt.html

Capital gains tax - software programs

Q Do you know of a software program that will calculate CGT? I have received scrip dividends and now need to go back about 15 years to find out the CGT liability.

A Until recently dealing with CGT was a fiddly nuisance. Fortunately there are now some very good portfolio programs that can help. **Fairshares** (recently acquired by **Updata**) looks after all aspects of CGT and portfolio management, including scrips going back 30 years. **Sharescope**, too, has a good CGT facility: select `Transactions`, then right-click and the `Capital Gains` option appears. Further information, if required, can be found at the proficient, and surprisingly jolly, **Inland Revenue** web site.

If you want to do your CGT calculations offline, but still on a computer, there are several good software programs available. The Consumer's Association produces **TaxCalc** which you install onto your hard disc from CD. It is easy to use - you just follow the screen prompts, type in the figures, and TaxCalc works out your liability/rebate. It also prints out your return on an IR-approved form. **Quicken** is another heavyweight in this area.

Q² I recently acquired shares in a company which was created following the demerger of another company in which I had shares. Is there a web site where I can look up the base cost of the shares in the new company so that I know what my CGT liability is?

A² According to Ben Melling, Tax Partner at Grant Thornton, where there is a 're-organisation' of share capital (e.g. a demerger), the basic rule is that the capital gains base cost of the original shareholding has to be apportioned between the shares held in the successor companies pro rata to their respective market values at the time of the re-organisation - normally the first day of dealings.

For example, for an investor holding shares in British Gas plc and subsequently ending up with one BG plc and one Centrica plc share for each British Gas share originally owned, the historic capital gains base cost of each British Gas share would be split between BG and Centrica in the ratio of their respective share prices when first traded as independent companies. The figures used for market value are:

1. The lower of the two prices shown for the company concerned in *The Stock Exchange Daily List,* plus 25% of the difference between them; or

2. The mid point of the highest and lowest prices at which bargains were struck on the relevant day.

Where the results of the two methods differ, the lowest figure is taken. The historic share price information is available from a number of sources, but in these cases you may find it easier to get the information directly from the companies concerned (e.g. from their annual report).

L Fairshares: www.updata.co.uk
Inland Revenue: www.inlandrevenue.gov.uk
Sharescope: www.sharescope.co.uk

3

Data
Sources

- Historic stock data
- Volume data
- Intra-day price data
- International stock and indices data
- Closing prices

Historic stock data

Q Do you know of any sites that provide historic closing prices for UK equities free of charge? Also for the FTSE All Share index on any given date?

A If you are going to be using historic prices often, I'd recommend subscribing to a data service such as **Sharescope** or **ADVFN**. They are not free, but in the grand scheme of things the charges are not significant. And this data can usually be imported into other programs such as Metastock.

But if you only want access to historic prices very occasionally, then **Yahoo** has a good service. Enter the EPIC code (suffixed with a '.L') choose the historic period and frequency (daily, weekly, monthly) and the table displays the open, high, low, close and volume data.

This can be downloaded direct to a spreadsheet for easier manipulation. If the data doesn't automatically parse itself into separate cells: highlight the column of data, then from the menu bar select, `Data > Text to columns`, select `Delimited`, click `Next`, check the `Comma` box and then click `Finish`.

For international markets, a good source is **DownloadQuotes.com**, which offers a huge range of historic data to download from over 30 different world markets, including the UK. This used to be a free service but now costs money. The charging structure is based on a monthly subscription per market (for the UK market it's 7.95 EUR), which provides unlimited access to the database.

You also asked about historic closing prices for the FTSE All-Share. Again, **Sharescope** carries historic data - in the case of the FTSE All Share Index back to Jan 1994. If you want a date before then, it is more difficult. Unfortunately the definitive source for Index data, **FTSE International,** only carries 3 months of historic data on its web site. However, if all you want are values for one or two days, I'd recommend calling FTSE International direct on +44 (0)20 7448 1800, and they'll give the values directly over the telephone.

L
ADVFN: www.advfn.com

DownloadQuotes.com: www.downloadquotes.com

FTSE International: www.ftse.com

Sharescope: www.sharescope.co.uk

Yahoo Finance: chart.yahoo.com/d

Historic price and volume data

Q Is there anywhere on the web that provides historic volume data for stocks, so that I can compare the volume traded on any particular day against the historic average?

A The answer to your question lies with an information provider called Track Data which has been supplying volume (and other) data to institutions for years. Track Data also has a retail product called **myTrack** which, while popular in the US, has not been heavily marketed in the UK, except as the technical platform for myBroker, the online broking operation of Options Direct.

MyTrack is a fascinating program that deserves to be better known. Part of its problem is a design which, even by the low standards of investment software, is convoluted to say the least. But it is worth fighting through the interface, for the goodies that lie behind.

Let's say you wanted to find volume data for Ultraframe on, for the sake of argument, 25th November 1999. The first step is to install myTrack on your hard disc. You can download it from either the myTrack or myBroker web site. Then open the program and follow the following steps. [Note that you will have to have an internet connection open, as the program has to access the Track Data database online.]

• Click on `FreeQuotes`, and input 'UTF-L' (this is the EPIC code for Ultraframe, suffixed with a '-L' to indicate it is a London traded stock). A little box should pop up with all the usual trading data.

• Hover over the code symbol, UTF-L, and click the right mousebutton. (The key to using myTrack is the use of the right mouse button.) A sub-menu will pop up with all sorts of features. The particular feature we're interested in is the `AIQ Historic Charting`.

• Select `AIQ Historic Charting`, and then `Option 1`. Up pops quite a decent OHLC bar chart of Ultraframe (if the chart seems a bit small, double click on the window title bar to expand to full-screen). Along the top are various time parameters for customisation; and by playing around with those (and setting `Periods=Daily`) you can get a chart including 25/11/99.

• Using the scroll bars at the bottom, the line cursor can be moved to a specific day – the date is indicated in the top left of the upper window. Position the cursor at 25/11/99, and it will be seen that the closing price that day was 387.5p and the volume was 47,481.

The above procedure would scarcely be worth the effort to find one value, however the myTrack program does offer many other features, and rewards perseverance and experimentation.

L myBroker: www.mybroker.co.uk

myTrack: www.mytrack.com

Intra-day historic index data

Q I regularly use the internet to research stock data. I have recently taken an interest in the daily movements of the major stock indices. I would like to download historical index data at an intra-daily level - ideally at minute intervals. Do you know of a web site that could provide this data - preferably free?

A That's quite specialised data, and I don't know of any web site which offers it – for free or otherwise. If you're using MetaStock or OmniTrader, the data sources for those programs may offer such historic data. The best option may be **Paritech**, a reseller of trading programs and data.

L Paritech: www.paritech.co.uk

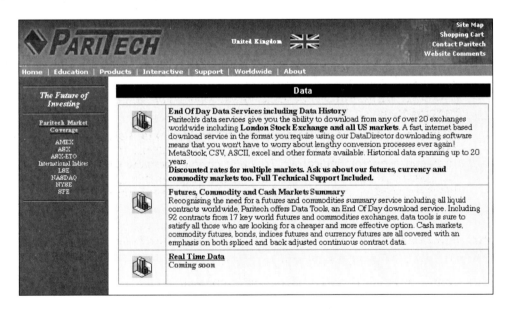

Historic international data

Q I would like to get hold of historic data for the German DAX Index, for as far back as possible. Is there an online service that has this data?

A The best source for international financial data is the imaginatively named, **Global Financial Data**. This offers a download file of the DAX Index from 1959 to the present day. Unfortunately, the service is not a bargain. A full subscription costs $7,500, partial database subscriptions cost $1,500-3,000, while individual file downloads cost $25-50 each. As I said, it's not cheap. But if you find you really need a specific data series, this is a useful source.

The range of data available at Global Financial Data is impressive. As well as the DAX index, they also carry 18 other stock indices from Germany, as well as stock indices from 104 countries. This includes the UK FT-Actuaries All-Share Index (with data from 1800). And for investors who find the year 1800 rather *too* recent to analyse the real long-term trends, there's also the UK FT-Actuaries All-Share Composite with a data range from 1693-2000. And if your advanced global analysis model needs the Argentinian Swan, Culbertson and Fritz Index (1938-58) – this is where you'll find it.

The service is not restricted to stock indices. There is also data on currency rates (from 1590), interest rates (from 1700), commodities (from 1500) and finally a data series allowing some decent long term analysis - inflation rates since 1264.

If you're looking for other economic data a couple of good sources are the **Financial Data Finder** at Ohio State University, and the database at the **Federal Reserve Bank of St Louis**.

Further data downloads are available at **The Financial Forecast Center**, which also, rather handily, makes forecasts for stock indices, money rates, exchange rates and economic indicators. If you're curious to know what the value of, say, the Nasdaq Index will be in October 2002 (2,394) this is where to find it. The forecasts must be accurate because they're generated from neural networks.

L Federal Reserve Bank of St Louis: www.stls.frb.org/fred/

The Financial Forecast Center: www.forecasts.org

Global Financial Data: www.globalfindata.com

Ohio State University (Financial Data Finder):www.cob.ohio-state.edu/fin/osudata.htm

UK closing price data

Q Now that MarketEye has gone, are there any other web sites from which you can download UK closing price data?

A Quite a few of the services from the old MarketEye site were transferred to the parent ThomsonFn site, but unfortunately the data download didn't make it. Here are your options at present*:

- Closing prices can be downloaded free from **Moneyextra**, but the service is restricted to FTSE 100 and FTSE 250 stocks.

- OHLCV data can be downloaded from **ADVFN** (£5 per month).

- OHLCV data is available from **Financial Express Prestel** (£90 per year).

- The service from **Downloadquotes.com** offers a good range of data (charge: unlimited access to UK historical file and end-of-day data: 7.95EUR/m)

- You could consider buying **Sharescope software and its data feed**. Sharescope allows you to export prices to external applications, including spreadsheets, which makes it useful not only as a data source but also for investment analysis.

Finally, I've received the following from a correspondent in Holland, which sounds interesting, although I haven't been able to test it myself yet.

"I use a program called StockBrowser (freeware from www.xs4all.nl/~ithiel). It downloads quotes from open sources on the internet, and with a Hauppauge WinTV card (approx £100) in my computer I can write Ceefax pages to disk, which the StockBrowser can then read. (This requires an additional package called BBC.zip, which can be downloaded after installation of the StockBrowser). The advantage is, of course, that Ceefax offers an extensive list of stocks and quotes. It takes my computer 5 minutes to write all Ceefax pages from BBC1 to disk (the pages with quotes), by reading multiple pages at a time. StockBrowser also offers an additional program called SB2Excel (freeware too), with which you can transfer the last quote and a small number of other items from the StockBrowser to an Excel spreadsheet (through DDE)."

L
ADVFN: www.advfn.com

Downloadquotes.com: www.downloadquotes.com

Financial Express Prestel: www.finexprestel.com

Moneyextra: www.moneyextra.com/stocks/data_downloads.html

Sharescope: www.sharescope.co.uk

ThomsonFn site: www.thomsonfn.com

****
*Update: MarketEye lives! Well, nearly. Go to www.thomsonfn.com, click on Global, and you'll find the old MarketEye site, unfortunately minus its data download feature, but still with useful price pages on futures, options, bonds and international markets.
****

Intra-day updating of portfolios with myTrack

Q Is there a way of creating a portfolio on a spreadsheet that can be updated throughout the day?

A Yes, **myTrack** can help out here. myTrack is a proprietary portfolio program which you install on your computer, and which then receives streaming prices via the internet. It is popular with many traders. One of its greatest features is the ability to link to an Excel spreadsheet and **import data directly into the spreadsheet**. This feature is not documented very well by myTrack, and it's quite possible that a large number of myTrack users are not even aware of it.

Installation is quite simple. First install the myTrack program (available from the web sites of **myTrack** of **myBroker** in the UK as a download, or a CD ROM). Then start MS Excel, with a blank sheet. From the menu bar select, `Tools > Add-ins > Browse,` navigate to the directory where myTrack is installed and select `mt.xla`. Then load the spreadsheet `mttest.xls` from the myTrack directory. Everything should now be ready.

To insert a function that calls market data, highlight a cell, and then from the Excel menu bar, select `Insert > Function >User defined,` and choose the data type required in the right window.

For example, select `mtLast,` click `OK,` and then input the reference of the cell containing a stock's ticker symbol (e.g. VOD-L for the London-traded Vodafone shares). The cell will henceforth update itself automatically with streaming delayed, or real-time prices (depending on your service level agreement with myTrack).

In the above case, the cell would have been updated with the stock's last traded price. But there's much more data that can be called, such as, bid/offer prices and sizes, change over the previous close, day high/low, volume traded and useful indicator which shows the direction of the last 5 tick movements.

From such a simple construct, it is possible to build simple portfolios that monitor individual share prices. But also some fairly sophisticated portfolios can be built as well. Of course, all the usual spreadsheet functions are still available so real-time portfolio valuations can be easily created. Another example is that the conditional formatting feature of Excel can be used to highlight certain prices (e.g. the cell can be highlighted in yellow, if its content matches specified criteria).

Fortunately, the data source covers a wide range of markets: US, UK, European stock markets, options, futures and currencies. A simple spreadsheet I've written (*uk_adr_trac.xls*: download from this book's web site) simultaneously compares the prices of UK ADRs trading in the US with their associated stocks trading on the London market, with the ADR prices converted into a real-time starting equivalent using the myTrack currency feed.

Recently, another program has announced that it also offers live updating of Excel spreadsheets. This is the beta version of **Personal Stock Monitor 5.1**, which is a program similar to **Medved's QuoteTracker**. They both offer a sophisticated front-end portfolio program, with data supplied by third party internet services (such as Yahoo). Personal Stock Monitor now offers a facility similar to myTrack in which spreadsheets can be created with constantly updated market prices. In fact, ticker symbols can be dragged and dropped into any compatible Microsoft DDE-aware application.

A question that may occur to some readers is, why bother going to all this trouble, when there are very many perfectly good online portfolio services available for free from many web sites? And it's certainly true that playing around with Excel functions isn't everybody's idea of fun. But investing successfully requires having an edge of some kind, and using the same tools that a million other investors are using, is not conducive to finding that unique edge. Creating your own spreadsheet portfolio program is not the only way to go about finding that edge, but for some it may be a good start.

```
Medved's QuoteTracker: www.quotetracker.com

myTrack (US): www.mytrack.com

myBroker (UK): www.mybroker.co.uk

Personal Stock Monitor 5.1: www.dtlink.com
```

Real-time share prices

Q Which web sites offer free real-time share prices?

A At the height of the web boom, free real-time prices were being thrown at investors like confetti. A financial web site that didn't have real-time prices was not a serious player in the macho web world. A few months later, old-style bottom-line economics hit home. Some sites that used to offer free real-time prices now only have 20-minute delayed prices or they charge a subscription for real-time prices e.g. **LondonMoneyMarket**. Other sites like EuropeanInvestor, MoneyWhispers, and UK-iNvest have completely shut up shop.

UK-iNvest was one of the more spectacular burn-outs in the dotcom meltdown. For a fascinating article on the rise and fall of GlobalNet Financial (its parent company), search under 'GlobalNet' at the **WSJ** web site and read the colourful tale of green Bentleys and express shipments of pet food from California for the London director's finicky American cat. The WSJ site is subscription-only, but you can get a two week trial period, which is worth taking up just to read this article.

So, which free real-time services are left?

Not many. The main service is provided by **ADVFN**. Not only are the real-time prices free, but they are also streaming – data is fed continuously to your computer, with no need for manual refreshing of the pages. Although the service is free, it is limited in the sense that only a certain number of users can use it at any one time. Working on a FIFO (first in, first out) basis, a new user logging on will knock out the user previously logged on the longest (who can himself then log on again, and go to the front of the queue).

Another free real-time service is offered by the new **City Comment**. This looks a very good site, with useful commentary, analysis and a stock market game. Finally, free real-time prices are also available at **Teletext**.

A quasi-free service is available from **RealTimeShares.com**. Here, real-time prices are free to users of the web site's own ISP. If you use another ISP (e.g. AOL) you have to pay £49 per year for real-time prices. Elsewhere, there are still quite a few sites offering real-time prices on a subscription basis: **Ample**, **LondonMoneyMarket**, **myTrack** and **ProQuote**.

L
```
ADVFN: www.advfn.com
Ample: ww.iii.co.uk
City Comment: www.citycomment.co.uk
LondonMoneyMarket: www.londonmoneymarket.com
myTrack: www.mytrack.com
ProQuote: www.proquote.net
RealTimeShares.com: www.realtimeshares.com
Teletext: www.teletext.co.uk
WSJ: www.wsj.com
```

Q Is it possible to get to real-time values for the FTSE 100 Index on the web?

A The FTSE 100 Index is calculated by FTSE International every 15 seconds from a live feed of stock prices from the London Stock Exchange. FTSE International then disseminates the data to information providers, such as Reuters, and other companies and web sites. Depending on the contract the company has with FTSE International, the data can then be further disseminated either real-time, or with a delay of usually 20 minutes. All the main financial web sites (e.g. **FT Investor**, **Bloomberg**, **OnVista**, **Yahoo Finance**) provide values for the FTSE 100 updated throughout the day, albeit with the delay of 20 minutes.

LondonMoneyMarket used to offer free real-time prices, but now you have to pay. **RealTimeShares** has free real-time prices but only if you use their own ISP. **ADVFN** has real-time index data but only as part of their subscription Level II services. An alternative is the US-based **TheFinancials.com** which covers global indices, commodities and currencies. Their indices pages includes real-time FTSE 100 data with the great addition of a real-time streaming tick chart, with technical analysis indicators such as MACD and RSI. Another option might be **myTrack**. Although a charge is levied for real-time stock prices, real-time index data is free in the basic package.

All the above real-time services have streaming data, which means that pages do not have to be refreshed manually to see the latest values. Be warned that they all use different ticker symbols for the FTSE 100 Index, for example: ADVFN [UKX]; myTrack [UKZ-L]; TheFinancials.com [UKX.L].

Where can I get intra-day data that I can feed into Omnitrader or Metastock? I live in London, but my TV reception isn't good enough for a teletext feed.

Paritech is very good for data. It provides a real-time data feed for London Stock Exchange and Europe (from eSignal) for around £85 per month. For a real-time charting system, try ir Dynamics.

L
```
ADVFN: www.advfn.com
Bloomberg: www.bloomberg.co.uk
FT Investor: www.ft.com/investor
LondonMoneyMarket: www.londonmoneymarket.com
myTrack (U.K.): www.mybroker.co.uk
OnVista: www.onvista.co.uk
RealTimeShares.com: www.realtimeshares.com
TheFinancials.com: www.thefinancials.com/indices/Quotes.html
Yahoo Finance: finance.yahoo.co.uk
ir Dynamics: www.ird.com
Paritech: www.paritech.co.uk
```

4 Fundamental Analysis

- Finding key financial data
- Cash flow statements
- Earnings forecasts
- Directors' dealings
- Charting fundamental data
- Sourcing research from brokers
- Independent company research
- Online conference calls
- CEO interviews

Q Which are the best sites for company data?

A If you are looking for data on a particular company, the web site to head for is **hemscott.NET** (select `Company Info`). Overall, the data is excellent, but the amount you get on any particular company will vary according to the contract which the company has with hemscott.NET. Generally, you get: company statements, 5 year summary P&L with balance sheet, brokers' consensus EPS forecasts, and further details on major shareholders, the company's advisers, directors, registrars and contact details. In addition if you subscribe to the hemscott.NET ISP service (which is free), you will have access to directors' dealing and detailed brokers' forecasts.

As a simple example, if you research Diageo on hemscott.NET, you find:

Old name: Guinness PLC (1997)
Activities: Distillation and marketing of Scotch whisky, gin and other spirits and the brewing and marketing of beer; food manufacture; fast food retailing.
Status: fully listed; Lon Opt; ADR
Index: FTSE 100
Sector: Beverages
Employees: 71,523
Turnover: £6,478m in the half-year to 31.12.01
Return on capital employed (ROCE): 28.9%
Pre-tax profit: £1,275m
Earnings per share (EPS): 24.1p
Interim dividend: 9.30p

One of hemscott.NET's useful features is that you can access its company database in a number of different ways: alphabetically by name, by industry classification (i.e. sector) or by whether the company is included in an index (e.g. FTSE 100). You can also see which companies have traded options or ADRs.

Another useful source of company data is **Wright Investors Services**, an American company which provides data on thousands of international companies. It is similar to hemscott.NET, but provides more analysis, including a company research report, and analysis of sales, share price and earnings. It also has an interesting table called the *Wright Quality Rating* in which each company is assessed according to financial strength, profitability and stability, and growth. The company's rating is then compared to the market or industry sector.

Finally, there is **Hoovers UK** - part of the larger US-based Hoover's Online. Like the two services above, it has summary company information, and also financials that can be interactively converted into other currencies - theoretically useful for comparison with international competitors, although in practice likely to be difficult because of differing accounting standards between countries. As yet, this site doesn't offer anything more than hemscott.NET, but it is one to watch as the service develops to become more like its parent site in the US.

L
```
hemscott.NET: www.hemscott.net
Hoovers UK: www.hoovers.co.uk
Wright Investors Services: profiles.wisi.com
```

Company web addresses

Q Do you know of any directory of company web addresses?

A If you're looking for the web site of a specific UK company, you could do worse initially than just taking a guess. A quick try of www.[companyname].co.uk will work in most cases. For example, the web address of Halifax is www.halifax.co.uk.

But if you're looking for a group of companies, or an inconveniently named one such as Royal Sun & Alliance Ins Group, a good site is **Plc Sites**, which lists sites of all UK companies alphabetically and by sector. Alternatively, the following all provide links to corporate web sites: **Hoovers UK**, **DigitalLook** and **Yahoo Finance**.

L DigitalLook: www.digitallook.com

Hoovers UK: www.hoovers.co.uk

Plc Sites: www.plcsites.co.uk

Yahoo Finance: uk.finance.yahoo.com

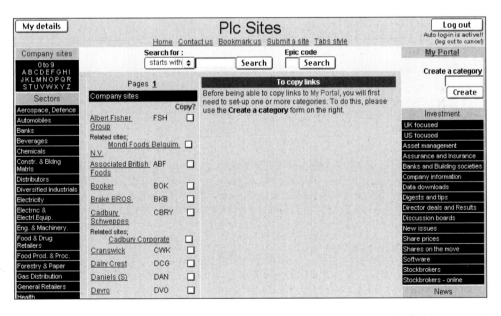

Company registrars

Q Are there any web sites where I can find the name and phone number of the registrar for a particular company?

A The quickest way to find this information is using the `Company Info` section of **hemscott.NET**.

Taking Majestic Wine as an example, if you click `Registrars` at the bottom of the left navigation column, you see that its registrar is Capita IRG – which happens to be the registrar for 70% of all UK companies. You do have to register with hemscott.NET to get this information, though.

L hemscott.NET: www.hemscott.net

HEMSCOTT NET	**Majestic Wine PLC**
Majestic Wine PLC	Registrars Details
	Capita IRG PLC
Company Map	
Summary Detail	Bourne House
Annual Report	34 Beckenham Road
5 Yr Summary P&L with	Beckenham
Balance Sheet	Kent
Daily Share Price	BR3 4TU
15 Minute Delay Prices	
Brokers' Consensus	
Detailed Broker Forecasts	**Tel:** (0870) 162 3100
Shareprice Graph	**Fax:** (020) 8658 3430
Advisers	
Directors	
Directors' Share Dealings	
Major Shareholders	
Registrars	
Contact Details	
Key Dates	sources and disclaimers | advertise with us
	21 May 2002
HEMSC TT Company Insight	Data Supplied by Hemscott Data Services
	For more information contact - netwebmaster@hemscott.co.uk
	Copyright Hemscott Group Ltd 2001
	HEMSC TT

Company reporting dates

Q Where on the internet can I find out when a company is announcing its results, preferably for the whole year ahead, so I can watch out for them? I know that *Investors Chronicle* lists them for the week ahead, and sometimes for the forthcoming few months, but I want to see the whole picture for the year. For example I want to know when Queens Moat Houses is announcing its figures and at the moment I have no idea at all.

A On a daily and weekly basis the best source for information on upcoming company results is the **AFX** news service. This provides a rolling diary of expected company results – interims, finals, AGMs, EGMs - in the week ahead. I'd also mention in passing that the same report also carries a timetable of economic figures due to be released. This report, released around 09h00 every morning, is usually titled, Forward Diary of Events. The AFX news reports are syndicated fairly widely on the web, and thus can be found (rather more conveniently) on many other web sites, including **ADVFN**, **Ample** and **nothing-ventured.com**.

hemscott.NET also has a diary of results due for the coming week, and links through to brokers' forecasts for each respective company listed.

For a longer-range timetable, for specific companies, the best source is also hemscott.NET – click on `Company info` in the left margin, then click the 'Q' to bring up a listing of all companies beginning with that letter (an alternative would be to go in via the 'Leisure & Hotels' industry classification). From that list, choose Queens Moat Houses, then click `Key dates` at the bottom of the left-hand margin. That shows you that the next year end is 31st December 2002, and also gives you the interim reporting date (6th September 2002), the date of its next AGM (3rd May 2003), and the date on which its annual report is expected (7th March 2003).

Offline, there are various financial calendars which list the reporting dates of listed companies. The one from *Square Mile Publications* is perhaps the best known, and is now in its 26th edition. It details:

• Dates of company announcements

• Key industry and calendar dates

• Previous years major financial indicators including sterling/dollar, bank base rates, prices of Brent crude and FTSE, Nikkei and Dow Jones indices

L
```
ADVFN: www.advfn.com

AFX: www.afxpress.com

Ample: www.iii.co.uk

hemscott.NET: www.hemscott.net

hemscott.NET: www.hemscott.com/hstoday/week_aheadndex.htm

nothing-ventured.com: www.nothing-ventured.com
```

Cash flow statements and company reports

Q There seem to be lots of web sites that provide company share price charts and details of 5-year profit and loss figures etc, but I can't find any which also give a cash flow statement? Do they exist?

A As you say, company data is now readily available from sites like **hemscott.NET**, **Hoovers UK** and **Wright Investors Services**, but, as you also observe, they do not provide cash flow statements. The best source for this is usually the company's annual or interim report, which can be found a number of ways.

The first place to look is the company's own web site - companies are getting better at offering their reports online. For example, if you are interested in Halifax, go to www.halifax.co.uk, click on Company Information, and then Results & Strategy. From there, you can download a PDF file to your hard disc and read it off-line.

If a company's own web site doesn't make its reports available, you might still find them at **Corporate Reports**, **CAROL** or **hemscott.NET**, all of which offer a large number of reports in one place. Their coverage is not comprehensive, however, which makes the exercise rather hit and miss. They might have the report you're looking for, but then again they might not.

There is a different tack you can take. Listed companies have to submit summaries of their final and interim reports to the **London Stock Exchange**, which then distributes the information via its Regulatory News Service (RNS). The summaries usually include cash flow statements, so the quickest way to access this data is to search on past RNS bulletins. The London Stock Exchange web site has a good searchable RNS archive – but to go back more than 6 months you need to register. **UK-Wire** carry RNS archives over a longer period.

Many investors still prefer the smeared-ink-on-dead-trees style of report, and with the online service as patchy as it is, who can argue. To receive a hard copy report in the post, request it direct from the company itself (by telephone, or from the company's web site). Alternatively, use **WI Link**'s *Annual Reports Service*. This service is provided via third parties like **FT.com**, **MoneyGuru** and **Yahoo Finance**. Wherever you see the spade (as in playing card) logo, company reports can be ordered directly online.

L CAROL: www.carol.co.uk

Corporate Report: www.corpreports.co.uk

FT.com: www.ft.com

hemscott.NET: www.hemscott.net

Hoovers UK: www.hoovers.co.uk

London Stock Exchange: www.londonstockexchange.com

MoneyGuru: www.moneyguru.co.uk

UK-Wire: www.uk-wire.com

Wright Investors Services: profiles.wisi.com

Yahoo Finance: finance.yahoo.co.uk

Earnings estimates

Q I'm trying to calculate the PEG ratio, used by Jim Slater and Motley Fool. But I need to find analyst's estimates of future earnings growth. Is there anywhere on the web that has this information?

A To recap briefly, the PE ratio compares the current price of a share to its historic earnings per share (EPS). If the PE is high, the share is deemed expensive. But the PE by itself takes no account of the growth rate of the company which, if high, may justify a lofty PE. That's where the PEG (price earnings growth factor) comes in*. It attempts to improve on the straight PE ratio by incorporating the forecast growth of the company. Technically, the PEG is calculated by dividing the company's prospective PE by the estimated future growth rate in EPS. So to calculate the PEG, you need those EPS growth rate estimates to hand.

Where do you get them? Well, they can come from anywhere, including yourself if you think you know the company well. But the usual source is brokers' forecasts. Since the PEG calculation is sensitive to EPS estimates, and as individual analysts' forecasts can vary widely, it's safest to use 'consensus' forecasts rather than the forecasts of any one broker.

A popular source of analysts' estimates is **hemscott.NET**. Click on `Company Info` on the home page, select a company (e.g. Marks & Spencer), and then click on `Brokers' Consensus`. You'll see the consensus EPS forecasts, calculated directly by hemscott.NET from data supplied by 17 brokers. Usefully, they are date-weighted (more recent forecasts have a greater weighting on the calculation than older ones). To help further in deciding the confidence weighting to apply to these figures, hemscott.NET calculates the standard deviation for all the brokers' estimates – a low figure implies greater confidence in the estimate. Figures are also given for the change in the consensus EPS from three months before.

An alternative source for estimates is **FT.com**, which uses data compiled by Multex. As well as the simple EPS forecasts, their figures also include a record of historical surprises and the estimates trend over the previous few weeks.

Other sources for EPS forecasts are **Yahoo Finance**, which has data from BARRA, and **Ample**. If you're really getting into this you might like to create your own algorithm for calculating consensus forecasts (for example, under-weighting, or ignoring, estimates from specific brokers).

L
Ample: www.iii.co.uk

FT.com (analyst forecasts): news.ft.com/news/companynews/multex/

hemscott.NET: www.hemscott.net

Motley Fool: www.fool.co.uk

Yahoo Finance: finance.yahoo.co.uk

*Further background on PEGs can be found at the **Motley Fool** site – input 'PEG' in the search box at the top of the page.

EPS, PE and PEG forecasts

Q My share selection system starts with forecasts of EPS, PE & PEG for the next 2 years. Finding lists of those shares with the highest/lowest forecasts for the whole UK market seems impossible. I have searched for a web site which lists all shares and provides forecasts in all 3 categories (in high to low order), without success. Does such a site exist or can you recommend an alternative solution to provide such fundamental data?

A Forecast EPS figures are fairly readily available for individual shares. For example, you can find them (by company) at **hemscott.NET** and **Yahoo**. But EPS (nor PER or PEG) numbers are not ranked.

The stock screening services at **ADVFN** and **iTruffle** allow you to screen stocks according to various criteria including EPS, PER and PEG. For example, at ADVFN you can generate a list of all stocks with a PEG greater than 0 but below 1. But this listing is not ranked, and to use the stock screener, you have to be a premium subscriber, so it is not a free service.

DigitalLook offers some pre-configured searches on UK stocks. These searches cannot be customised, but you can list stocks with the lowest PE or PEG values.

Your best bet may be **Sharescope**, which is not a web site, but a proprietary program that runs on your PC. Sharescope has a monthly subscription charge (around £12), but is one of the best bargains on the market. For each stock Sharescope displays a number of parameters, including EPS, PE and PEG, and the whole market can be sorted on any of these parameters. At the time of writing, for instance, a search for stocks with a PEG value between 0 and 1 brings up a list of 340 companies.

L ADVFN: www.advfn.com

DigitalLook: www.digitallook.com

hemscott.NET: www.hemscott.net

iTruffle: www.itruffle.com

Sharescope: www.sharescope.co.uk

Yahoo Finance: finance.yahoo.co.uk

Bulk download EPS forecasts

Q Is there a site that will allow me to download EPS forecasts for lots of companies at once in spreadsheet format, in the same way that downloads of closing share prices are available?

A Consensus earnings forecasts are fairly widely available on the web now, but as yet there is no free online service which allows you to get a bulk download of all the forecast figures.

The best option for this is probably the portfolio program **Sharescope**. Sharescope carries 1-3 year forecasts for profits, EPS, dividends and turnover. All data can be exported in CSV format to be subsequently imported into a spreadsheet like Excel. The Sharescope interface is fairly spreadsheet-like to start with (columns can, for example, be sorted in ascending or descending order), such that, depending on one's analysis, it may not even be necessary to use an external spreadsheet.

L Sharescope: www.sharescope.co.uk

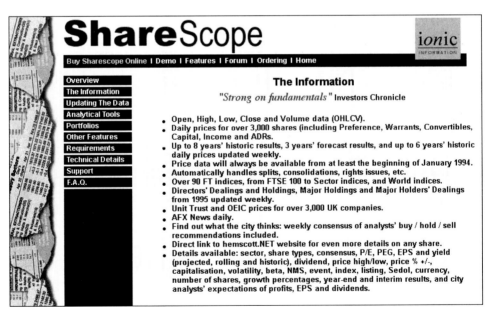

Directors' dealings

Q Which are the best online sources of information on directors' dealings?

A Whenever a director of a listed company buys or sells shares in that company, the London Stock Exchange has to be informed, and it then disseminates the news via its Regulatory News Service (RNS). The most direct way to follow directors' dealings, therefore, is to monitor RNS announcements, either on the Exchange's own web site, or on one of the news sites that carries RNS information, including **UK-Wire**, **Sharepages**, **ADVFN** and **hemscott.NET**.

RNS announcements about directors' dealings usually have the words 'Director Shareholding' in the title. So if you search on the RNS for 'Director Shareholding', or just 'Director', you should find all the relevant announcements. Some web sites have pre-configured searches that allow you to get straight to directors' dealing information for a particular company. A good example of this is UK-Wire, where DDs can be found at the `Category > Director's Dealing` section.

The above is fine for monitoring the latest breaking news, and also, because the web sites above also maintain archives of news, for researching historical dealings in specific companies. However, it is not all that convenient for keeping a general eye on what's going on. Fortunately, there are a couple of sites that present the information in a friendlier format. The first of these is **DigitalLook** which has a page that summarises DDs for all companies over the previous 7 days and which tells you how many dealings there have been in each company. For instance, as I write, I see that on the 20th May a director of media group Trinity Mirror bought 2,000 shares at 438p. For the record, 4 days later the bid price is 440p. It is difficult to get this type of overview from individual RNS announcements. In addition, the page that has the directors' dealings has a table of **institutional dealings** in the same company. The other useful service is from **Citywire**. Instead of hitting you over the head with thousands of RNS announcements, its journalists just report the important ones.

A combination of Citywire, DigitalLook, and UK-Wire is fine for monitoring directors' dealings. If you're only interested in a few companies, Citywire and DigitalLook both have services alerting users to new developments by email. There is also a more sophisticated service available for a fee from **Citywatch**.

The question is - can any of the above really help you make money? Personally, I've no doubt that DDs are *on occasion* a spectacularly successful indicator, and also that they can be useful as a confirmation signal for other research, but I'm sceptical that they can demonstrate consistent profitability. Search on 'directors' dealing' at **Motley Fool** and look at the articles of 6 Dec 2000, and 22 July 1999.

L
```
ADVFN: www.advfn.com
Citywatch: www.citywatch.co.uk
Citywire: www.citywire.co.uk
DigitalLook: www.digitallook.com
hemscott.NET: www.hemscott.net
London Stock Exchange: www.londonstockexchange.com
Motley Fool: www.fool.co.uk
Sharepages: www.sharepages.com
UK-Wire: www.uk-wire.com
```

Charting fundamental data

Q Where does a fundamentalist go on the net to find a decent chart? I would settle for an earnings line against price (see Peter Lynch's books) but would really like something more sophisticated. It is almost as if charts are reserved for technical analysts and those with additional interests are assumed to have no use for them!

A This is a good point. Many web sites now offer stock charts, but unfortunately none of them allow the charting of fundamental data. The reason, I imagine, is a technical one. From a simple database of OHLCV (open/high/low/close/volume) historic price data, it's possible to generate a huge range of charts with exotically named technical indicators. Whereas fundamental data is far more fiddly, requiring many different databases with non-homogenous data. So I'm afraid there's no easy answer to your question.

A couple of web sites that come close - but not very close- are **MoneyGuru** and **Comdirect**. In their company profiles they offer 5-year charts of a few accounting ratios (e.g. sales/turnover, debt/equity, quick ratio), but the charts are not customisable. Both these sites get their data from Teledata Börsen, so unsurprisingly the information is fairly similar.

However, the best information is available from non-UK sources. An excellent source of fundamental data is the Connecticut-based **Wright Investor Services**, which carries data on companies from many different countries including nearly all listed UK companies. For example, if you were researching the WPP Group, you'd be able to find several pages of sales, price and earnings analysis at Wright. On the first page *Company Profile* there's a 5-year chart of share price against earnings and dividends. An interesting feature of Wright is that they have an expert system that translates many of the figures into a plain English commentary. A good example of this can be seen on the *Research Report* page. This expert system also compares the company with three competitors – in the case of WPP, Havas Advertising, Publicis, and Cordiant Communications Group.

Where UK companies have ADRs trading in the US, other American websites can be helpful. One of the best is **Quicken**, and one of its best sections is the company *Evaluator*. Input the ticker symbol 'WPPGY' (WPP Group) and a six-page analysis report is automatically created covering: growth trends, financial health, management performance, market multiples, intrinsic values and finally a summary. As with Wright, Quicken also employs an expert system to translate the data into plain English, and these are illustrated with 10-year charts of the ratios such as ROE, ROA and ROIC.

L Comdirect: www.comdirect.co.uk

MoneyGuru: www.moneyguru.co.uk

Quicken: www.quicken.com

Wright: profiles.wisi.com/profiles/UnitedKingdom.htm

Wright (company extension):
www.corporateinformation.com/definitions.html

Company research - brokers

Q Are there any brokers offering online research on UK companies?

A Many traditional brokers now provide research to their clients over the internet. Judged on speed and cost, it is clearly a better medium than print. Unfortunately, the research is rarely available to non-clients.

The new generation of online brokers can be divided roughly into four categories depending on the research they offer to their clients.

1. The first category is plain and simple – **no research is provided at all**. The flag-bearer of this group is **iDealing**, offering just a straight-forward execution-only dealing service at a low price.

2. The next category includes those brokers that offer some information, usually in the form of **snapshot company profiles**. This includes, **E*Trade**, **StockAcademy** and **TD Waterhouse**. As well as company profiles, **Charles Schwab** and **Sharepeople** also offer information on brokers' forecasts.

3. The third category of broker includes **Hargreaves Lansdown**, **IMIWeb** and **SELF trade**. In addition to the basic company data, these brokers also offer **links through to third party research**. In the case of SELF trade, they provide the weekly six tips from *Investors Chronicle*, while IMIWeb have an arrangement whereby their clients can buy reports from Moneyguru. Hargreaves Lansdown has set up a separate web site to offer access to research from a number of different sources, including Peel Hunt, Seymour Pierce and Moneyguru, as well as research from its own analysts.

4. The final category consist of brokers which offer their own **in-house research** to clients. In most cases, the research comes from the analysts working for the parent investment bank. Just recently, **Barclays Stockbrokers** launched a new service which enables clients to access summary research recommendations on 130 leading UK companies. **Comdirect UK** also offers access to research on 700 international companies, courtesy of its sister company, Commerzbank Securities. **DLJDirect** has one of the most comprehensive offerings: as well as research from CSFB, there's also access to research from Peel Hunt, IDEAglobal, Investors Chronicle and Best Signals. In each case clients must qualify for the research through various asset value or trading activity criteria. (Note: DLJDirect is in the process of being bought by TD Waterhouse, and so its service may change following the acquisition).

The broker that has trumpeted its research the most has probably been **Merrill Lynch HSBC**, which offers reports from both Merrills and HSBC. This is no small offering, as, combined, the houses apparently produce 9,000 research notes a month, covering companies, sectors, strategy and global economy. The most popular reports are the morning analysts notes. Since launching the service 49% of all downloaded reports have been in the telecom sector.

Clients of **nothing-ventured.com** can access research in the form of recommendations and comments from a group of experts on what they call the *Panel*.

Given the great amount of research now being created, an obvious development is the growth of research aggregators. One such service is **Multex** which offers a portal for access to a range of research from many different sources. Another useful service is one that monitors the performance of the stock picks by analysts, and other pundits. Unfortunately, there's no comprehensive service in the UK.

Before getting too excited about brokers' research reports becoming widely available, it's well to be aware of their limitations. Increasingly investment banks are earning their money from corporate work, and not from broking commissions. And their research, apparently, is reflecting this situation. Fund managers are conducting more research in-house, and treating brokers' recommendations with a pinch of salt – knowing that the brokers don't want to upset potential corporate clients by producing nasty sell recommendations. Recent research in the US found that of 8,000 stock recommendations, only 29 were *sells*. Examples of this can be seen directly with the **Yahoo Finance Stockscreener**. Filtering on the Average Analyst Recommendation criteria, over 2,200 stocks are found as buys or strong buys. Conversely, only 50 stocks are found as sells or strong sells. This might be fine if all brokers were forecasting the general market to rise strongly this year, but as they're not, there seems to be a certain inconsistency here.

Barclays Stockbrokers: www.barclays-stockbrokers.co.uk

Charles Schwab: www.schwab-worldwide.com

Comdirect UK: www. comdirect.co.uk

DLJDirect: www.dljdirect.co.uk

E*Trade: uk.etrade.com

Hargreaves Lansdown: www.h-l.co.uk

Hargreaves Lansdown (research): www.analystinsite.co.uk

iDealing www.idealing.com

IMIWeb: www.imiweb.co.uk

Merrill Lynch HSBC: www.mlhsbc.co.uk

Moneyguru: www.moneyguru.co.uk

Multex: www.multexinvestor.com

nothing-ventured.com: www.nothing-ventured.com

SELF trade: www.selftrade.co.uk

Sharepeople: www.sharepeople.com

StockAcademy: www.stockacademy.com

TD Waterhouse: www.tdwaterhouse.co.uk

Yahoo (stockscreener): screen.yahoo.com/stocks.html

Company research - independent

Q Is it possible to get company research online from independent research houses?

A From its early days the web has been good at providing share prices and company data. Furthermore, company reports are now generally available in electronic format, or, failing that, hard copies can be requested online. *Company research,* however, has been slow to join the party. And much of what passes for research, is in fact just comment – not necessarily backed up by diligent analysis. One reason for this might be that the research providers have, understandably, been reluctant to subject themselves to the kamikaze economics of internet broadcasting.

But this might now be changing. As doubts over the value of brokers' research have risen, the demand is there for more objective research from truly independent organisations. To answer this demand, quite a few small research boutiques have set up with online services. Most of these services tend to specialise in either small companies, or in a small niche sector, where they can add value following stocks that might be ignored by the larger brokers and fund managers. The main research boutiques are listed below.

The questions that need answering include, what is research, and are investors willing to pay for the pure dope?

Financial sites may despair of the tight-fisted reluctance of investors to pay for online information; but why should investors open their wallets when there is so much for free, and so little evidence to show that superior research leads to consistent out-performance?

None of the research sites listed below are doing anything revolutionary. Indeed, the majority of them are not strictly internet operations at all – they are just old-fashioned newsletters, using the web as a convenient delivery medium.

L
Equity Development: www.equity-development.co.uk

Equity Growth Research: www.equitygrowth.net

Equity Investigator: www.equityinvestigator.com

Growth Company Investor: www.growthcompany.co.uk

Investors Chronicle: www.investorschronicle.co.uk

Investor Information: www.investorinformation.co.uk

iTruffle: www.itruffle.com

MoneyGuru: www.moneyguru.co.uk

Ovum Holway: www.holway.co.uk

RedSky Research: www.redskyresearch.com

t1ps.com: www.t1ps.com

thewrongprice: www.thewrongprice.com

Q Is it possible to listen to company conference calls on the web?

A Every six months (and every three months in the US) listed companies release reports summarising the current state of their business. These reports obviously have a big impact on the performance of the share price. But the trouble in the past has been that not all investors had access to these reports at the same time. This unfortunate state of affairs however suited many in the financial industry. *Selective disclosure*, as it's known, allowed companies to reward analysts at favoured brokers, and for brokers to pass this on in turn to their favoured clients. A cosy arrangement. Criticisms of the practice could be rebutted with arguments on the logistical problems of effecting simultaneous disclosure to all investors.

The internet changed all that. In 2000, the SEC in the US proposed *Regulation FD* (Fair Disclosure), a rule that would punish companies for disclosing information to stock analysts before releasing it to the general public. A great step forward. (A good article in the **Motley Fool** pointed out that the SEC fought some very strong special interest groups to introduce this, and it thus behoves us as investors to take advantage of it).

Coinciding with the release of the reports, companies often host *conference calls*, in which executives outline the corporate strategy and performance, and answer questions from analysts. These conference calls (often simultaneously broadcast over the web) can be an excellent way of seeing beyond the dry figures, and getting a real feeling for the pulse of the company. A good place to find these broadcasts is at the **Motley Fool** site which has an excellent *Conference Call Calendar* at quote.fool.com. A similar calendar can be found at **Yahoo Finance**. Many corporate web sites host their own broadcasts – an excellent example is **Microsoft** where you can listen to the Chief Geek himself. The biggest US site is **Best Calls** – which is completely dedicated to conference calls, and also has a good explanation of what they're all about in its Fact Sheet.

In the UK, **Yahoo Finance** has a company presentation calendar which includes some video clips. **iTruffle** has a fair number of company presentations in the smaller company sector. The main operator in the UK, however, is **RAWfinancial.com** which specialises in providing video presentations to fund managers, but now has a service for individual investors as well.

L
Best Calls: www.bestcalls.com

Itruffle: www.itruffle.com

Microsoft: www.microsoft.com/msft/speech.htm

Motley Fool (Regulation FD):
www.fool.com/Specials/2000/sp001212b.htm

Motley Fool (conference call calendar): quote.fool.com

RAWfinancial.com: www.rawfinancial.com

Yahoo Finance US (conference call calendar): biz.yahoo.com/cc/

Yahoo Finance UK (conference call calendar): uk.biz.yahoo.com/140/

CEO interviews

Q I've heard that there are some sites that have interviews with CEOs. Do you know of any?

A The internet now offers a great array of services to track company news, and also analysts' comment on that news. But sometimes there is no substitute for getting the news direct from the man, or woman, at the top of the company itself. Fortunately there is an increasing number of online services that offer exactly that.

One such is a newsletter, **The Wall Street Transcript** (TWST), which for almost 40 years has been interviewing company CEOs. Although US-based, it has recently increased its coverage of UK companies, with transcripts of many of the interviews available online at its web site. Recent interviews have included: Hamleys, nCipher, BHP Billiton, Kuoni Travel and Pittards. The TWST interviews can also be seen at **Yahoo Finance** – which may be a preferable source as they are presented rather better there.

Another site that has occasional interviews with CEOs is **t1ps.com**.

L t1ps.com: www.t1ps.com

Yahoo Finance (TWST interviews): uk.biz.yahoo.com/171/

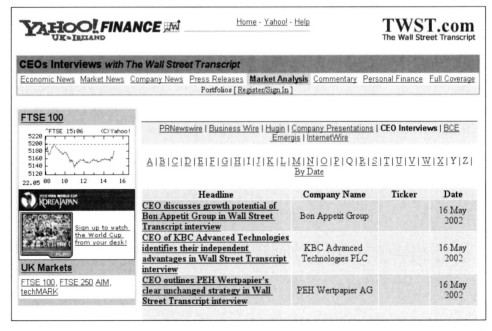

5 Technical Analysis

- Best sites for online charts
- Sites that provide streaming charts
- Drawing trend lines on charts
- Chart alerts
- Candlesticks, and point and figure charts
- On balance volume
- Golden cross alerts
- Signals from abnormal volume
- Relative Strength indicator
- Coppock Indicator
- Charts for industry sectors
- Comparing Nasdaq and FTSE charts
- How to rebase a chart online
- The problem of bad data
- Where to get technical analysis commentary

Online charts

Q Is there a straightforward interactive charting site which will enable me to plot moving averages of a stock?

A As your question implies, some online charting services have become so sophisticated that ordinary investors who are not experienced technical analysts find them overwhelming and difficult to use.

Some of the simplest charts can be found on **Bloomberg** and **Yahoo**. However, neither of these offer customisable moving averages, which for the purposes of this survey I'll take as a basic requirement.

The next place to look, therefore, is **OnVista**. Its charts offer a wider range of technical indicators (including some of the more esoteric indicators like Williams %R and Commodity Channel Index), and the user can add features by choosing from a range of display options.

More sophisticated still are the charts at **Ample** and **FT Investor**. With so many chart parameters possible, it can take a while setting each chart up. Both sites have taken account of this and built in a feature which allows you to save chart settings and apply them to other charts later without having to reconfigure.

The most advanced online charting programs currently available are the *Chart Analyser* at **nothing-ventured.com** and the interactive charts at **Downloadquotes.com**. These are both Java charts, which means, among other things, that changes to the chart parameters are displayed immediately on the chart. The nothing-ventured.com Java chart is interesting to play around with but is pipped by the one at Downloadquotes.com. It may be over-the-top for many investors, but it's a very impressive program.

L Ample: www.iii.co.uk

Bloomberg: www.bloomberg.co.uk

Downloadquotes.com: www.downloadquotes.com

FT Investor: www.ft.com/investor

nothing-ventured.com: www.nothing-ventured.com

OnVista: www.onvista.co.uk

Yahoo: finance.yahoo.co.uk

110

Streaming charts

Q Where can I find streaming charts (preferably with candlesticks and tools) for the Dow 30 Industrial Futures index?

A Almost every financial site worth its salt has a charting program, and most of them work the same way: the user inputs various parameters, clicks `submit`, a request is sent to the remote server, data is sent back and is displayed as a graph on the screen. The important point is that after the remote server has sent the data to your machine, that is the end of the communication, no further data is sent, and in most cases the remote server doesn't know whether your computer is still displaying the graph or not. The significance of this is that **the chart itself is not updated with new data**. Leave the computer running for 6 months, and the same chart will just sit there, oblivious of any movements in the markets.

For most web pages, it doesn't matter if they don't update themselves. But for some, especially those to do with financial markets, it can be inconvenient. There are ways round the problem. The easiest, not to say essential, trick is to keep hitting the `F5` function key to refresh the web page. Beyond this, some web pages are built to **automatically update** themselves every few minutes – partly in the interests of displaying up-to-date information, partly to present more banner ads. The problem with this is that it's not always obvious which pages are automatically updating, and which aren't.

In all the above cases, the remote server is passive, and only sends new data when requested to do so by your computer. With **streaming data**, on the other hand, the remote server fires a *continuous* stream of data to your computer, without waiting for a request. This can be very useful, as it means you can be fairly sure that the information on your screen is current (within the obvious constraints of the actual service you're using). A good example of a web page that uses streaming data is the FTSE 100 trigger page at **Sharepages**.

The streaming data method can also be used to produce charts which update themselves automatically. One of the best examples is *LiveCharts* on the **Lycos Finance** (formerly Quote.com) web site. Input 'VOD', and you can see a streaming chart of Vodafone trading in the US market. Unfortunately, streaming charts are rarely free, but with Lycos you can get a free month's trial.

Elsewhere, streaming charts are available on non-web proprietary systems. **myTrack**, for instance, offers intra-day streaming charts for UK and US securities. Other streaming chart services are offered by **Updata** and **IRD**. **Proquote** offers streaming charts on all UK stocks and indices as well as US indices. Dow, Nasdaq and S&P futures are due to be added soon.

L
```
IRD: www.ird.com
myTrack: www.myBroker.co.uk
Proquote: www.proquote.net
Lycos Finance: finance.lycos.com
Sharepages: www.sharepages.com
Updata: www.updata.co.uk
```

Stock index moving averages

Q Do you know where I can obtain comparisons of the moving averages for the main UK indices? For example, a chart comparing the 50 day and 200 day moving average for the FTSE 100?

A The best source of such a chart is **Ample**. From the home page, input 'UKX.L' in the `Quote search` box, and then click `FTSE 100` and then `Chart`. This will bring up a simple line chart of closing FTSE 100 values. Change the time frame to `5 years(daily ticks)`, the graph type to `Hi-Lo-Close`, and under the Advanced Plotting options, select `50 tick SMA` in the first moving average box, and `200 tick SMA` in the second, and then click `Plot`. You will see from the resulting chart that there was a fairly accurate sell signal when the FTSE Index was at 6,400 in November 2000 as the short-term moving average (50-day) moved below the long term moving average (200-day).

The purpose of a moving average is to identify a general **price trend**, without being confused by short period price fluctuations. And the point of using two moving averages (a short and a long) is to try to spot when the **trend direction changes**. Referring back to the FTSE 100 chart on Ample, you can see that both the short and long term moving averages were falling in October 2000, while the underlying index was actually increasing. It wasn't until the 50-day SMA moved down below the 200-day SMA that the downtrend (in a technical sense) was really confirmed.

Moving average calculation

The calculation of the moving average is quite straightforward. For example, the 50-day simple moving average on day 150 of the year, will be calculated as the sum of all the share prices on days 101 to 150, divided by 50. This produces an average price for the 50 trading days up to day 150. The following day (day 151) the same calculation is made but using the 50 share prices on days 102 to 151. And so on. Thus, for every day, one can plot a share price, and also the trailing average of its 50 previous share prices (its *moving average*).

As you can imagine, calculating these averages manually is not much fun. And, indeed, in the old days, technical analysis didn't involve much more than point & figure charts – which could be maintained by hand. But computers have led to a delightful proliferation of weird and wonderful technical analysis indicators.

Like most technical analysis, the study of moving averages assumes that a stock's historic price behaviour has something to say about its future performance. Whether it really does, of course, is the topic of one of the most popular religious wars in finance. If unbelievers can suspend their disbelief for a moment, we can all probably agree that if a stock's historic price behaviour *is* significant, then its most recent price movements will be more significant than those a long time ago. In other words, the movement of a share price yesterday, has more to say about its likely performance tomorrow, than the share's behaviour one year ago.

If this is indeed the case, then the calculation of the moving average (as described above) is somewhat flawed, because all historic share prices were given the same weighting. There are several methods to compensate for this, most of which give greater weight to the most recent prices. The most common method is the calculation of an *exponential moving average*, normally abbreviated to EMA to distinguish it from the simple moving average (SMA).

Exponential moving average

To see how exponential moving averages work, return to Ample and open a new browser window (`Ctrl-N`). If the new browser doesn't display an identical chart to the original, copy the original page URL into the clipboard, switch to the new window, paste the URL into `Location box`, and hit `Return`. In the new window, in the bottom `Advanced Plotting` options, change the moving average options to `50 tick EMA` and `200 tick EMA`. Now by `Alt-Tab`'ing between the two windows (or re-sizing and displaying both windows on the same screen, if your screen is large enough), you can compare the two moving average types.

At first glance, there's not much difference. But look closer at the period from the end of 1998 to the beginning of 1999, when the FTSE 100 rebounded from 4,600 to 6,600. Using the SMA as a buy signal (short-term moving up through the long-term), would have got you into the index at a level of around 6,100 – when most of the trend was over. However, the EMA would have got you into the index at around the 5,500 level.

That does not imply that the exponential moving average is automatically always better than the simple moving average. Sometimes it works, and sometimes it doesn't work – like so much of technical analysis. Further information on moving averages can be found at the Metastock web site.

Ample: www.iii.co.uk

Metastock (TA glossary): www.equis.com/free/taaz/index.html

113

Trend lines

Q Do you know of a web page that will allow me to add trend lines to its charting system?

A Interactive Java charts are required for drawing trendlines. Two good examples are the Chart Analyser at **nothing-ventured.com** and the interactive chart at **Downloadquotes.com**.

In the US the popular technical analysis program, **Metastock**, has a great charting web site with excellent Java charts. For example, input 'VOD' (ticker symbol for Vodafone), and trend lines can be drawn on the resulting chart by simply dragging the mouse. Unfortunately, this service is limited to US stocks – Vodafone works in this case (as would a hundred other UK stocks) because it trades ADRs in the US.

Another alternative would be **myTrack**, for both UK and US stocks, which includes the great AIQ charts, offering interactive trend line drawing.

L Downloadquotes.com: www.downloadquotes.com

Metastock: www.equis.com

myTrack: www.mybroker.co.uk

nothing-ventured.com: www.nothing-ventured.com

Chart alerts

Q I have found several US sites that scan for chart patterns, and provide tips and alerts based on technical analysis. These include bollingeronbollingerbands.com, hardrightedge.com, and litwick.com. Do you know of any sites that provide a similar service for UK stocks?

A The web sites you mention are good. I also like **Barchart.com**, **Sixer.com** and **AvidTrader**. A good list of online services like these can be found at the Stock Pick Blanket page of **The Security Blanket**.

There aren't many similar services in the UK. The closest is probably **Investtech**. It doesn't yet have alerts, but is a clever service nevertheless. Also, the premium section of **ADVFN** has daily lists of chart breakout stocks.

The best services however are probably not on web sites. For example, **Omnitrader** and **AIQ** are two popular expert trading system programs that identify trading opportunities and work with UK data. A popular UK equivalent would be **Updata**.

L ADVFN (chart breakouts): www.advfn.com/cmn/tl/movers.php3

AIQ: www.aiqsystems.com

AvidTrader: www.avidinfo.com

Barchart.com: www.barchart.com

Investtech: www.investtech.com/uk/

Omnitrader: www.omnitrader.com

The Security Blanket: www.thesecurityblanket.com/tradingideas/

Sixer.com: www.sixer.com

Updata: www.updata.co.uk

Q Do you know of any web sites which offer candlestick and point & figure charts?

A When I used to work for a Japanese broker, a huge package would be delivered every month containing the updated, definitive candlestick chart books for Japanese stocks. As the word spread, clients would be left hanging on the phone as brokers jumped over desks to grab their copies and write their names on the front covers – rather like the first day at school. Such was the importance of these charts that a salesman would feel naked without them.

Developed in Japan, **candlestick charts** are now widely available in the West, thanks to pioneers like Steve Nison, (author of *Japanese Candlestick Charting Techniques*). The charts first started appearing in programs such as **MetaStock**, but are now available on many web sites including **Ample** and **FT Investor**. FT Investor, by the way, has by far the widest range of chart types on offer, including: OHLC, Candlestick, Mountain, Bar Charts, Dot, Close, and Logarithmic. It even has a chart type called *Hide Price*, which is intriguing. As the title suggests, you get a chart, with . . . nothing. Perhaps it's for stocks that have fallen so far that investors would rather not see the gruesome details.

Like candlesticks, **point & figure charts** have been around for a long time. When computers arrived, OHLC bar charts began to take over, but no doubt there are still some investors who construct p&fs using pencil and paper in the, possibly justified, belief that it gives them a better feel for price movement. The main attraction of p&fs is that they cut out the 'noise' of OHLC charts, and allow general price trends to become more apparent.

P&f charts are now included on various proprietary charting programs, but have not yet made an impact on the web. In fact, I know of no UK web site that offers them. The best US site is **StockCharts**, which offers a great range of charts including p&f. Their charts can be configured for variable box and reversal size, logarithmic or traditional plots, trend lines can be drawn and the charts can be expanded full size (with no loss of definition). Unfortunately StockCharts only has data for US stocks, but don't forget that whatever works for US stocks also works for UK ADRs (UK stocks trading in the US). For example, input 'VOD' as the ticker symbol, and you'll get a p&f chart for Vodafone. If you want to learn more about candlestick and p&f charts, there are some excellent web-based tutorials at **Chart Patterns**, **MetaStock** and **StockCharts**. The StockCharts site also carries some TA columns from experts like Mitch Harris who specialises in p&f. There's probably no better way to understand p&f charts than to read the archive of his comments. Conveniently, each chart recommendation is linked to a current chart, so the subsequent accuracy of the forecast can be assessed.

L
```
Ample: www.iii.co.uk
Chart Patterns: www.chartpatterns.com
FT Investor: www.ft.com/investor
MetaStock: www.equis.com
Stock Charts: www.stockcharts.com
Stock Charts (TA columns): www.stockcharts.com/commentary/
```

On balance volume

Q In previous articles you've referred a few times to a technical indicator called 'On Balance Volume'. Could you explain what this is and where it is available on the web?

A If a share price rises 10% in one day, that might seem like an important increase. However, if that rise was accomplished on very low turnover - say, just 30% of the average daily turnover, the true strength of the share price may be questionable. This is because in thin trading (low turnover) it can be easy for a few small orders to affect the share price; and those few trades should not be interpreted as representing a significant change in market view. Conversely, if a share price rises on unusually high volume, this can be a good indicator that there is significant buying activity and that the share price rise is meaningful.

The lesson from this is that knowledge of price movements by itself is not always enough. It's also important to know what the accompanying volume was. And the problem with top ten *mover* lists (i.e. of shares increasing or decreasing in price), is that the rankings can be dominated by shares that have drifted up or down on insignificant volume. Which begs the question - *what is significant volume?*

On balance volume (OBV) is a technical indicator that tries to answer this by relating price action to turnover activity. It is a momentum indicator which tracks volume flowing *into* a share (driving it up) or *out of* a share (driving it down). The indicator can be used in a number of different ways. An underlying premise is that it can be used to monitor smart money flowing into a share, anticipating a sharp increase in the share price itself. It can also be used to confirm significant share price movements. The best way I can explain this is by using an example from **Ample** or **FT Investor**, both of which include the OBV indicator.

For this example we'll use the charts on Ample, and look at the daily closing price of AstraZeneca in 2000. At the bottom of the web page, select `On Balance Volume`, in the first indicator box, and then click `Plot`. After the page has been re-drawn you'll see a new chart, below the volume chart, with a line that fluctuates roughly between −50m and +50m. This line is a running total of share volume: if a share price increases on a day, that day's share volume is added to the cumulative OBV, if the share prices falls, the volume is subtracted from the OBV. That's it, quite simple.

Looking at the Astra Zeneca chart, you can see that from June to October 2000, its share price rose strongly. Furthermore, over this period, the OBV also rose fairly steadily, indicating that the share price rise was supported by volume flowing *into* the share. This was a good sign. The share price then fell sharply to the end of October 2000, but staged a recovery from the beginning of November to the beginning of December. The question at the time would have been whether this was a real recovery, a prelude to further price increases, or merely a technical bounce with the June-October uptrend decidedly broken. In this case, reference to the OBV may have helped. We can see that during November 2000 although the share price rose from around 3150 to 3600, the OBV moved very little, in fact it decreased. The lesson here was that the share price increase was not supported by the OBV indicator.

Personally, I find the OBV quite useful in this *non-confirmation* role. In other words I am distrustful of price movements that are not supported by supporting volume activity. The role of the OBV in confirming price movement is possibly less useful. For example, if a share price is in an uptrend, there are many indicators that will confirm that. And as to whether the OBV can be used to actually anticipate price movements, by revealing early flows of the *smart money*, I am sceptical.

OBV calculation

Because the OBV is quite a simple indicator, it can be interesting to calculate it yourself. To illustrate this, I've created a demonstration spreadsheet (`obv.xls`: download from this book's web site), with historic share price data from AstraZenca downloaded from **Yahoo Finance**. The calculation of the OBV indicator is in column D, and the two charts display the share price and the OBV, which should match those from the **Ample** web page.

I can imagine some people wondering what on earth the point is doing this on a spreadsheet, when, as I said, the OBV indicator can be freely seen on many web sites. There are several reasons. First, I am suspicious of all black box calculations, and prefer to thoroughly understand an indicator before using it. If you use an indicator and it fails, you won't have learned much unless you understand why it failed – and to understand that, a knowledge of the indicator's 'inner workings' is required.

One of the features of technical analysis is that it tends to be self-fulfilling, in that the accuracy of an indicator increases with the number of people following it. Classic examples of this would be support and resistance lines. And acting on common, black-box indicators (such as OBV) from free web sites may reassuringly dictate that one trades with the herd. But these technical indicators are not tried and tested over the centuries. Many have been devised in just the last few years (thanks to computers). It may be that the accuracy of some indicators can be improved by adapting them for specific circumstances. On the second sheet of the spreadsheet, I've calculated an *adjusted OBV* indicator that uses daily share price highs and lows, instead of closing prices, to identify *up* days and *down* days. In this case, I don't think it improves the indicator very much. But there are plenty of other refinements that could be tried.

Ample: www.iii.co.uk

FT Investor: www.ft.com/investor

Yahoo Finance: www.yahoo.co.uk

Golden Cross alerts

Q Do you know of any free web site that monitors charts for a 'golden cross' buy signal and sell signals, or are they all expensive subscription sites?

A For readers who don't already know, a *Golden Cross* is a technical indicator that aims to identify when a price is changing direction, either from trending downwards to upwards, or vice versa. This is monitored by tracking two moving averages (a short-term and a long-term) of the stock. When the short-term moving average (MA) moves up through the long-term MA the chart is said to form a Golden Cross. This is a **buy signal**, as the chart is indicating that the price is moving into an uptrend. A *Dead Cross* occurs when the short-term MA moves down through the long-term MA – which is a **sell signal**. If you want to read more about this, I'd recommend John Murphy's definitive book *Technical Analysis of the Financial Markets*.

On the definition given, the Golden Cross might seem a fairly easy way to make money. But, it's not quite as straightforward as that. In the description above I was deliberately vague about the exact parameters to be used for the moving averages. In practice, there's a huge range of different moving average combinations that can be used. Commonly a 10-day period is used for the short-term MA, while 20-day is used the long-term MA. But this is not always the best combination. There is also a choice of whether to use simple moving averages, exponential or another type. One combination of moving averages may give very good buy and sell signals for trading, while another combination may give terrible signals.

For many traders, there is no short-cut for choosing the best combination. Long experience with a particular stock and patient experimentation with different parameters may eventually identify a combination that can be traded more profitably than others. In some cases, the long experience can be replaced by testing on historic data. Programs such as **MetaStock** allow users to back-test trading signals (including those generated by moving averages), to assess their profitability. This is very useful but can still take a long time, as there is such a large number of possible parameter combinations. Fortunately, there's another program, **TradeStation**, that automatically optimises parameters for trading systems. In this case, the program would iterate through all parameter combinations and identify the most profitable for a specific stock.

If you don't want to do this work yourself (and TradeStation is not cheap), there are a number of programs that automatically scan the market looking for trading opportunities; an example is the popular **OmniTrader**. Unfortunately this type of service is definitely in the *value added* category, and most will have a charge. The closest free service is **Investtech**, which, while not highlighting Golden Crosses specifically, does monitor other technical opportunities.

In the UK you could consider buying **Sharescope** software which, while not free, is a great program and hardly expensive. Sharescope has recently introduced a new feature called *Data Mining*, which allows various, fairly advanced filters to be constructed for the UK market. It includes the ability to filter for stocks forming Golden Crosses as buy signals.

This type of technical analysis was a strong feature of the **Indexia** programs. Now that Indexia has been acquired by **Updata**, it's likely that Updata will also include this type of analysis soon.

However, be aware that scanning a whole market for Golden Crosses may not be very effective. This is because each stock will have its own specific set of parameters to optimise the strength of trading signals, which argues against scanning all stocks with just one set of parameters.

If you really want to get into this type of analysis you may find the US an easier market to trade, from the point of view of access to information (and the ability to short stocks on Dead Crosses). A couple of good sites that produce trading signals are **Barchart** and **Sixer**.

Barchart.com: www.barchart.com

Investtech: www.investtech.com

MetaStock: www.equis.com

OmniTrader: www.omnitrader.com

Sharescope: www.sharescope.co.uk

Sixer.com: www.sixer.com

TradeStation: www.omegaresearch.com

Updata: www.updata.co.uk

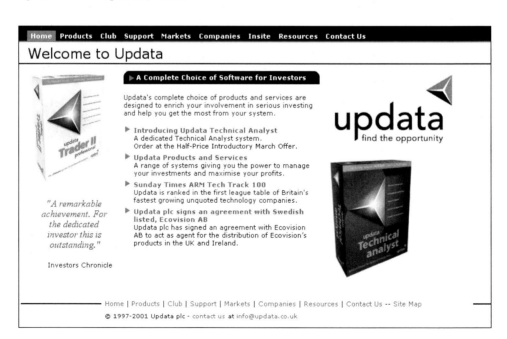

120

Abnormal volume

Q Do you know of any web site that alerts you to abnormal volumes being traded in stocks i.e. volumes way above the average?

A In a previous article I explained the technical analysis indicator, *On Balance Volume* (OBV). The idea behind the indicator is that **share price movements themselves are not significant, unless the activity is supported by a corresponding increase in the share's trading volume**. If a share price rises, but the share's trading volume remains in its normal range, the price increase is considered insignificant and unlikely to continue. Whereas if a price is supported by an increase in trading volume, then the price activity is deemed significant. The OBV quantifies this in a simple calculation, but it is just a statement of common sense when you think about it.

Turning the above concept around, an abnormal increase in a share's trading volume can be seen to signify a potentially interesting opportunity. On an individual share basis this can be monitored fairly easily. A web site such as **Comdirect** gives figures for a share's average daily turnover for the previous 20-day or 52-week period.

For example, in the case of Inveresk [IVS], its average turnover for those two periods is £30m and £23m. If you see that Inveresk has traded over £80m in one day – the position as I write – it is reasonable to deduce that something's up!

If you follow a small portfolio of shares closely, you soon get to know what the normal turnover ranges for each share are and can spot anything out of the ordinary quickly. To make this monitoring even easier, some web sites (such as **ADVFN**) have services that will automatically alert you to a share hitting a pre-configured volume level.

What you really want, of course, is a service that monitors the whole market, and identifies those shares displaying *abnormal* trading volume. Unfortunately, this type of service is usually considered a premium service, and attracts a fee. ADVFN offers such service in the *Premium Section* of its *Lists*.

For example, at the time of writing there are six stocks with trading volumes over their previous 52-week high for volume (including: Bell Group [BEL] and NMT Group [NMT]).

For further examples of this service we have to leave the web, and go to specialist software applications such as **Updata** and **Sharescope**. **myTrack** also has a useful set of market scans including: most active stocks hitting daily or 52-week prices highs.

L ADVFN: www.advfn.com

Comdirect: www.comdirect.co.uk

myTrack: www.mybroker.co.uk

Sharescope: www.sharescope.co.uk

Updata: www.updata.co.uk

Q Is there anywhere on the internet where I can find the RSI of a company's share price, for 1 month, 3 months and 12 months, which is *not* in graphical form?

A A deceptively simple question, but one that turned out to be much trickier to answer than I expected. Of course, many web sites now offer charts with the RSI (Relative Strength Index) - a technical indicator that attempts to highlight whether a share is over-bought or over-sold. But none of these charts allows examination of the underlying data, which is the nub of your question.

The web site that comes closest is **Investtech.com**, which ranks stocks with the highest and lowest RSI values. Additionally, it also indicates high (over 70) and low (below 30) RSI values on its price charts by colouring the price plot red and green respectively, which is a novel idea I haven't seen used elsewhere. But no historic data.

Another site that comes close, for US stocks at least, is **Barchart.com**. This site has an extraordinary collection of technical data, including current values for the 9, 14, 20 and 50 day RSI – but, again, no historic data.

That leaves a couple of reliable programs that aren't strictly web sites. First is **myTrack**. Let's say we are looking for historic RSI values for Vodafone. Type the symbol 'VOD-L' (note, this is the symbol for Vodafone used in myTrack) in the portfolio, right-click on the symbol, and select `AIQ Historical Charting`. Right-click on the chart, select `Indicators`, scroll down to `RSI Wilder` and select that. Note that different time parameters can be chosen for the RSI. A standard RSI chart should now appear at the bottom of the screen. Hover the mouse pointer again over the chart and right-click, this time selecting `Cursor Bug`. If you now hover the mouse pointer over the RSI chart, an indicator top right will display the date and RSI value for each day.

A similar capability exists on **Sharescope**. Some investors may prefer this over myTrack, as it is more directly focused on UK stocks. In a similar fashion to myTrack, select a stock in Sharescope, switch to the chart page, right-click on the chart, select `Add Indicator`, and then `RSI` (again, there is a choice of time parameter). The RSI chart appears, with the historic RSI displayed in the program's bottom status bar, where specific days can be chosen by dragging the mouse over the chart.

L Barchart.com: www.barchart.com

Investtech: www.investtech.com

myTrack: www.mybroker.co.uk

Sharescope: www.sharescope.co.uk

Customising RSI parameters

Q Are there any charting services on the web which offer RSI with periods that can be customised? All the chart services I've seen only offer an RSI indicator with a fixed period of 14 or 21, whereas I need periods of 5 or 9.

A As you say, while RSI indicators are common on many web sites, nearly all have a fixed period. Two sites with customisable RSI periods are **ADVFN** and **Reuters**.

Reuters, which until now has had a rather muddled approach to the web, might finally be getting its act together. Its recently re-designed web site is beginning to offer a critical mass of useful information to investors, especially now that it is integrating the brokerage research service of Multexinvestor into the Reuters main web site. The web site now offers share price data, company profiles, aggregation of brokerage research and analysts forecasts. In addition, it has an advanced charting service which, while not particularly advanced by today's standards, does at least offer an RSI indicator with periods that can be customised. While traders and active investors will still prefer the more sophisticated data services from ADVFN, this re-vamped Reuters web site could become the service of choice for many ordinary stock investors.

L ADVFN: www.advfn.com

Reuters: www.reuters.co.uk

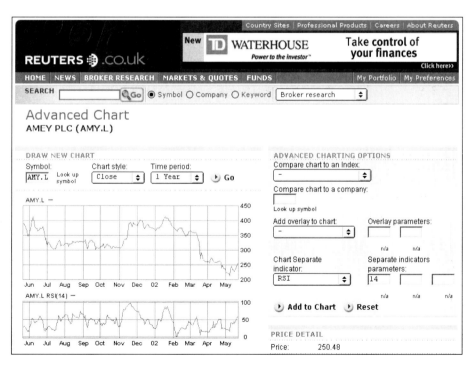

The Coppock Indicator

Q I want to produce spreadsheets to create my own Coppock indicators for FT 30, FTSE 100, UK Government Securities, FTSE Gold Mines, Dow Jones Industrials, Hang Seng, Nikkei 225, etc. and thus need last 36 months closing indices for these markets. Do you know where can I obtain this historic data?

A The best source for historic data like this is **Yahoo Finance**. It has a historic data service where daily/weekly/monthly closing prices for stocks and indices can be downloaded. If Yahoo doesn't have a specific data series, you might have to use a premium charge data service such as **Download.com** or **Global Financial Data**.

For readers who don't already know, the *Coppock Indicator* was devised in 1962 as an oscillator to identify significant bottoms in the stock market. *Investors Chronicle* created its own revised version in 1963.

The basic indicator itself is fairly easy to calculate. To illustrate this, I've created a spreadsheet with a demonstration calculation (`ftse100-coppock.xls`: download from this book's web site). The FTSE 100 data for the calculation was downloaded from **Yahoo Finance**. First the rate of change over 11 and 14 months is calculated (the percentage movement in the index over those two periods). A moving average is then taken of the sum of the two rates of change. Note that the moving average is not a simple moving average but a front-weighted (or *exponential*) moving average. The Coppock Indicator calculated here is the standard version proposed by Edwin Coppock, not the revised IC version.

Don't forget, the absolute value of the Indicator is not interesting; rather, it's the change in direction of the oscillator that you are looking out for. Don't forget also that the calculation of such technical indicators is not carved in stone. The best investors take indicators such as this as a starting point, and adapt and improve them as they see appropriate.

L Download.com: www.downloadquotes.com

Global Financial Data: www.globalfindata.com

Yahoo Finance: finance.yahoo.co.uk

Yahoo Finance (historic FTSE100 data):
uk.table.finance.yahoo.com/k?s=^ftse&g=d

Long-term index charts

Q I'm looking for a long-term (50+ years) chart of the Dow Jones Industrials Index. Can I find this on the web?

A Yes, there are a number of sources of long-term charts. First you might like to look at **TradingCharts.com**, which although it only has a two-year perspective, includes a very detailed current technical report of the DJIA. Good quick sources of long-term (roughly 30 years) charts can be found at **Martin Capital** and **Moore Research Center**. These include stock index, interest rate, currency, commodity and economic charts.

A truly long-term chart of the DJIA can be found at the Historical Chart Gallery of **StockCharts.com**, which covers a period 1900-2001. The long-term chart does at least appear to support the view that equities go up in the long term. So, that's all right then. Or, is it? Closer study of the chart reveals the uncomfortable fact that although the plotted line starts bottom left of the picture, and ends top right, there are long periods (notably 1966-82) when the Index did very little indeed. This suggests that long-term in the case of equities should mean something of the order of 20 years - not the five-year view that many investors and pundits implicitly take.

Further, the postulate, *equities go up in the long term* is not strictly correct. The majority of companies go bust in the long-term. What does appear to be true, as evidenced by the long-term charts, is that equity *indices* go up in the long term, not necessarily individual equities themselves. Most indices are continually renewed animals: weak members are ejected, and replaced by new strong companies. As a consequence, the constituents of the DJIA, or the FTSE 100, indices are very different from a few decades ago.

Another good site with long-term charts is **Lowrisk** with charts (from 1942) of the S&P500 dividend yield and PE ratio – again, all pretty bearish. There's a chart that compares the recent fall in the S&P500 Index with previous bear markets. The current level of 1,000 makes it equivalent to the fall experienced in 1987; a fall to 800 would equate to the 1973-74 bear market, or to 600 would match the fall in the Nikkei Index. A further selection of long-term charts can be seen at: **Cross Currents**, **Decision Point**, **Dr Edward Yardeni** and **LongWaves**.

L
Cross Currents: www.cross-currents.net

Decision Point: www.decisionpoint.com

Dr Edward Yardeni: www.yardeni.com/finmkts.asp

LongWaves: csf.colorado.edu/forums/longwaves/

Lowrisk: www.lowrisk.com

Martin Capital: www.martincapital.com/charts.htm

Moore Research Center (long-term charts): www.mrci.com/pdf/

StockCharts.com (Historical Chart Gallery): stockcharts.com/charts/historical/

TradingCharts.com (Dow Jones technical chart): futures.tradingcharts.com/chart/DW/W

TradingCharts.com (commodity charts): www.tfc-charts.w2d.com/chart/

Charting sectors

Q Is there a website where I can view charts of sectors of the stockmarket (ie. banks, telecoms, media etc)? At the moment I can view the FTSE or the FTSE 250 charts but can't find any for sectors.

A Lots of web sites provide charts which allow you to compare a company's share price performance with the performance of the major indices, but very few allow you to benchmark against an index of the sector which the company operates in. Two that do are **Ample** and **Comdirect**. A better service, though, is on offer at **FT Investor** where you can plot a chart of a share against any one of 53 sector indices.

One of the few sites that allows sector charts to be plotted individually is **ADVFN**. For example, on ADVFN input the symbol 'UB04' to get a chart of the mining sector.

L ADVFN: www.advfn.com

Ample: www.iii.co.uk

Comdirect: www. comdirect.co.uk

FT Investor: www.ft.com/investor

Nasdaq and FTSE 100 chart

Q I want to compare the performance of the Nasdaq Index against the FTSE 100 over the last two years. Is there a web site where I can plot their charts together?

A The best charting service for this type of thing is **FT Investor**. From the home page, click FTSE 100 (in the left column), and then click interactive charting. This will create a simple one-year chart of the FTSE 100. In the controls at the bottom, change the time frame to 2 years, and select Nasdaq, in the index comparison box. You'll notice that there's quite a good range of market indices that can be plotted against each other, including: DJIA, S&P500, FTSE All Share, DAX, and CAC 40.

Don't forget, if you want to save this chart, position the mouse pointer over the chart, right-click and select Save picture as… from the pop up box. Alternatively, select copy, switch to another program (e.g. MS Word) and select Edit > Paste from the menu bar, which will paste the graphic directly into the program.

If you want to see a really scary chart, take a look at the Nasdaq chart at **Lowrisk**. This is the web site of a US newsletter, *Walker Market Letter*, and the page compares this year's Nasdaq collapse with the meltdown in the Japanese Nikkei index from 1990. The chart shows the Nasdaq superimposed over the Nikkei, with both indices' timeline shifted to start from the date of their respective pre-crash highs. The similarity between the patterns of the two indices decline so far is quite eerie. In the unlikely event that Nasdaq continues to mimic the Nikkei, the former would have another 500 points to fall yet, and would not rebound above 2600 before the year 2010. A cheery thought.

The same page also compares the 2000-2002 bear market to previous Nasdaq falls in 1973, 1983, 1987 and 1989. This year has seen a far more precipitous fall than any known before, although it still needs to fall a further 500 points to match the crash of 1973-74.

L FT Investor: www.ft.com/investor

Lowrisk (Nasdaq): www.lowrisk.com/nasdaq-bear.htm

Rebasing charts against the FTSE 100 Index

Q Many of the charts presented in Investors Chronicle have the FTSE 100 index 'rebased'. Can you explain what this is and why it's necessary?

A If a company's share price rises, say, 30% over a period, that might be thought of as quite good; but if the general stock market had increased 60% over the same period, the performance wouldn't seem so good. It's therefore quite common when analysing the share price performance of a company to compare it against an appropriate benchmark. Such a benchmark might be a general market index (such as the FTSE 100), a sector index, or another company's share price in the same industry.

OK, you might think, that's pretty straightforward, where's the problem?

The trouble is that measuring comparative performance is a little more involved than just laying one chart on top of another. It usually requires some of the data to be rebased in order for the comparison to make any sense.

To illustrate this I've created a spreadsheet (`tsco_ftse100.xls`: download from this book's web site) to compare the performance of Royal & Sun Alliance [RSA] against the FTSE 100 index as a benchmark. In the spreadsheet, the date appears in column A, the RSA share price in column B, and the FTSE 100 Index in column C, to the right of which are a series of charts. These charts are for illustration purposes only – time has not been spent formatting them to the best configuration.

Problems of using the same Y-axis

The first chart displays a simple plot of the closing price of RSA over the last 5 years; starting at around 350 in November 1995, the share price rose to just over 800 in March 1998, before falling to a low of 300 in March of this year and to end at around 500 today. So, over the whole period, an increase from 350 to 500 represents a rise of about 42%. Is that good? There are many ways to judge this, but we will compare its performance over the period against the market (as represented by the FTSE 100 index). Our first attempt to compare the two data series is shown in Chart 2, where something seems to have gone awry. At the very top of the chart is a pink line (FTSE 100) fluctuating in a range 4,000-6,000, while at the very bottom of the chart is a blue line (RSA) which to all intents and purposes looks pretty much a horizontal line. If this is supposed to compare the performance of RSA against FTSE 100, it's not doing a very good job. What's wrong? The problem is that the two data series have very different absolute values and ranges (RSA: 300-800; FTSE 100:4,000-7,000), such that when they are plotted on the same Y-axis the RSA data gets lost on a Y-axis that has a range 0-8,000.

Two Y-axes

One solution to this is to plot both series on the same chart, but using two Y-axes (right and left), one for each data series. The result is displayed in Chart 3. The RSA data series (blue) can be measured against the left axis, while the FTSE

128

(pink) is measured against the right axis. This chart is certainly better than the previous one, as this time both lines fill the vertical space equally. And if the graph resolution was adequate we could discover the exact price of RSA and the FTSE 100 on any day over the period should we want to. But what we still don't have is a sense of the relative performance. For example, if one data series had fluctuated in a narrow 10% price band over the whole period, while the other data series had fluctuated up or down over 90%, you would not immediately be able to appreciate that by merely looking at the lines on the charts, without mentally calculating the price ranges on the axes. And it is this **relative performance** that we are really interested in. So some further tweaking is required, and this is where rebasing comes into the picture.

Rebasing one data series

A solution is to rebase one of the data series to the starting point of the other series - in this case, rebase the FTSE 100 data to that of RSA. Col D of the spreadsheet shows how this rebasing is calculated. Effectively, the whole of the FTSE 100 data is moved to start at the initial price of RSA (356), and Chart 4 displays what happens when we plot RSA against the FTSE 100 data that has been rebased to that of RSA. This is getting closer to what we want. You can see the actual share price of RSA on the Y-axis, and also its performance relative to the FTSE 100. One feature shown up on this chart – not previously discernible – is that RSA strongly out-performed the Index in the early part of 1998.

Rebasing both series to 100

A refinement of this chart is to rebase both data series to start at 100 (the calculations are shown in columns E, F on the spreadsheet). As can be seen in Chart 5, the result looks identical to the previous chart, but the absolute share price axis has been replaced with an indexed one, allowing the percentage performance to be read directly from the chart. For example, RSA peaked in March 1998, at around 220 (representing a percentage increase of 120%), and closed recently at about 125 (representing a rise over the whole period of 25%); whereas the FTSE 100 can be seen to have risen 80% over the period.

Turning to the net, web sites treat price performance comparisons in slightly different ways, so it's important to appreciate exactly what type of chart you're looking at. For example, if you look at an RSA chart on **ADVFN** over 5 years compared against the FTSE 100 (note: line, rather than bar, charts are best to use for relative performance charts), they employ the two-axis approach as used by *Chart 3* in the spreadsheet. By contrast, **Ample** rebases the FTSE 100 Index to the starting price of RSA (*Chart 4* style). This is fine, but it means you can't simply read off the percentage performance. This can be done at **Moneyextra**, which has rebased both data series to 100 (*Chart 5* style); although rather confusingly they add "%" signs to the Y-axis, which makes a 50% price increase read like 150%. The best comparison charts are probably at **FT Investor**, which rebases both series to 100, but then shifts the starting point to zero, making it very simple to directly read the exact percentage performance at any point.

ADVFN: www.advfn.com

Ample: www.iii.co.uk

FT Investor: www.ft.com/investor

Moneyextra: www.moneyextra.com

Bad data

Q I use a charting facility to time trades, but more and more frequently I'm seeing off-the-scale trades which compress the 1 day and 10 day trading range into a meaningless straight line. What causes this and is there an internet charting source that doesn't have this problem?

A Unfortunately this can be a problem with some online charting packages. Before criticising them too much, it is worth remembering that until very recently if you wanted interactive stock charts you had to subscribe to an expensive proprietary charting service. Today, a huge range of online charting packages is now freely available on many web sites. That is the good news. The bad news is that the quality of data is not always of the highest order. And the old adage, you get what you pay for, is as true as it always has been. If uncompromising quality is a priority for you, you may have to bite the bullet and pay up for a service that offers clean data.

The reasons for odd prices occurring in data series are many. Sometimes they result from special trades, sometimes they are simple mistakes. Whatever the cause, they are the bane of investors using charts. An example I am looking at now is a 3-month OHLC bar chart of Vodafone on **FT Investor**, where, around 21 Sep, a suspiciously elongated bar peaks at 340p. Admittedly, dodgy data is not a new phenomenon introduced by the internet; it's always existed, even on expensive charting services. At least on the web, you have the ability to check one service easily with another. In this case, I compared the FT Investor chart with a similar 3-month charts on **Ample**. This shows Vodafone had a daily high of about 257 – well below the 340 suggested by FT Investor.

Does this mean that one should ditch FT Investor as no good?

No. All free online charting services will occasionally have similar problems. But as mentioned above, at least with the internet you have the option of switching to other web sites when necessary; the corollary being that it is dangerous to rely on just the one online service. But, careful – other web sites won't necessarily be better. It depends on where they source their data. If, for example, you look at the 3-month bar chart for Vodafone on **Motley Fool**, you will find the same dubious data for the same day. This is because the Fool buys its charting service from BigCharts.com – the same company that FT Investor uses. So, not only should the shrewd investor know of several alternative charting web sites, it's also useful to take note of the original source of the charts (this is usually indicated in small print below the chart).

L Ample: www.iii.co.uk

FT Investor: www.ft.com/investor

Motley Fool: www.fool.co.uk

Technical analysis commentary

Q I used to get the technical analysis weekly report on UK-iNvest. Since being taken over by ADVFN, it has disappeared. Is there another site giving a similar TA overview?

A Many sites with TA commentary have closed, notably MarketEye, UK-iNvest, TheStreet.co.uk, investorevolution and UnionCAL. Of those that remain:

• **Sharecast** has a frequent, but not regular, technical analysis commentary; **FT Investor** has the occasional article; **David Schwartz**, the market historian, provides daily TA comment.

• **GNI**, has a great series of market reports on its web site. It also has live commentary throughout the day, which includes frequent technical observations.

• The spread betting firm **Financial Spreads** has a daily market comment, but the technical comment is fairly basic.

• There are some subscription sites that provide TA commentary: **Chartanalysts**, incorporating the Fuller Markets report, specialises in point & figure. **Investtech.com** has an interesting daily commentary generated entirely by a computer program.

• *Shares* columnist Zak Mir provides a daily market outlook from a TA perspective, on **t1ps.com**. He also contributes to **CityComment**.

• Stockcube (which runs the **Chartanalysts service**) has launched a web site called **ShareStar** with technical analysis aimed at the UK investor.

• **TradingCentral.com**, a French company which follows US & European markets, has a strong TA emphasis. In its *Trading Ideas* section, it provides recommendations throughout the day, like - '*We now buy Reckitt Benckiser at 1081p with a target at 1200p and a stop order at 1030p at the close'*. It also has a fun section called *Ask our analysts*, where you can pose questions directly and get a quick reply. The vocabulary of TA is fairly anglicised so you shouldn't have too much trouble understanding references to e.g. *le double top*. The service costs around 200 Euros, but it's professional level (80% of revenues come from banks and brokers) and for hard-core traders could be well worth it.

L
```
Chartanalysts: www.chartanalysts.com
CityComment: www.citycomment.co.uk
David Schwartz: www.schwartztrends.com
Financial Spreads: www.finspreads.com
FT Investor: www.ft.com/investor
GNI TA commentary (onewaybet.com): www.onewaybet.com
GNI: www.gni.co.uk
Investtech.com: www.investtech.com/uk/
Sharecast: www.sharecast.co.uk
ShareStar: www.sharestar-uk.com
t1ps.com: www.t1ps.com
TradingCentral.com: www.TradingCentral.com
```

Technical Analysis Plain and Simple

by Michael Kahn
FT Prentice-Hall, 1999, paperback, 230 pages

So many TA books are abstract or academic in style and completely unsuited to ordinary investors. This one is different. It describes the key concepts simply and clearly. Then it explains commonly used charting patterns, and how you can use them in trading situations to make money. There's little to choose between this book and Alistair Blair's above (they're both good) but this is, perhaps, a notch or two up on the difficulty scale.

Gi price £18.69 (rrp £21.99), Code 10562

Technical Analysis of the Financial Markets

by John Murphy
NYIF, 1998, hardback, 542 pages

There are two books that compete for the title 'bible of technical analysis' and this is one of them. Edited by John Murphy, it covers everything you'd ever want to know about moving averages, line charts, Fibonacci ratios, Elliott Wave, candlesticks, head and shoulders, tops and bottoms, and every other branch of TA. It's probably not the book to buy if you're completely new to TA, but if you've read a primer or two and have decided that this approach appeals to you, at some point you're going to want this in your library. Recommended by the Society of Technical Analysts.

Gi price £39.99 (rrp £49.99), Code 10044

Other popular technical analysis books

Note: we have ≥350 books on TA. Please ask if you don't see the one you want.

All New Guide to the 3-Point Reversal Method, by Michael Burke, 1990, Gi price £14.95, Code 0927

Bollinger on Bollinger Bands, by John Bollinger, hb, 2001, Gi price £31.44 (rrp £36.99), Code 13847

Come Into My Trading Room, by Alexander Elder, hb, 2002, Gi price £31.88 (rrp £37.50), Code 14556

The Elliott Wave Principle, by Robert Prechter, hb, 2000, Gi price £19.99 (rrp £24.99), Code 9944

Encyclopedia of Trading Strategies, by Jeffrey Katz, hb, Gi price £33.14 (rrp £38.99), Code 12709

How Charts Can Help You in the Stock Market, by William Jiler, pb, Gi price £14.20, Code 1301

Japanese Candlestick Charting, by Steve Nison, hb, 2001, Gi price £48.59 (rrp £53.99), Code 14229

The Magic of Moving Averages, by Arthur Scot Lowry, pb, 1998, Gi price £17.94 (rrp £21.10), Code 9697

Martin Pring's Intro to Technical Analysis, CD&pb, 1998, Gi price £16.54 (rrp £19.99), Code 12838

Point and Figure Charting, by Thomas Dorsey, hb, 2001, Gi price £37.83 (rrp £44.50), Code 0869

The New Fibonacci Trader, by Robert Fischer, CD&hb, 2001, Gi price £50.58 (rrp £59.50), Code 13935

The Psychology of Technical Analysis, by Tony Plummer, hb, 1993, Gi price £33.15 (rrp £39.00), Code 0895

The Seven Chart Patterns that Consistently Make Money, pb, Gi price £12.33 (rrp £14.05), Code 11027

Technical Analysis from A to Z, by Stephen Achelis, hb, 2000, Gi price £25.49 (rrp £29.99), Code 13047

The Truth of The Stock Tape, by W.D. Gann, hb, 1923, Gi price £31.50 (rrp £35.00), Code 0502

For more information on these books, or to place an order, visit www.global-investor.com or call +44 (0)1730 233870.

6   Trading

- How to choose a broker
- Running two brokerage accounts
- Commission charges
- Liquidity and Normal Market Size
- Market Makers
- Level II quotes
- Trade definitions
- Trade prices and broker dealing
- Significance of buy/sell volumes
- Using limits and stops
- Guaranteed stop losses
- Day trading and Direct Access trading
- Volatility - not such a bad thing
- Going short
- Uses of hedging
- Trading outside normal market hours
- Developing a trading system
- Trading simulators

Choosing an online broker

Q How do I decide which online broker to open an account with?

A A few years ago, listing the selection criteria for online brokers would have been an academic exercise because the choice was so small. Now that there are over 30 online brokers, it's a more challenging and worthwhile exercise.

In fact the question I get asked more than any other is - *which broker do you recommend?* It is difficult to answer as it really does depend on what type of investor you are. However, it is possible to lay down a set of criteria for choosing a broker, which will, at least, help to filter out the completely unsuitable ones.

At the moment, online brokers split into two types: those whose dealing system is **fully automated**, and those whose system is largely an **email system**, with human intervention. In theory, trades through the former are faster and less error-prone than trades through the latter (although that statement may cause a ripple of sardonic laughter among the country's existing online traders).

An obvious factor to look at when considering brokers is the level of commission charges. However, unless you are an extremely active trader (in which case, charges are of the *utmost* importance) don't get too obsessed by charges. There are many other questions to ask, including:

• is there a minimum dealing size?
• do you have to leave a minimum cash amount in your account?
• which types of orders does the broker accept? (e.g. market, limit, stop, gtc)
• does the broker only cover UK markets or international markets too?
• which securities can be traded? (shares, bonds, warrants, gilts, options)
• is there any research available?
• is there a choice in how you contact the broker? (telephone, fax, letter, email)
• how much interest is paid on cash balances?
• can you trade on margin?
• what online account reports are available?
• is the account insured?
• how can money be transferred in/out of the account?

These factors will be of differing importance to different investors. Some sites like Ample, which used to provide a summary of brokers, now have their own sharedealing service and so are less inclined to advertise rivals, but **FTYourMoney** and **Motley Fool** still provide a good round-up of brokers. For a more in-depth ranking look at **BlueSky**.

Final advice: open accounts with 2 brokers (not 1).

L BlueSky: www.blueskyratings.com

FT YourMoney (Brokerfinder): ftyourmoney.ft.com/FTym/brokerfinder

Motley Fool:
www.fool.co.uk/personalfinance/discountbrokers/discountbrokers1.htm

Expatriate online accounts

Q I am a British expat living in Hong Kong who would like (but has so far failed) to find a share broker who I can use to buy/sell UK shares on the net from HK?

A In recent years banks and brokers have had to introduce new account-opening procedures to comply with money-laundering legislation. The intention of the new guidelines may be laudable, but they have had the unfortunate side effect of making it difficult for non-UK residents, and temporarily non-UK residents, to open stock broking accounts. This affects not only foreign nationals, but also British expatriates living abroad.

The problem is compounded by the fact that brokers seem to interpret the legislation in different ways and hence they all have different guidelines. The best advice I can give is to shop around, using the broker rankings at **BlueSky** as a starting point. In general, all brokers are trying to restrict their new accounts to UK residents, but they have different ways of verifying residency. In some cases they may want to see a recent utilities bill. If you own, or rent, a house in the UK, this may be something you can easily provide, even if you are currently living in Hong Kong. However, even if you do find an accommodating broker, there's no assurance that it won't change its procedures next year.

Spread betting

There may be an easier option, and that's to open an account with a spread betting firm. Spread betters have many accounts with people overseas, and this should be no problem. The major spread betting firms are: **Cantor Index**, **City Index**, **Financial Spreads**, **IG Index** and **Spreadex**. Most of these offer both spread betting and CFDs.

ADRs

Finally, if you're thinking of trading the larger UK shares, don't forget that many trade as ADRs in the US, and can therefore be traded through a US broker. This can be much cheaper than trading the shares in the UK, and a sensible option for both UK and non-UK resident investors (unless you hold the bizarre belief that it's a patriotic duty to pay 0.5% stamp duty on share purchases). See page 182 for more information on ADRs.

L BlueSky: www.blueskyratings.com

IG Index: www.igindex.co.uk

City Index: www.cityindex.co.uk

Cantor Index: www.cantorindex.com

Financial Spreads: www.finspreads.com

Spreadex: www.spreadex.co.uk

Online broker regulation

Q I have an account with an online broker. What would happen to my portfolio if the broker went bust? On a less dramatic scale, is there anything I can do if my online broker executes an order badly?

A Answering your questions in turn - the short answer to the 'my broker's gone bust' scenario is that the whole UK financial industry is heavily regulated, and there is a range of monitoring and compensation schemes to protect the investor.

The longer answer is that this is a complex area, and I'd recommend that every investor look at the **FSA** web site, which has plenty of information on investor protection, in addition to much sensible advice for all investors.

Of course, the lessons of Barings, Equitable Life and others, stand as a warning that sometimes, despite all the regulation, things go wrong. And this places the onus squarely back on you, the investor, to approach every financial decision with a quiver full of risk-assessment arrows. Being aware of, and managing, risk is not something you can completely delegate to others. Among the sensible precautions you should take is the fairly obvious one that you should limit your exposure to any one financial institution. This is consistent with advice I have given elsewhere recommending having accounts with more than one stockbroker.

You also asked whether there is anything you can do if your online broker executes an order badly. All online brokers in the UK operate in exactly the same regulatory environment as offline ones. Therefore, complaint procedures are the same. If you have a problem, raise it first with your broker. An argument could be made that the new online brokers are more sensitive, for the moment, about their public profile than the old established brokers, and thus they might be more flexible in dealing with client issues.

If you want to take matters further, then the appropriate body would be the **FSA**. Further useful resources are **APCIMS**, and **The Financial Services Compensation Scheme**. The latter is a rescue fund for UK private clients and it is probably a good idea for all investors to take a quick look at its web site.

L APCIMS: www.apcims.org

FSA: www.fsa.gov.uk

FSA: www.fsa.gov.uk/consumer/consumer_help/

The Financial Services Compensation Scheme: www.the-ics.org.uk

Q What happens if I open an account with an online broker, but then cannot connect to its service at a time when I really need to trade?

A This is a good question. Both the internet infrastructure and brokerages' own computer systems are being improved all the time, but there is always the chance of a system breakdown (which, chances are, will happen just when the market is crashing). The best, although not perfect, solution is to open two brokerage accounts. One broker might offer bargain basement dealing commissions, but very little support (including no telephone service), while the other will, ideally, have a more comprehensive service, albeit at a higher rate. Trades could then be divided between the two. An alternative would be to have one account with an online stockbroker and another account with a spread betting firm.

Your question highlights the wider issue of confidence in online trading systems. The new world of computers and the internet offers tremendous power to the individual investor, but there *are* dangers in blazing any new trail. The guiding rule in the short (and most probably long) term must be *caveat emptor*. Or, to put it another way, do everything you can to cover yourself, because if a mistake happens, you cannot assume that the regulators will be there to help.

In practice this means checking every stage of the trading process and minimising the risks. One example is to open multiple brokerage accounts, as described above. Another is to establish accounts with more than one ISP (internet service provider) – you don't want to be prevented from trading just because your ISP is too busy one day. And, of course, do think about backing up your computer data. For those with a second computer around, consider setting up a parallel system to your main computer – if the latter goes down anytime, you don't want to spend ages hunting around for usernames and passwords and re-configuring investment programs.

Transferring shares between nominee accounts

Q I have read your recommendation to open accounts with more than one stockbroker, but as most of them use nominee accounts, if I buy shares through one broker can I sell through another broker?

A While it *is* possible to transfer shares from one nominee account to another, it may take anything from 3-14 days (depending on the efficiency of the brokers involved), and there will also be an administration charge. The delay makes life difficult if you want to deal quickly, because the broker you want to sell through will usually insist on having the stock before executing the sale. i.e. you will not normally be allowed to go short on the stock.

A partial solution is to split an order in the first place. If you are buying 10,000 shares, allot 5,000 to one broker, and 5,000 to another broker. From a risk diversification viewpoint, this might be a good idea anyway.

An alternative is to use brokers which offer **personal membership of Crest**, because then the shares will be registered in your name and you won't have to wait for a transfer between broker nominee accounts. Not all brokers offer the personal membership of Crest service, so if you are interested in it, make sure you check with a broker before opening an account.

Using two brokers can be useful for other reasons too. Suppose that you are holding shares in GlaxoSmithKline (GSK) and a news story comes out after the London market has closed which you think will affect the share price adversely. Ordinarily, there is not much that you can do until the market opens the following day, and when it does the chances are that the price will have moved significantly before you have chance to deal. If you have a US broking account, however, you can take pre-emptive action.

You can't, of course, sell your London shares directly in the US, but what you can do is go short on an equivalent value of GSK ADRs. The effect of this short trade will be to immediately neutralise your exposure to GSK. If the shares subsequently collapse, the losses on the GSK shares in London will be offset by the gains on the short GSK ADRs in New York.

It would not be necessary – or sensible – to keep such a position open for a long period. Soon afterwards, when both the UK and US markets are open at the same time, the (hedged) position can be unwound by simultaneously selling the GSK shares in London and buying back the GSK ADRs in New York.

The intention and net effect of all this is to protect your holding in a share, even when the share price fell on news announced after the London market was closed. Fortunately, because dealing costs in the US are low, this hedging action is relatively cheap.

Slow brokers

Q I'm exasperated by the slow speed at which my online orders get executed. From what I read in the papers, I'm not the only one experiencing this. Is there anything I can do?

A When the markets are busy, this can become quite a problem, with all online brokers seeming to suffer at least intermittent periods of digital indigestion. The longer term solution is evidently for the brokers to invest more on IT and support staff. If you want to become a trading activist then pressure can be put on the broking industry by contributing to bulletin boards, contacting the increasing number of media vehicles and complaining to the **FSA**. Apart from that, the options are limited. Resorting to the telephone may be the only alternative, although on occasions the service here might be even worse.

It's always a good idea to think about opening an account with two brokers, one online, another with a more established broker that doesn't offer an online service and isn't experiencing the high customer acquisition rates of the new boys on the block. Personally, I find share dealing in the UK frustrating, and often deal in the US market instead. It may not be possible to trade Pacific Media or Scoot.com in the US, but you can trade larger UK companies like Arm Holdings, Vodafone, Cable & Wireless and GlaxoSmithKline. Plus the Americans have one or two companies that aren't bad themselves.

L FSA: www.fsa.gov.uk

Q I've been using the same stockbroker for 20 years, but am thinking of moving to an online broker as the commissions seem to be much lower. Is this a good idea?

A One of the great benefits online trading has brought is a reduction in commission costs. All investors stand to save, but the scale of savings will depend on the kind of investor you are, as the case studies below illustrate:

Investor A trades once a year, buying shares to a value of £5,000. The commission on this deal from the standard old-style, full-service broker would be around £80. This represents a cost of 1.6% on the starting capital of £5,000. If an online broker was used for the same trade, the cost would be around £10 – which represents a cost of 0.2%.

Investor B trades 12 times a year, each bargain being £5,000. Remember, trading 12 times a year is only making six separate investments – each investment involves a buy and sell trade. For the purposes of this example, we'll assume that no profit or loss is made on the share price. The cumulative cost of using a full-service broker will be £960. That means 19.2% of the starting capital of £5,000 disappears in commission, compared to a total commission cost with an online broker of £120 - 2.4% of the starting capital.

Investor C trades 36 times a year, again, with bargains of £5,000. This might sound absurdly hyperactive to you, but really it is only trading three times a month. The cumulative commission cost with the standard broker has now soared to £2,880 - 58% of the starting capital! Put another way, the investments have to increase 58% just to cover the cost of commission. By contrast, the online cost would be £360 – 7.2% of the starting capital.

# of trades	Full-Service broker	Online-UK broker
1	£80 (1.6%)	£10 (0.2%)
12	£960 (19.2%)	£120 (2.4%)
36	£2,880 (58%)	£360 (7.2%)

The figures do *not* say: *ditch your long-standing broker, we've all got to go online*. If you are a non-active, buy-and-hold investor, you don't need to be overly concerned with commission costs. But as soon as you start trading actively, commission costs kick in with a vengeance, and it will be difficult to ignore the economics of going online. Don't forget either that commission represents just **one component** of the transaction costs - the others, *stamp duty* and the *bid/offer spread*, are also significant.

In the last few years, many equity portfolios will have enjoyed equity returns of 20% plus; in which case a percentage point here or there on transaction costs may not seem terribly important. But if annual equity returns fall to single figures, then the importance of controlling trading costs would become paramount.

Liquidity and Normal Market Size

Q I've heard of some shares being referred to as 'illiquid'. I imagine this has something to do with volume or turnover, but does this affect me as an individual investor and where can I find information about this on the web?

A Liquidity refers to the ease with which a particular share can be bought or sold. It is influenced greatly by the daily share volume (the number of shares bought and sold in a day). In general, if you are thinking of trading a FTSE 100 stock then poor liquidity should not be a problem. But if you are looking at a smaller stock (perhaps AIM or OFEX listed) then this might be something to watch out for.

For example, around 50 million shares are traded in BP every day. With a share price of approximately £6, that means shares with a total value of £300 million are traded daily. Hence, if you're thinking of buying (or selling) BP shares with a value of, say, £50,000, you shouldn't have too much trouble executing the order. Share volumes can usually be seen on charts accompanying the price data. If you look at the chart for BP on **Ample**, daily trading volumes are shown in the lower box, and you will see that the average has been around 50 million shares daily.

For comparison, we'll look at NetBenefit [NBT] – an AIM listed stock. (If you still have the Ample chart for BP open, simply change 'BP-.L' to NBT.L in the browser location box to quickly switch to viewing a chart for NetNenefit). You can also see that the trading volume is small and sporadic, on some days no shares being traded at all. Average daily volume is around 35,000 shares, which with a share price of 12p gives a daily turnover of approximately £4,200. If you wanted to buy shares with a value of £10,000 in this company, on a quiet trading day, your order could be over twice the total turnover for the day. And this could affect the price you pay for the shares.

Market makers and normal market size

When you give an order to a broker, he in turn goes to a market maker who quotes a bid/offer price, say 54-56. This means that the market maker is willing to buy shares at 54, and sell them at 56, so if *you* want to buy shares (from the market maker), you'll get them at 56. But the market maker's prices are only valid up to a specified number of shares. The full quote might be, '54-56, good for 10,000', meaning the quoted price holds for all orders up to 10,000 shares, but for orders over that size another quote is required.

The reason for this is that market makers like to protect themselves: when they sell you shares, they have to be able to deliver them, which means they must either already own the shares or must go out into the market and buy them. If they quote a price *whatever* the size of the order, they might find that when they start buying in the market, the price is forced up by the high demand and they actually lose on the trade. The share limit associated with each quote, called the *Normal Market Size* (or sometimes, the *Quoted Market Size*), is their protection.

Note that market makers don't decide what the NMS of each stock is. The London Stock Exchange does. It conducts a quarterly review of all NMS levels, and sets the NMS accordingly. Market makers are obliged to offer a quote up to the NMS level for each stock on which they are a designated MM. If you want to see the LSE's reports, by the way, you can download them from its web site, and also read a more technical explanation of the calculation of NMS.

Where can you look up NMS figures? They are usually displayed on brokers' web sites, but are also on **ADVFN**. For example, the NMS for BP is 200,000; which means that any quote is good for an order up to that size (around £1.2m). However, NetBenefit has a NMS of just 2,000. Therefore, if you wanted to buy 6,000 shares of this company, there are a couple of points to watch.

- First, you would have to be **careful in executing this order**: if your broker charged into the market with a large order over the NMS, the market makers would see him coming and would (unhelpfully) move the offer price up accordingly.

- Second, it is **unlikely that you would be able to give this order online**, as most brokers do not accept online orders that are over the NMS. In this case, you would either have to telephone the broker, or try staggering the order in units below the NMS.

You also need to be aware of NMS when *selling* stock. Supposing you build up a holding of 10,000 shares in Company X over a period of one year, buying in parcels of 2,000 shares well below the NMS of 3,000. If, at some point, you decide to sell all 10,000 shares, you cannot assume that you'll get the market maker's quoted bid price, because the deal size is over three times larger than the NMS. You might receive a much lower price.

The lesson from all this is to be aware of the liquidity of shares you trade in. If liquidity is poor, it will affect the execution of large orders. Analysis of a stock's historical trading volumes (you can download a file from **Yahoo Finance**) is worthwhile, and can be useful not only to determine a share's average volume, but also how thin it might get on the worst days.

Note that just because a share has a high volume on some days, it doesn't necessarily mean that the share is liquid for individual investors. It may be that large blocks of shares are merely being shuffled around between institutions. In the `Equities/CityDesk` section of **Sharepages** there's a breakdown of a stock's trading by large block trades (measuring institutional activity), small block trades, inter-market maker activity and delayed settlement trades. There's also a running indicator of the day's volume as a percentage of the average daily volume. On the same site, if you switch over to the `Equities/Analysis` section and select `Volume Spikes` from the drop-down box, there's a list of shares exhibiting extraordinary volume that day, relative to their normal volume. Obviously, this usually represents a surge of interest (either positive or negative) in the company.

ADVFN: www.advfn.com

Ample: www.iii.co.uk

London Stock Exchange (NMS Quarterly Review):
www.londonstockexchange.com/techlib/nms_default.asp

Sharepages: www.sharepages.com

Yahoo Finance (historic data download): chart.yahoo.com/d

Q Is there an online site that will give me the number of market makers that deal in a chosen share?

A Briefly, shares on the London Stock Exchange are traded in three ways-

1. Since 1997, the largest stocks (FTSE 100, plus 100 of the larger FTSE 250 stocks) are traded using an electronic order book called **SETS**. On this system all trading is automatic with bargains being matched by computer.

2. Non-SETS stocks are traded using **SEAQ**, which is a system for continuously distributing market makers' bid and offer prices.

3. Finally, there's **SEATS PLUS**, which is a combination order and quote-driven system for AIM stocks and other listed stocks that don't have competing market makers for trading on SEAQ.

There are therefore two basic methods of trading. One is an *order-driven* system (SETS, SEATS PLUS), where there are no market makers, just member firms placing firm orders. The other style is called *quote-driven* (SEAQ, SEATS PLUS), where competing market makers post bid and offer prices.

A consequence of this is that there are no official market makers for SETS stocks. For SEAQ and SEATS PLUS stocks, market makers must register for stocks they want to make quotes for. Unfortunately the London Stock Exchange doesn't release a list of these registered market makers by stock. To get further information on a stock you need access to a Level II quote service. For example, with reference to the Level II screen on **ADVFN** you would be able to see that JJB Sports is traded on SEAQ and has nine market makers.

Further information on trading systems can be found on the London Stock Exchange web site. (A summary of trade types is also given on pages 264-267 of this book).

ADVFN: www.advfn.com

London Stock Exchange (trading systems explanation): www.londonstockexchange.com/trading/market/

Level II quotes

Q I've heard increasing talk of something called Level II quotes. Are they something that can be found on the web, and is there an explanation of them that I can read?

A Most investors trading online see Level I quotes, as displayed by many web sites like **Yahoo Finance**. Level I quotes show the best current bid and offer prices on a stock. So a Level I quote for Vodafone might be: 108-109, where 108 is the current highest bid in the market, and 109 is the current lowest offer in the market.

But apart from the bid at 108, there may be **many other bids and offers in the market** (below 108 and above 109), and that is where Level II quotes come in. Level II quotes display all these other bids and offers (with size) as well as just the best bid and offer.

Level II quotes are going to become increasingly common, and an essential tool for many investors. By far the best explanation I have come across is on the **ADVFN** web site. Besides Level II, the page also has good explanations on the different methods of trading between SEAQ/AIM and the SETS order book. For example, the **current price on SEAQ** is calculated as the mid-price of the current best bid and offer, while the **current price on SETS** is defined as the last traded price. There is also a description of the mysterious procedure of the opening and closing auctions, and a useful overview of the role of market makers.

While Level II quotes have been available to institutional investors for some time, only recently have individual investors had access to them. Currently **ADVFN**, **GNItouch**, and **Proquote** provide them, but only to premium subscribers. Unfortunately, there are no free services yet.

L ADVFN (Level II explanation): www.advfn.com/cmn/help/level2.php

GNItouch: www.gnitouch.com

Proquote: www.proquote.net

Yahoo Finance: finance.yahoo.co.uk

144

Trade definitions

Q When I'm reading messages on bulletin boards I quite often come across references to 'market maker to market maker trades', or 'block trades'. Where do I find this information, and where can I find out what the different types of trades mean?

A When trading, many investors look at the current best bid and offer prices (*Level I quotes*), while more active traders may prefer to look at the depth of the market using *Level II quotes*. Combined with this, most traders will look at the last actual traded price, and see if it is closer to the prevailing bid or offer as an indication of buying or selling pressure. The more active traders though will want to look at not just the last traded price, but at the recent history of actual trades, their size and the time of the transaction (in the US this data is called the *Time & Sales*). This information, in combination with Level II quotes, gives the trader a good idea of the action in a particular stock. Good web sources for this trade history are **Ample**, **ADVFN** and **hemscott.NET**.

Whenever trades are transacted they are reported to the Exchange, and that information is made available through various information vendors. But there are many different types of trades, depending on who is transacting with who, and how the trade is implemented. Each type of trade has a unique code, the explanation of which can be seen on the **London Stock Exchange** web site. For example, the Exchange defines a block trade as being *at least 75 times the NMS for a security with an NMS of 2,000 shares OR above 50 times the NMS for a security with an NMS of 1,000 shares*. At the moment, I think it is only ADVFN that reports the trade type for each transaction in the trade history.

L ADVFN: www.advfn.com

Ample: www.iii.co.uk

hemscott.NET: www.hemscott.net

London Stock Exchange:
www.prices.londonstockexchange.com/glossary.asp#tradetypes

Trade prices

Q Is there are any way that I can check what the market price of a stock was after I've dealt with a broker?

A I assume that you want to check that the broker got the best price for you in the market? A very reasonable thing to want to know.

In the old days (pre-internet, when dinosaurs roamed the wilderness that was the Stock Exchange trading floor) an investor might call a broker and ask for the current price in, say, British & Commonwealth – companies used to have names like that in those days.

The broker might reply that the stock's quote was 64-67; meaning the market makers were buying at 64 and selling at 67. If an investor wanted to buy, he would instruct his broker to buy at 67, or, if feeling competitive, would give a buy order with a limit at 66 or even 65.

Alternatively, if the investor had a good relationship with the broker, he might ask to deal *within the spread*; meaning for the broker to use his discretion to try to buy at less than the quoted price of 67 (or sell at more than the quoted 64 for a sell order). In this case, the broker might take a little time to finesse the order, but with luck would come back with the good news that he had been able to buy at, say, 66.

Everyone was happy. The client particularly so, as not only had he bought at a better price than the rest of the market, but he also had the satisfaction of dealing with a broker who was both adroit and obviously had useful contacts.

But when the client was originally quoted the market price of 64-67, he had **no way of telling if that was really the current price in the market**. Discrepancies could occur for many reasons. For one, there might have been many different market makers for the stock, who at any one time might have been quoting slightly different prices. And, very occasionally, it was not unknown for some brokers to try to put one over on the client. If the broker knew the client well, he would know what the client was thinking of doing in the market, and possibly quote a price of 64-67 to the client, when the more representative market price was in fact 64-66. This, at its most charitable, allowed the broker to later display an uncommon skill at dealing inside the spread.

But now we have the internet.

When I am trading on the net, I open a browser window with the order input screen of an online broker, which will also tell me the current price of the stock I am thinking of trading. In addition, I have a second browser window open displaying real time prices from another broker. And I might have further browser windows open with real time prices from services such as **ADVFN**. Just before placing the order I will be switching quickly between all screens using the `Alt-Tab` keys (Windows only), and checking the current price through different services. And then when I give the order to trade, I'll be monitoring the real-time price on several different web sites. (By the way, when switching between browser windows like this, always remember to hit the `F5` button. This re-loads the page, and makes sure you're looking at the latest data.)

It is not (yet) practicable to monitor several share price services and then deal with the service offering the best price. But this simultaneous viewing of prices from different sources does allow you to monitor the efficiency of your broker's trade execution. If, over time, you realise that your broker is not executing your orders well, switch to another.

Having traded in the market, and received an execution confirmation, you might like to check the prices of other trades being executed for the same stock. Good services for trade histories are available from **Ample**, **ADVFN** and **hemscott.NET**; which display a table with information on the last few trades including data on: trade code, trade price, time of trade volume and the bid/ask prices at the time of trade. If you really want to track your own specific trades, try giving orders in odd lots. For example, trade 3,003 shares, not 3,000, so you can more easily identify your trade in the trade table.

ADVFN: www.advfn.com

Ample: www.iii.co.uk

hemscott.NET: businessplus.hemscott.net/backpage/

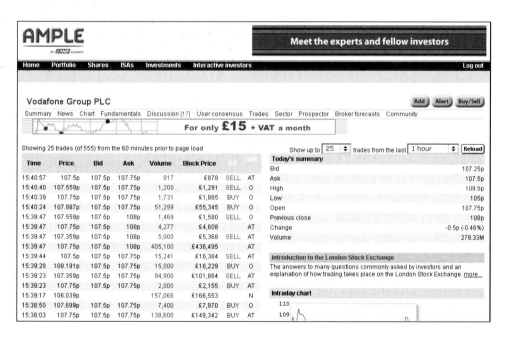

Volumes for buy and sell trades

Q Can you tell me which is the best web site for information on traded volumes and on the split between buy/sell trades?

A Several web sites provide a record of trade histories (sometimes called *Time & Sales*) including **ADVFN**, **hemscott.NET** and **Ample**. Most of the data is delayed by the usual 15 minutes, although ADVFN has real-time Times & Sales.

All the web sites, except hemscott.NET, indicate if the trade is deemed a *buy* or a *sell*. The Ample site calculates a total turnover (by value) attributable to buy trades and sell trades – but this is only for the trades displayed on that particular page (which will not necessarily include all the trades so far that day). ADVFN displays a cumulative total of shares traded for buy and sells.

More sophisticated analysis of buying/selling activity can be seen on the `CityDesk` page of **Sharepages**, where for each stock the cumulative percentage of trades attributable to buying and selling activity is calculated. In addition, it also calculates the buying/selling percentage split for large block trades (mainly institutional dealing) and for small block trades. Analysis of any discrepancy here can be interesting.

For example, at the time of writing, GlaxoSmithKline was down 3.9%, and Sharepages was showing buying/selling activity as 39/37% for large block trades and 44/49% for small blocks. Both sets are fairly evenly split, although it's interesting to note that only 76% (39+37) of large block trades are accounted for – Sharepages ignores trades not at the bid or offer prices. Which suggests, unsurprisingly perhaps, that there were a number of large block trades transacted inside the spread. Finally, in its `Analysis` section, Sharepages ranks stocks in order of greatest buying activity and selling activity.

None of the sites offer charting as such for volume split into buy/sells. But the charts at **FT Investor** and **Ample** are very good with a number of volume-related indicators such as OBV (On Balance Volume).

The theory (in brief) behind all this share transaction monitoring is that trades occurring close to the prevailing offer price indicate *buying activity* - on the grounds that a buyer has been forced to accept the higher offer price, rather than post a lower bidding price and wait to be hit. Buying activity therefore represents buying pressure, which indicates that the force on the stock price will be up.

But is this true?

A casual analysis of the behaviour of stock prices, seen through the filter of this buying/selling activity, suggests that there is no direct causal relationship between indicative buy/sell activity and subsequent price performance. And analysis of the aggregated buying/selling activity on Sharepages reveals many stock prices that have fallen during a day when activity was predominantly *buying*, and vice versa.

Why is this?

There may be problems with the theory and with the methodology. Regarding the latter, trade data from the Stock Exchange, and subsequently via the web sites, may not be consistent or accurate. The reporting and monitoring of trades by the Stock Exchange is not perfect, so sometimes the **recording of trades is delayed**. If reporting of a trade is delayed, the price may not reflect the current market (i.e. the current bid/offer levels). Other types of trades can also be at variance with the current market for reasons other than simple delays. A list of all the different types of trades that may occur on the London Stock Exchange can be found at its web site or on pages 264-267 of this book. All these different trades can confuse trading activity analysis.

An interesting discussion of trade analysis can be found on the **Motley Fool** bulletin boards. In one of the messages, a user has posted an analysis of the predictive ability of trade activity monitoring – by comparing each buy/sell indicator with the subsequent trade movement for Emblaze. The result was that the buy/sell indication was correct 37% of the time. Obviously a great deal of further analysis would be required for truly rigorous research – but there's no doubt that if there is a relationship, it is a fairly complex one, and that simple monitoring of this activity is not a short-cut to trading riches. Which should come as no surprise to experienced investors.

ADVFN: www.advfn.com

Ample: www.iii.co.uk

FT Investor: www.ft.com/investor

hemscott.NET: www.hemscott.net

London Stock Exchange (glossary of trade types):
www.prices.londonstockexchange.com/glossary.asp#tradetypes

Motley Fool BB:
boards.fool.co.uk/Message.asp?id=2010001011075000&sort=id

Sharepages: www.sharepages.com

Limits and stop losses

Q

Do any online brokers have a system which allows you to set limits and run stop losses automatically? Say for example I was following a company that currently had a price of £1.00 and I wanted to set a limit to buy the shares at £0.90 and then run a stop loss of 15%. This would allow me to go to work and not worry about missing a deal. I have tried doing this with my current broker but it has proved to be unreliable.

A

It is possible to set **limits** on orders with most brokers. This is the simple order whereby if a stock is currently trading at, 90, you can instruct your broker to buy at limit 86. If the stock trades down to 86, the broker should buy at that price or less. These types of orders can be given online, albeit they are only *good for the day* – meaning that if they are not executed on the day they are cancelled, and if you want the order to carry forward to the next day, you have to re-enter it. Few online brokers offer a *GTC* facility (*Good till cancelled* orders remain valid over several days until executed).

Stop orders are very useful but are more difficult, and few online brokers in the UK accept them – an exception is **Comdirect**. This type of order allows trailing stop losses to be set up that will protect a portfolio (i.e. sell if the prices drop) without having to monitor the market continually. Conversely they can be used to set an entry point to buy a stock (for example if it breaks out of a trading range on the upside).

Note: for buy orders, limits are always set *below* the current price, while stops are placed *above* the current price. For sell orders, limits are set *above* the current price, while stops are placed *below* the current price. For example, if a share price is currently at 60, a buy order may be placed with a limit at 55, *or* a stop at 65. The limit order would *only* be executed if the share fell to 55 or below. Whereas, the stop order would *only* be executed if the share increased to 65 or above.

If your broker doesn't allow stop orders, what are the alternatives?

Firstly, even if you can't place these orders online, you may be able to **give the order offline** if you have a good relationship with your broker. (One argument for not immediately ditching your old offline broker when you open a new online trading account.)

Secondly, **many UK stocks also trade in the US** (as securities called ADRs). Although UK brokers may not accept stop orders, they are standard practice in the US markets, and if the stocks you are interested in *are* listed in the US, it might be an idea to trade them there.

Finally, another alternative might be to **use spread betting or CFDs**. Both of these, while perhaps fairly new to some investors, offer greater flexibility in trading over ordinary shares. Shorting is possible, and also orders can sometimes - depending on the broker - be given with limits and stops.

L

Comdirect: www.comdirect.co.uk

150

Guaranteed stop losses

Q Do any brokers offer guaranteed stop losses?

A For those who don't already know, guaranteed stop losses are stop losses in which the broker guarantees to get you out of the stock at the stop price even if, in practice, the market price descends so fast that he is unable to execute the sale at that price.

You might wonder why such a guarantee is necessary. After all, isn't that what happens with ordinary stop losses? To which the answer is an emphatic no. When you place an ordinary stop loss, there is no certainty that the broker will be able to execute it at the stop price. For example, if you hold a stock with a current price of 60, and you place a stop loss order with the stop at 50, the stock will be sold when the market price falls and touches 50. However, if the price is falling very quickly and liquidity is poor (as might be the case with a small cap company, or a larger company in the midst of a general market meltdown), there's no assurance that when the sell order is triggered, it will be possible to sell at 50. If the market is falling very fast, the sell order may be executed at 45 or below, which makes your stop loss rather ineffective.

Guaranteed stop losses would solve the problem because, in the example above, the broker would treat your sale as having been executed at 50 even if it was in fact executed at 45. The 5p difference would be his concern, not yours. Unfortunately, apart from **Comdirect**, hardly any stockbrokers offer even simple stops in the UK market, and **none offer guaranteed stop losses**.

One way of controlling the *stop-loss-that-isn't-a-very-good-stop-loss* problem is to incorporate a limit into the order. For instance, you could place a stop at 50 but also have a contingent limit at 47. This translates as an instruction to sell if the price touches 50, but not to sell anything below 47. In this way, you would avoid being caught by very short-term price movement that then quickly reverse themselves. But it is a fine balance. If the market really is tanking, then it might be better to just get out of the market quickly, rather than trying to finesse the thing. In our example, you would rue the limit at 47 if the stock fell past that with no trade possible and leveled out at 30.

Which brings us back to guaranteed stop losses, and their frustrating non-availability from online stockbrokers. The answer, if you really want guaranteed stop losses, is to use **spread betting or CFDs**, where simple and guaranteed stop losses are available from some brokers. There is a price to pay for the extra level of comfort, usually in the form of higher commission (on CFDs), but you may feel that it is a price worth paying.

L Comdirect: www.comdirect.co.uk

Day trading

Q Is day trading possible in the UK, and do I need any special software for it?

A Strictly, the term *day trading* means to open and close positions within a day without holding a position overnight, but it is commonly used to mean just very active trading - which might well involve holding positions overnight.

In answer to your question, and using the strict definition first, it *is* possible to day trade in the UK – but there are problems. The main problem is the **cost of trading**, which is made up of:

- **commission** on the opening and closing trades

- **stamp duty** at 0.5% on purchases

- the **bid/offer spread** of the market makers

- possible **execution slippage** (the difference between the price you thought you were going to get, and the actual trade price)

These costs mount up, and for small deal sizes, in/out transaction costs might be around 3%, which requires a fairly hefty move in the stock price to make a profit after covering costs. Other problems might be access to real bid/offer quotes in the market, and a rather clunky trade execution process. Despite these disadvantages, there are some day traders in the UK. But they are more likely to be *swing traders* (or *range traders*) than genuine day traders, and may, or may not, close out positions within a day.

Day trading US stocks

An alternative to day trading UK stocks is to trade in the US market using a simple account with an online US broker. This has a number of attractions:

- the **trading costs are much lower** (well below 1%)

- many stocks – particularly the hi-tech ones – are **very volatile**,

- **access to market prices** is better

- the **trade execution systems are more efficient**

No special software is required here as everything is available via a simple web browser, and the brokers will usually supply research and data (including real time prices) as part of the service.

Direct access trading

Finally, there is *direct access* trading of US stocks. This method cuts out brokers and offers direct access to the Nasdaq market and use of a Nasdaq Level II quote screen (where the bid and offer order books can be seen). Order routing can be to market makers, SOES (Small Order Execution System) or to the increasing numbers of ECNs (Electronic Communications Networks) such as Island. This is the real thing, traders glued to their screens all day, doing it for a living.

The high profile manifestation of DAT trading is the network of day trading centres (or should that be centers) in the US where traders go every day to rent a booth with equipment supplied by a broker. The attraction of these centres is as much social as technical. Unfortunately, or otherwise, they don't exist yet in the UK; but is it too far fetched to imagine the imminent advent of *Thomson Day Trading Holidays – 14 days of sun, sea and stop-outs in a Florida trading booth*?

An alternative to the trading booth is to use your computer at home. For this, special software is required to view the Level II quotes and for placing orders. Trading commissions can be very low (almost negligible), but the proprietary software is expensive (up to $300 per month). There's no shortage of internet resources on this topic. Good starting places are **DayTradingStocks** and **Rookie DayTrader**, with many links to further resources (the former lists over 200 'day trading' sites). Also check out some bulletin boards, **Raging Bull** and **Silicon Investor**. The latter even has a board called *Daytrading and Stock Trading Addiction*.

Direct Access Trader: www.directaccesstrader.com

myTrack: www.mytrack.com

InvestIN: www.investin.co.uk

DayTradingStocks.com: www.daytradingstocks.com

Raging Bull: www.ragingbull.com

The Rookie DayTrader: www.rookiedaytrader.com

Best types of stock for day trading

Q Are there any web sites that give the volatility of stocks? I'm looking for stocks to day trade.

A Volatility has had a bad press. It is often held to be a *bad thing* - financial advisors warn investors away from it. This may be good advice for casual investors. But for active investors – particularly day traders – volatility is the essential ingredient that generates profits.

Every trader should develop their own trading system, and their choice of stocks to follow will be subjective. However, there are a few guidelines that one can lay down regarding the suitability of stocks to actively trade.

- You want stocks that trade in a **wide range** (low to high) during the day.

- The stocks must be **volatile**. This is not quite the same as the above. A stock that bounces between 20 and 25 six times in a day, is preferable to a stock that moves once from a low of 20 to 27.

- The stocks must be **liquid** (high trading volume). This reduces the costs of getting in and out of positions.

There are no web sites (in the UK) that provide information on all the above. **Comdirect** is good for finding the volatility of individual stocks. **ADVFN** has a very useful table of stocks with the smallest bid/offer spreads – for day traders, this is more useful than merely knowing the trading volume.

Alternatively, you can create your own customised filter for selecting stocks. As an example of this, I've created a spreadsheet (`ftse100-daytrading.xls`: download from this book's web site) that can act as a model. The spreadsheet contains high/low/close/vol and volatility data for all FTSE 100 stocks. The data was exported from **Sharescope** - although any data source could be used. From the universe of 100 stocks, the 30 stocks with the highest turnover (share price x volume) were exported to a separate worksheet. On this sheet, the day's trading range (low to high) is expressed as a percentage of the low price. This figure is then multiplied by the stock's volatility, and the spreadsheet ranked in descending order by this final figure. The result is a table of stocks ordered by their suitability for day trading. The top ten stocks turned out to be: ARM (by a wide margin), Standard Chartered, WPP Group, BT, BHP Billiton, Kingfisher, M&S, Pearson, Reuters, BSkyB.

Notes:

1. The initial **selection of 30 high turnover FTSE 100 stocks was arbitrary**. Any criteria could be used; the purpose was to limit the initial universe of stocks to high liquidity stocks. The stock data used was for one day (5 Nov 2001). It's quite possible that certain stocks had unusual behaviour that day. To be more rigorous, the analysis would be repeated over several days.

154

2. There are many ways of calculating, and expressing, **volatility**. Normally, therefore, one would want to know exactly how Sharescope calculated its volatility figure before using it for, say, calculation of an absolute figure such as the theoretical value of an option. But in this case, we're only using it as a relative measure.

3. The top ten stocks listed above, are **not necessarily the best stocks to day trade** – they are merely ranked in terms of suitability. From this list further analysis would then be required. After all, to day trade you need a methodology to follow. If that methodology depends on the analysis of a trading range, the charts in the above list could be analysed individually to identify those stocks exhibiting a strong range pattern.

ADVFN: www.advfn.com

Comdirect: www.comdirect.co.uk

Sharescope: www.sharescope.co.uk

Q I would like to be able to profit by going short on shares that I think are going to fall. What is the best method and instrument for doing this?

A If you have traded CFDs, futures, options or other derivative-like instruments, the concept of shorting will be familiar to you and should present no problems. However, if your investing experience is limited to buying some shares (and hoping they go up) then shorting may be one of those topics that you occasionally come across but you've never quite got round to understanding. This is a shame. In a roaring bull market - when we're all geniuses - it's quite easy to make money. But in a sideways or falling market, investors need more guile, and they need to exploit the full range of investment tools and strategies – including *shorting*.

Until recently, shorting in the UK market was an obscure and fiddly activity. But this is changing. There is now quite a range of tools to use for the adventurous shorter. The obvious approach when thinking about shorting is to **sell short the share itself**. The viability of this depends on your relationship with your broker, and also on the specific characteristics of the share itself. So, although it may be the purest approach to shorting, it will rarely be the easiest or cheapest for the ordinary retail investor.

Spread betting

The choice for most individual investors for shorting is likely to be spread betting. For my money, the best way to understand shorting is to open an account with a spread better, short a stock, and place a stop loss to limit your losses to twenty or thirty pounds. (Ideas on which stocks to short may be found at the `Signals` section of **Investtech**, or **Bloomberg's** *Money Flow Report*. You may lose the money, but in that one trade you will understand more about shorting than reading any number of academic articles. And, of course, there's a 50% chance you may even make money.

Don't worry too much initially about choosing the right spread betting firm; all their services are fairly similar. Open an account with one, and when you start getting more active (and also when you understand your own requirements better) open an account with one or two other spread betting firms, and directly compare their services.

CFDs, Universal futures and ADRs

Similar to spread betting are CFDs, which can also be used to take simple short positions in UK equities. Recently, LIFFE has introduced its *Universal Futures*, which are futures contracts on individual stocks. Liquidity may be low in the early days, but volume should steadily grow and these could be a useful alternative for shorters (although contracts at the moment are limited to just the largest international stocks).

Finally, don't forget ADRs in UK stocks trading in the US which can be shorted very easily with an ordinary US broking account. If I want to short, or temporarily hedge, one of the larger UK stocks (such as Vodafone or Reuters) I would normally use this method.

Shorting may seem an odd activity to many traditional investors. Almost unpatriotic. Unfortunately, patriotism and investment rarely go together, as shareholders in Marconi and Marks & Spencer know. When even companies like these see their share prices melt away, even the most conservative investor might accept that shorting provides a useful weapon in an investor's armoury.

There are not many books solely devoted to shorting. The main one in the UK market has been Simon Cawkwell's, The Profit of The Plunge, which has recently been updated and re-published by **t1ps.com** as Evil's Big Book of Boasts. Cawkwell is a celebrated shorter who writes for t1ps.com under the nom de plume Evil Knievil. His book is a colourful reminiscence of his shorting adventures, out of which he has, according to his own account, made a great deal of money.

Books on spread betting and CFDs will give you better step-by-step instruction on how to construct a short trade. Elsewhere, the only serious book on shorting I know of is an American one, The Art of Short Selling by Kathryn Staley.

Bloomberg (Money Flow report): www.bloomberg.com/uk/tv/moneyflow/

Investtech: www.investtech.com/subscr/uk/

t1ps.com: www.t1ps.com

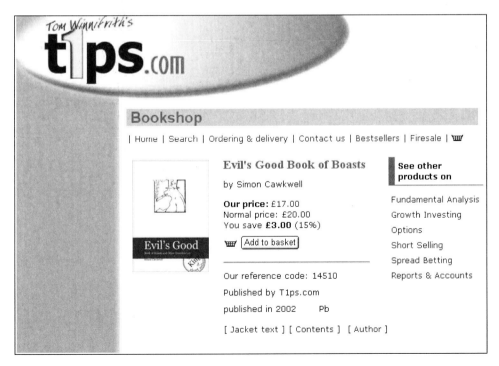

Hedging

Q I own Vodafone shares, which have fallen almost 30% in the last few weeks. Is there any way that I could have protected myself against this fall? I have heard about hedging, but don't know exactly what it is.

A Hedging is a process of protecting the value of an investment by taking a temporary action in the market to neutralise any negative impact on your principal investment. An example would be buying put options on a stock, to temporarily protect a primary holding in that same stock. But hedging is not without risks, and is not for everyone.

Strictly, long-term investors should not be concerned with relatively short-term fluctuations of share prices. They might reason: if a share price has fallen 30%, then it was probably over-valued and the fall is just a natural – and sensible – correction back to a solid fundamental valuation. In the case of Vodafone, the long-term trend is strongly positive, and the share price remains above its long-term moving averages.

However, whether one is a long-term investor or not, the temptation to second-guess the market is very strong. After a few winning trades, epithets like *Master of the Universe* pop into the mind when looking in the mirror in the mornings. During these periods, an investor may think: *although I'm a long term bull of this stock, in the short-term I think it's going down, and I'm going to do something about it*. In which case, what are the choices?

High cost of trading equities

The easiest solution is to sell the stock, stay in cash over the period of the anticipated weakness, and then buy back again after the stock has fallen and is beginning to recover. The main problem with this is the cost involved: after accounting for the brokerage commission, sales tax, and the market-makers' bid-offer spread, the total cost might be 3%.

Imagine that a stock falls 20%. Let's say that you anticipated the fall and sold your holding 5% off the recent high (it's never possible to get into an investment at the bottom and out at the top, however good you are). After it's fallen, you buy back into the stock 5% above the low. The two transactions could have incurred 3% costs, in which case you will only have saved yourself 7 percentage points on the whole 20% fall.

Options

An alternative way to hedge your stock holding against a fall would be to *sell call options* equivalent to the holding. The attraction is that you will receive cash for selling the option. However, this is not strictly a hedging activity, and would not protect the investment for a large fall.

A further alternative, therefore, would be to *buy put options*. In theory, this is the ideal use for put options – this is what they were designed for. In practice, however, their use can be expensive (just as an insurance premium is expensive), and also options prices don't always behave as one might expect if there are dramatic changes in market conditions. But if you want to try the options route, the best service is **Options Direct**.

Spread betting

If not options, then what else? An interesting alternative may be to use spread betting (or CFDs). This allows for the easy shorting of stocks, with the added advantage of no brokerage commissions or sales tax. There is still a cost involved, usually represented in the bid-offer spread, but that cost will usually be far lower than the cost of selling a stock holding and then buying it back again. The theory here is to sell short an amount equivalent to your (long) stock holding. Any losses you subsequently incur on your stock will be offset by gains on your short position.

ADRs

Finally, the cheapest method of hedging a FTSE 100 stock is probably to short the associated ADR trading in the US market. Commission costs can be as low as GBP6.00 for a trade up to GBP200,000, no sales tax, and narrow bid-offer spreads.

Options Direct: www.options-direct.co.uk

Q I have a full time job and do not wish to mix it with my trading activities. Is there an internet site which will allow me to place my trades out of hours on the basis that they would be carried out immediately the markets open?

A Yes, most online brokers allow orders to be input at any time, which will be *good for the day*. For example, if you input an order on a broker's web site at 20h00 on Tuesday evening, it will be valid until market close on Wednesday, the following day. If the order is a *market* (at best) order, it would be transacted at the market open on Wednesday.

Warning!

Although it is possible to place a market order outside market hours, it is extremely imprudent. It is also unwise for the majority of investors, for a related reason, to try to deal as the market opens. In fact, many experienced investors will not deal in the first hour, or more, after the market opens.

This is because share prices can be very volatile just after opening, particularly for small cap stocks. Market makers hear the same news that you do, and first thing in the morning will adjust their prices precisely to anticipate any rash orders coming into the market from inexperienced investors. If a positive news story on a stock breaks after trading hours, buying the stock at market open the following day will commonly result in trading at the day's high price for that stock. Even if it sometimes doesn't, **the unpredictability of prices at market open makes it generally too risky to sensibly trade**.

If you do decide to place an order outside of market hours, **make sure you use a limit order** instead of a market order. A limit order instructs your broker to deal at a maximum price if buying a stock, or a minimum price if selling.

Spread betting

You could consider opening a spread betting account, because the spread bet market has longer market hours than the underlying stock market. Many investors have accounts with both stockbrokers and spread betters, and use both in combination for short or long hedging.

US account

Another alternative is to open an account directly with a broker in the US, and to trade that market in the evening, London time. I must admit I find it odd that more UK investors do not have a US trading account. Perhaps it is perceived as too risky? But if you looked at the portfolios of those investors who think it is risky, you'd probably find a clutch of technology stocks languishing 70% or more below their purchase price. In which case, one has to wonder what working definition of risk many investors use? Personally, I find the opportunity cost of being restricted to the increasingly narrowly focused UK market just too great.

Delayed settlement

Q I have been looking at the Sharepages web site and noticed that a large number of trades are made on an extended settlement basis, i.e. T+25 days rather than the more usual T+5 days. Can you explain the significance (if any) of this?

A By special arrangement with their broker, investors can sometimes settle trades 25 business days after trade date, instead of, as you point out, the more usual five days (although the standard settlement period has now moved to 3 days). The attraction is that investors can gain abnormally large exposure to a stock and then quickly sell it, without having to produce all the funds to cover the initial purchase.

Stocks with a high proportion of T+25 (extended settlement) trades are usually the more **speculative, and thus volatile, shares**. **Sharepages** maintains a list of these stocks on its 'Smoke Signals' pages, accessible from the `Equities` link in the left-hand menu. If a stock starts falling after a succession of extended settlement trades, it can fall quickly as investors rush to close their positions without the funds to be able to really settle their trades. Having said that, extended settlement is likely to become less common in the future as more trading goes online, where settlement tends to be standardised and extended settlement is not usually possible.

L Sharepages: www.sharepages.com

Trading systems

Q Are there any online trading systems that give specific buy/sell recommendations?

A If you're interested in technical analysis (TA) I'd recommend that you take a look at the **Metastock** web site. It carries the full transcript of the excellent *Technical Analysis From A To Z* by Steve Achelis. This latter work includes descriptions of over 100 separate TA indicators – from Absolute Breadth Index to William's %R and Zig Zag.

Over 100 indicators! There may be many investors who have a passing interest in TA, but not the time to mug up on the topic seriously. Fortunately there are programs available, sometimes called *trading systems*, that do all the hard work. These are expert systems that filter the whole market through a set of TA criteria, to identify trading opportunities (i.e. they produce a list of stocks to go long on, and also to short).

One of the most popular programs is called **OmniTrader**, which is often used in combination with MetaStock. Other similar programs are: Trading Expert Pro from **AIQ Systems**, **TC2000** and **Indigo Investor**.

OmniTrader and AIQ are probably the two most popular programs; they both support real-time prices, and cover the UK market. Further feedback on users' experiences can be found by keyword searching (e.g. 'omnitrader', 'aiq') bulletin boards such as **ADVFN**. There's also a good web site called **Trade2Win** which is a useful resource for information on TA and trading systems. UK distributors for the above programs are usually listed on the respective web sites, or you can try **Paritech** - a large Australian reseller of trading programs which has an office in the UK.

I'm currently reading the latest edition of *Trading Systems And Methods* by Perry Kaufman - the 700-page bible of trading systems. The book analyses all aspects of technical analysis, and the respective indicators' effectiveness for incorporating into trading programs. Definitely not an easy read, but a must for anyone seriously interested in the topic.

L ADVFN: www.advfn.com

AIQ Systems: www.aiqsystems.com

Indigo Investor: www.indigoinvestor.com

Metastock: www.equis.com

OmniTrader: www.omnitrader.com

Paritech: www.paritech.co.uk

TC2000: www.tc2000.com

Trade2Win: www.trade2win.co.uk

Trading systems redux

Investtech.com

Recently we looked at trading systems such as OmniTrader. These are programs that automatically filter the whole market using technical analysis to identify trading opportunities. Besides those programs, which require installation on a computer, there are also web sites that provide a similar service. Most of these are US-based, but there is an interesting service from Norway that covers nearly all the European markets, including the UK, called **Investtech.com**. It describes its service as *automatic pattern recognition and trend detection*. Each day the web site prepares a technical report on the market, and individual stocks, with annotated charts.

The fascinating thing is that virtually the whole report – including the text commentary – is **written automatically by a computer**. The site claims that by this process it removes the subjective element of analysis. Whether this is true or not, it's certainly a bravura performance. As well as offering copious lists of stocks (ranked by highest/lowest RSI, bullish trends long-term, bearish trends broken up etc.), it also identifies daily the top buy and sell stock recommendations.

At the time of writing, one of its top buy recommendations is Reed International, on the grounds that *it's within a rising trend and continued advance within the current trend is indicated*. Its top sell recommendation is Lorien.

Of course, it would be idiotic to base any trading decision on the basis of these recommendations alone. But this site is attracting increasing attention, and, as is the way with technical analysis, it tends to be self-fulfilling.

US markets

In the US a similar service is offered by **Sixer.com** and **Barchart.com**. The latter also has a great number of tables listing stocks hitting 52-week highs/lows, volume leaders and all the usual technical reports, but the most interesting part is their `Signals` section. Every stock is analysed using 13 technical indicators, and assigned a numeric weighting according to their attractiveness. All stocks are then ranked in a table, with their ratings of yesterday, last week and last month also displayed. Individual stocks can also be analysed in some depth, with the expert system creating an automated technical opinion. For example, Cisco is currently rated a short, medium and long term sell. After you have recovered from the statistical assault, seemingly scientific systems such as this can be deceptively attractive. In this case, they are good enough to also offer an analysis of the back-tested profitability of their various indicators. In the case of Cisco, the 50/100-day MACD oscillator has proved the most profitable indicator, while the 50-day Parabolic time/price indicator would have proved an unfortunate choice.

Barchart.com: www.barchart.com

Investtech.com: www.investtech.com

Sixer.com: www.sixer.com

Q Are there are web sites where I can practice trading stocks?

A If investing in the market recently has been too much of a white-knuckle ride, you might prefer to paper trade for a while using a trading simulator, or get your thrills vicariously through an online trading competition.

An example is the Virtual Trader competition at **CityComment**. The idea is to simulate trading in a live market, and it doesn't do a bad job. It has an interesting feature allowing the setting up of leagues for that extra competitive spirit – and also further blurring the boundaries between stock market investing, sport and gambling. These leagues however can be useful for investment clubs or devotees of specific web sites to compete against each other.

Of course, in these types of competitions there is rarely any incentive to invest in safe companies such as utilities, particularly if one can short stocks. The trick is usually to gear up to the maximum and go for the high beta stocks, or better still warrants – if they're allowed.

An American company, **SimVest Solution** specialises in creating simulated trading environments for broker web sites. Its own site has a list of the company's clients where these simulations can be found.

If you want to get a lot more serious with your practice, try downloading the simulators from the `Trading Platforms` section of US web site **CyberTrader**. *CyberX* is for ordinary investors; but if life seems dull, download *CyberTrader* – an advanced program for day traders. As their own literature states, *this is not for everyone* - but serious fun for a few.

The above competitions and trading simulations can be very useful for paper trading. However, be warned that investors usually come a cropper, not due to some technical mistake (which could have been refined through paper trading), but through **trading emotionally** (cutting profits and running losses!) which no amount of paper trading can guard against. Therefore the best type of practice trading is real trading, but with limited risks and costs. The best option is probably to open a spread betting account with **FinSpreads** or a currency trading account with **FXTrade**. In both cases, very small deal sizes are allowed.

L
```
CityComment: www.citycomment.co.uk

CyberTrader: www.cybertrader.com

FinSpreads: www.finspreads.com

FXTrade: fxtrade.oanda.com

Nasdaq (Head Trader): www.academic.nasdaq.com/HeadTrader/

SimVest Solution: www.simvesting.com
```

7

US
Markets

- Why the US?
- The top ten US web sites
- Best sites for commentary on US markets
- Sources of market tips
- Sources of broker forecasts
- Setting up an account with a US broker
- Direct Access trading
- Where to get free real-time prices
- Historic stock data
- Nasdaq stock price downloads
- US economic data: the Beige Book
- Using ADRs
- US stock index futures

Why the US?

Q I would like to ask why you write so much about the US market?

A Fair question. It's certainly true that I do mention quite a few US web sites. I'd guess that on average 20-30% of the sites I mention are US, or international. But that proportion represents the profile of the feedback I get from readers fairly closely. Why is the interest in the US market so high? It might be for a number of reasons:

As markets become more international and integrated, investing opportunities arise in many places. This is especially the case when many **UK companies also trade in the US**. Even if you don't invest in the US, it can be useful to know what's happening to UK companies trading over there (see **CNN** for news). Conversely, **American stocks also trade in Europe**, and their early afternoon movements in London can provide a clue to the direction of the US market when it opens.

Quite a few UK investors prefer trading exclusively in the US markets. This is especially the case for active traders. The **transaction costs can be much lower** - no stamp duty, lower commissions, and tighter bid/offer spreads. The **research material is superior**, helped by the more rigorous company reporting requirements. And the online broking sites are far in advance of those in the UK (e.g. the ability to use stop orders). In addition, I suspect many UK investors with day jobs enjoy trading a live market when they get home in the evenings.

Another factor is sector diversification. The UK stock market today is lacking representation in many sectors (e.g. bulk chemicals, automobiles, software). And, as someone pointed out, if you want to buy a company like Microsoft, you have to buy Microsoft!

Successful investing is all about having an edge. An edge in knowledge, or perhaps an edge in execution efficiency. Whether we like it or not, the US markets are in many ways more advanced and sophisticated than those in the UK. Therefore knowledge of the US markets, can help to give an investor an edge in the domestic market.

L CNN (ADRs): cnnfn.cnn.com/news/worldbiz/adr/

CNN (early morning call): cnnfn.cnn.com/markets/morning_call/

Top ten US sites

Q Which are the best investing sites in the US?

A I recently compiled a list of the Top Ten web sites in the UK; now it's the turn of the US. As before, the list is highly subjective – investors with special interests in, say, day trading will find better sites - but for investors new to the US market it provides a good introduction to the best that's on offer.

> **CBS MarketWatch** (www.marketwatch.com). This should be the first port of call for any investor in the US market. Excellent news, data and charts (the latter courtesy of www.bigcharts.com, which MarketWatch bought a little while ago, thereby allowing us to combine two sites in one for this Top Ten).

> **Lycos Finance** (finance.lycos.com). Good general portal site for data and charts; check out their fantastic *LiveCharts*. If you're thinking of becoming active in the US market and want a superior subscription service, this site is one to consider.

> **Datek** (www.datek.com). One of the foremost online brokers for day traders, but also offering a free real-time streaming prices gizmo. This is when trading gets serious. While here, it's also worth mentioning **Island**, www.isld.com which is one of the major new rivals to the established exchanges and which is owned by Datek. And also to mention www.3dstockcharts.com, which takes price data from Island and boldly goes where no price data service has gone before.

> **MoneyCentral Investor** (www.investor.com). A very professional general portal site, owned by Microsoft. Highlights are the articles in the *Insight* section, and also the Research Wizard in *Stocks*. A similar site to this is www.quicken.com, better for some things, but MoneyCentral wins overall.

> **SmartMoney** (www.smartmoney.com). The online counterpart of the Dow Jones magazine. First rate articles, but the attraction here is the charts and calculators: pop a purple pill, hit the Tools tab and take off.

> **ClearStation** (www.clearstation.com). Great for TA and trading systems.

> **PricewaterhouseCoopers** (edgarscan.pwcglobal.com). The Benchmarking Assistant is an analysis tool that (in their own words), 'performs graphical financial benchmarking interactively'. Perhaps not immediately useful in a trading environment, but a clever idea nevertheless.

> **Hoovers** (www.hoovers.com). The premier site for fundamental data on US companies. Also includes a nifty stock screener (found near the bottom of the page on the SiteMap).

> **StockTools** (www.stocktools.com). Good general portal site with links to real time prices and historic data.

> **Zacks** (www.zacks.com). Famous for collating brokers' forecasts. Skip the fussy home page, input a ticker symbol (e.g. AMZN) to the box at the top, select Estimates, hit go and see those downgrades.

US links sites

Q Which are the best sites for finding information on US companies?

A I am often asked which is the best web site for investors. The answer, I'm afraid, is that there isn't one. There are many web sites that are good in particular areas, but not one that is the best across the board. In addition, a good web site for one investor will not necessarily be useful to another. To get the best of all worlds, therefore, you have to shop around. But this can take time. Of help here can be web site *aggregators* which provide intelligent links to third party services.

In the US there are a great many services like this, of which the best is probably **WSRN**. Input the ticker code for Dell (I'll leave you to work out what that is), and prepare to be overwhelmed by a huge amount of information on the company, collated from third party sources. If you are new to the US market, and want to find information on companies, this is a good site to start. I see they've just introduced a couple of new reports – diagrams of companies' partners and competitors, where each partner (competitor) is represented as a planet orbiting the reference company. It's a good idea, although I don't think they have it working properly yet. Hopefully, we'll see more of these visualisation innovations in the near future.

L WSRN: www.wsrn.com

Q Which are the best US sites for market commentary?

A Market commentaries available for free from a wide range of sources are a tremendous resource for ordinary investors. Below, I have listed what I regard as the top 10 online commentators, mainly on the US and international markets, covering equities, options, technology stocks and economics.

Thom Calandra (cbs.marketwatch.com). Consistently interesting commentary on the US markets.

John Dorfman (www.bloomberg.com/columns/). A legendary US commentator, covering specific stocks. There's a great recent article on the out-performance of stockbrokers' sell recommendations over their buy recommendations.

Paul Erdman (cbs.marketwatch.com). Big picture stuff from the renowned economist and author.

Ken Fisher (www.forbes.com/columnists). Global market strategy from the veteran *Forbes* columnist and author of *Super Stocks*.

Herb Greenberg (www.thestreet.com/comment/). Found vilification and then fame as the one commentator to consistently question the figures coming out of Lernout & Hauspie, the Belgian voice recognition company. Search on the keyword 'Lernout' to get the whole story.

Jim Jubak (moneycentral.msn.com/content/data/jubakjournal.asp). Interesting international portfolio analysis and dubious stock picking from the main commentator on the Microsoft's MoneyCentral Investor hub.

Adam Lashinsky (money.cnn.com/commentary/bottomline/). CNN and Money markets commentator.

Dean LeBaron (www.deanlebaron.com). The founder of Batterymarch Financial Management records a daily video commentary with his views on life, the markets, and anything else that pops into his head. This isn't the place to find stock tips, but it's quirky and thought provoking.

John Murphy (www.stockcharts.com/commentary/Murphy/). Excellent (illustrated) technical analysis commentary from the author of the seminal *Technical Analysis of the Financial Markets*.

Bernie Schaeffer
(www.schaeffersresearch.com/schaeffer/bernie_schaeffer.asp). Technical analysis of stocks, indices and options from the author of "The Options Adviser". Interesting analysis on the open interest in the Nasdaq 100 cubes [QQQ].

The effectiveness of many of the above as successful stock pickers can be checked at **Validea.** At the time of writing Validea's site www.validea.com is down, but hopefully will return soon.

Collective tips

Q What's the point of sites which simply report tips from ordinary users?

A Let me answer your question by taking a rather circuitous route: *what are the valuable assets of Reuters?* A few years ago the answer might have been its unique reporting of financial news - its 'products'. But it now has competitors who supply similar information, so that can't be its competitive advantage. Maybe its expensively installed monitors and leased lines give Reuters an edge? But that is being eroded as more and more traders use PCs connected to the internet. If its strength lies neither in its products or distribution, what else is there? Its clients.

Of course, there is nothing new in defining a business's competitive advantage by its client base, but the traditional assumption is that the advantage lies solely in the business's ability to target the clients. In other words, in one-way communication. In fact, it's more subtle than this. Reuters, for instance, collates and interprets financial market data, but the financial markets themselves are merely an agglomeration of thousands of individuals, many of whom are themselves clients of Reuters. The clients of Reuters *are* the financial markets, and that opens up new possibilities.

If a business has a client base with which it can truly interact, it has the opportunity to become an intelligent conduit of information flow *between* the clients themselves. That is more valuable than merely recording a market and broadcasting its activity, which can easily be replicated. Does Reuters appreciate this? Perhaps, consciously or sub-consciously. Its Instinet operation is an example of a platform for direct information flow between clients.

This brings us round to your question. Web sites are beginning to cotton on to the value inherent in their client base. At a low level, they provide bulletin boards for users to interact with each other, but they are also doing more interesting things. For example, **ClearStation** solicits recommendations from subscribers and then monitors their performance, giving figures for average percentage gain and percentage winning trades. Figures that would be meaningless for just a few tips, but their subscribers obviously take this pretty seriously with the most active posting over 1,000 recommendations.

Another site, **ChangeWave** is a more exclusive operation where membership is by invitation only. In their own words, the Alliance is *the world's first open source, investment research network*, comprised of, *New Economy professionals*, and claims a five-year aggregate return of 2,700%. Members post tips which are then filtered and then disseminated back to all members.

This is an interesting area with powerful ramifications that might be catalysed by the internet. Or perhaps not. Or not quite yet. Several companies jumped in at the height of the internet, such as www.mutualminds.com, www.iexchange.com and www.stockjungle.com, none of which is still operating. StockJungle had the rather worrying strap line, '*Who knows more about investing than you? No one.*' and offered $50 for top tips for a fund that it ran.

L ChangeWave: www.changewave.com
ClearStation: www.clearstation.com

Q I subscribe to t1ps.com. Can you recommend similar services that cover the US markets, and also tell me if there is a site that rates their performance?

A **The Security Blanket.com** is a good reference source for US online newsletters Three worth looking at are: **Indexskybox.com**, **OptionInvestor.com**, and **SignalWatch.com**. As far as performance rating is concerned, **The Hulbert Financial Digest** ranks 160 newsletters and tracks the performance of 500 of their recommended portfolios.

Also of interest is **Validea.com**, which monitors stock recommendations given by gurus, analysts, magazines, web sites, television and its own users. The current top ranking guru on Validea is Mark Edelstone whose recommendations appear in *Forbes*, *Investors Daily* and *Barrons*. Edelstone gets a 5 Light Bulb rating due to his last 21 ideas producing a 3-monthly average return of 32%. Another in the top ten is Thom Calandra of MarketWatch who weighs in with a prolific 179 picks, which generated an average 14% return over the same period.

The analysis of these gurus goes much deeper than simple rankings. Their returns over 1-week, 1-month, 3-months and 1-year are compared with the S&P500 (with a relative chart graphically representing this), their recent ideas are listed, as are their top and bottom picks, and finally a rating is applied by the web site's community. The results can be filtered - you can search for tips on a specific sector, or a specific stock, and get all tips from all sources.

When it comes to magazines, the most successful stock pickers according to Validea over a 3-month period are **Technology Investor**, followed by **Money**, **Individual Investor** and **Redherring**. Whereas the star columns are Stock Focus (**Forbes**) and Stock Selector (**Bloomberg Personal**). The leading web sites are MSN MoneyCentral and worldlyinvestor.com. While the top TV sources are **CNBC** and **Bloomberg**.

One interesting section on Validea is **Guru Analysis**, which distils the analytical techniques of 9 famous gurus and automatically assesses a stock according to the individual gurus' criteria. For example, companies are rated Pass/Fail on 7 Ben Graham criteria, including: Sector, Sales, Current Ratio etc. There's also a stock screener, which allows the markets to be scanned for stocks satisfying the selection approach of, say, Peter Lynch or Martin Zweig. All rather clever.

L
```
The Hulbert Financial Digest: www.hulbertdigest.com
Indexskybox.com: www.Indexskybox.com
MSN MoneyCentral: www.investor.com
Nasdaq: www.nasdaq.com
Option Investir: www.optioninvestor.com
The Security Blanket.com: www.thesecurityblanket.com/tradingideas/
SignalWatch: www.signalWatch.com
Validea.com: www.validea.com
worldlyinvestor.com: www.worldlyinvestor.com
```

************* STOP PRESS: Validea's web site seems to have been closed! Hopefully it will return shortly. *:***********

Q Where is the best place to find brokers' estimates for US companies?

A Many US web sites carry brokers' forecasts, but the majority get their information from the same source - **Zacks** - so this is the best place to look. It works very simply: for example, if you go to the Zacks home page and enter 'DELL' into the top box, then select `Estimates` from the drop-down box, you'll see a list of forecasts from all covered brokers (in this case 25 of them). The list includes the brokers' recommendation, estimates for fiscal year and quarterly EPS and 5-year EPS growth. All the estimates are ranked in reverse date order – i.e. the latest estimates listed first. Some analysis of these figures is also included. Zacks calculate the consensus of estimates made over the last 120 days and also the last 30 days.

EPS forecasts

When it comes to broker's forecasts of EPS, it's not so much the absolute figures that count, but rather the change in those estimates over time. In this case, the 120-day consensus estimates for Dell are $0.91 and $1.11 for Jan 2001 and 2002 respectively. Whereas the equivalent 30-day consensus figures are: $0.90 and $1.06. And, as for many other companies, this recent downward revision in estimates has been reflected in the share price.

Brokers's recommendations

From the estimates page, if you click on `All reports for Dell`, you find an enormous amount of further information on the stock. The first page summarises some of the figures already seen, including brokers' recommendations. In the case of Dell, 7 brokers recommend it as a *Strong Buy*, 10 as a *Moderate Buy* and 9 as a *Hold*. Zacks calculates an average recommendation weighting, and monitors how this figure changes week by week. Another page lists detailed analysts' recommendations – instead of grouping the recommendations into convenient buy/hold/sell categories here, the original equivocal broker-speak language is used (e.g. *long-term attractive*). Again, these are listed in reverse data order, so, in the case of Dell, you can see the recommendations over the last three months move from *buy* to *outperform* to *neutral*.

Stock screening

A useful service on Zacks is its `Screening` program, which allows the company's universe of stocks to be filtered on any combination of over 90 criteria. If 90 different criteria sounds rather overwhelming, you can use pre-defined screens, one of which is a filter for the 25 stocks with the greatest increase (and decrease) in their *Average Broker Recommendation* rating.

Brokers' research

Zacks also provides links to brokers' original research, in a service similar to that provided by **Multex**. As with Multex, there is a mixture of free research and reports priced at around $10-25, although the range of research available is probably wider at Multex. If you want to see most of the information on just one page, Zacks has a page, *The Whole Enchilada* which offers just that. As well as company financials, there's a summary of brokers' recommendations (including changes from the previous week), EPS growth comparisons with the industry, and a representation of EPS estimates as a histogram.

Other sites

Many other web sites carry estimates data from Zacks. One is **Yahoo**, which, being summarised cleanly on one page, is arguably more digestible. There is less detail, but the page is very good at representing the trend in EPS estimates and brokers' recommendations; as well as earnings growth comparisons with the industry and market and history of earnings surprises. However, the figures are not quite as up to date as those on the source Zacks site. For example, Yahoo has consensus EPS estimates for 2001 and 2002 at $0.91 and $1.11, which are the 120-day averages, and slightly higher than the more recent 30-day figures. Yahoo also has a (simple) stock screener, which you can use to identify stocks with brokers' recommendation ranging from strong buy to strong sell (in the former category, currently 415 stocks are listed as strong buys).

Besides Zacks, another company collating brokers' forecasts is BARRA. Although mianly targeted at institutions, some of its data is available on public web sites, including **FT.com**. At the home page of FT.com, enter 'DELL' into the `Get quote` box, and select `analyst estimates` from the resulting company profile page. You'll see forecasts from 29 brokers (4 more than Zacks), but with far less detail - just EPS estimates for fiscal years to Jan 2001 and 2002, plus a summary recommendation. Also, the forecasts are listed alphabetically - less useful than reverse date order. Consensus estimates are calculated, which in the case of Dell are currently $0.92 and $1.12 (Jan 2001, Jan 2002); and which, as with Yahoo, do not appear to represent the most recent consensus of the last 30 days.

Other services in this area are: **First Call**, **I/B/E/S**, and **Thomson Financial Securities Data**. All three are owned by the acquisitive Thomson Financial, but traditionally these services have been oriented towards the institutional market. For the moment its main individual investor service is **Thomson Financial Network**, which offers access to research and FirstCall reports as part of a charged-for premium service. However, there's free access to an estimates snapshot.

Finally, don't forget that many US brokers also follow UK stocks, such that many of the above services will also cover the larger stocks like Vodafone, GlaxoSmithKline and BP.

```
First Call: www.firstcall.com

FT.com: www.ft.com

I/B/E/S: www.ibes.com

Multex: www.multex.com

Thomson Financial Network: www.thomsonfn.com

Thomson Financial Securities Data: www.tfsd.com

Yahoo Finance: finance.yahoo.com

Zacks: www.zacks.com
```

US trading accounts

Q I've read of UK investors opening accounts with US online brokers to trade American stocks. Is this easy to do? How should I decide which broker to use?

A Yes, this is a straightforward procedure. First, you need to select a broker - there are now almost 100 online brokers in the US to choose from, although not all of them will accept non-US clients. A good starting point is **Gomez Advisers**, independent consultants who rank online brokers according to certain criteria. Another useful site is **Motley Fool**, which has an excellent section on selecting UK online brokers, and links to its parent US site where you can find good information on US brokers. There are quite a few other sites that contain rankings of brokers' services, or bulletin boards with feedback from clients; for example, **SmartMoney** and **Cyberinvest**.

One of the criticisms leveled at brokers has been that their online service can be very slow when markets are busy. Further information on this can be found at the **Keynote Web Broker Trading Index** where weekly reports are available on the speed and accessibility of brokers' web sites. Hopefully these types of independent analysis of brokers' services will soon be on offer in the UK as well.

Having selected a broker, the next stage is to contact them (by telephone, post or, best of all of course, via the web site) and ask them to send **account opening forms and a W-8 form**. The latter form is to identify you as a non-US resident, and will exempt you from paying US taxes. These forms must be completed, signed and returned by post - it is not possible to open accounts purely via the web. Having returned the forms, your account will then be activated with the broker, but you will not be able to trade until you have deposited cash into your account. There are many ways to do this, but the simplest is to ask your bank to transfer funds from your sterling account in the UK to the dollar account with the US broker. You don't have to set up a separate dollar account with a bank.

L Cyberinvest: www.cyberinvest.com

Gomez Advisers: www.gomezadvisors.com

Keynote Web Broker Trading Index: www.keynote.com/measures/brokers/

Motley Fool: www.fool.co.uk

SmartMoney: www.smartmoney.com/brokers/

174

Direct access trading

Q Can you explain what direct access trading is?

A To understand what direct access trading is, and why it exists, you need to know a little about how order execution works in the US, and the key word here is 'fragmentation'. In the UK, the London Stock Exchange provides the main forum for trading stocks. Over the pond, however, stocks can trade on a number of exchanges: the NYSE, Nasdaq, or one of a number of smaller exchanges.

Recently the picture has become more complicateed (and interesting) with the rise of so-called **Electronic Communication Networks** (ECNs). These are independent competitors challenging the established exchanges, quite often backed by large brokers or investment banks who have taken a stake in this fledgling industry on the chance that it represents the future of stock trading. Examples of these new ECNs include **Island**, which was set up by Datek and is one of the largest, Reuter's **Instinet** for institutional investors, and **Archipelago**. Most ECNs are electronic bulletin board systems, on which members post buy or sell orders (size and price) for everyone else to see. The race is now on for these ECNs - like any marketplace - to gain critical mass by boosting their trading volumes.

Order routing

The result is that behind the scenes **the handling of stock orders is not as simple as it once was**. In theory, US investors wanting to buy or sell a stock have to decide how and where they want the order to be executed. And the decision might vary for different stocks. In practice, they just indicate whether they want to buy or sell a stock, with any further price instructions (e.g. for limit or stop orders), and their broker does the order routing. That might mean crossing the order in-house (i.e. matching a buy and sell order on the same stock from two different clients), or it might mean the broker passes the order to a market maker, who gives them a kick-back for the order flow; or the order might be passed to an ECN. A useful reference page which describes the order routing procedures for most of the new ECNs is at Alan Farley's swing trading web site, **HardRightEdge**.

Hang on a minute, what was that bit about kick-backs - isn't that illegal?

Not necessarily, but it is controversial. If you've ever wondered how US brokers make a profit with commissions as low as $6 a trade, one answer is to be found in these *cash for order flow* arrangements between certain brokers and market makers. This is nothing new, but recently there has been more public comment about it, and in one case Datek decided to rebate the cash received to its clients.

Although these order processing methods may sound a bit arbitrary, with plenty of scope for the poor, duped investor to lose out, in general it doesn't work like that. There are regulations governing how trades are processed, and, more importantly, the competitive pressures of the marketplace keep things in line. Whatever method is used, in most cases the client will get pretty much the same price, it may just take a little longer sometimes.

Speed of order execution

But there's the rub; *it may just take a little longer*. And for some investors, notably active investors, that's not good enough. For them, especially day traders, they need to trade very quickly. They need to be able to see accurate real-time prices, spot a specific bid or offer, hit exactly that price and then, importantly, know that they've dealt within a second. This type of service cannot be offered by the standard online brokers, partly because of the methods of order routing described above, and also in part due to the client interface technology. Clients of ordinary online brokers usually access the service via a web site using a browser, which is not ideal for dealing in fast-moving markets.

Direct access brokers

To meet the needs of active investors, new services have evolved, including direct access brokers, which offer greater control over how orders are executed. These services do not generally use the web, but instead use special software that is loaded on the trader's computer. The trader can automatically search the whole market for the best price, or can identify (*preference*) a specific market maker or ECN. Examples of these direct access brokers are: **CyberTrader.com** (owned by Charles Schwab), **Tradecast**, **myTrack**, **Tradescape.com** and **DirectAccessTrader**.

Hybrid brokers

Drawbacks of direct access systems are that they are more costly than normal online brokers, and the complex software interface can be rather daunting. But one of the most interesting current developments is the growth of hybrid broking services – offering direct access features to ordinary investors. **Datek** has released *Direct Trader* to all its clients. This is a very impressive service, with many of the features of direct access, but at a cheaper price, and a much simpler interface. Another good service is from **Interactive Brokers**, and **E*Trade** has also released Power E*Trade. Many of these new hybrid services use Java with the (slight) disadvantage that the application has to be fully downloaded each session, but they are fully cross platform, allow trading from any computer and removing the burden from the user of upgrading software on their own computers.

Although direct access systems are more powerful than most investors need, it is the growth area of the market, with ordinary investors increasingly signing up for the advanced services - hence the interest being shown by the big brokers in either developing their own DAT systems or in buying up existing players.

L

CyberTrader.com: www.cybertrader.com

Datek: www.datek.com

DirectAccessTrader: www.directaccesstrader.com

E*Trade: www.etrade.com

HardRightEdge: www.hardrightedge.com/work/orderrouting.htm

Interactive brokers: www.interactivebrokers.com

myTrack: www.mytrack.com

Tradecast: www.tradecast.com

Tradescape.com: www.tradescape.com

Free real-time US stock prices

Q

Do you know of a web site that gives free real-time US stock prices?

A

A couple of years ago, it was difficult to avoid free real-time prices on US web sites. But times have changed, and now the free services have all but disappeared. One of very few remaining sources is **FreeRealTime**, which has a rather tedious registration procedure (demanded by the exchanges), but at least the quotes are free. They also offer an annual subscription service costing $80, which does not display the banner ads.

A similar service is available from **Wall Street City**. This is superior to the FreeRealTime service in that there is a real-time chart, technical indicators such as momentum breakout and also historic quotes can be downloaded.

An excellent trial service is offered by **Lycos Finance** with access to free streaming Nasdaq stock and charts. The fee-based services are also very good. If you're happy to pay for a more flexible service, then the best real-time services, along with Lycos Finance, are **Money.net** and **IQ Chart**.

Investors interested in Nasdaq stocks can also look at real-time prices on the **Island** web site. Island is one of several independent exchanges (called *ECNs*) in the US trading Nasdaq stocks, so prices will not necessarily reflect the whole market. Island is now the largest ECN, having overtaken Instinet at the end of 2001. The US broker, **Datek** offers a great free applet with streaming real-time prices from four ECNs.

Of course, most brokers offer real-time prices to their clients, which will usually be sufficient. And if you don't have a US broking account, then the usefulness of real-time prices – with no way of taking action on the data – is dubious.

L

Datek: www.datek.com

FreeRealTime: quotes.freerealtime.com

IQ Chart: www.iqchart.com

Island: www.island.com

Lycos Finance: finance.lycos.com

Money.net: www.money.net

Wall Street City: www.wallstreetcity.com

Historic US stock prices

Q My shares in UK-quoted Airtech were bought by Nasdaq quoted Remec. Although I have been able to find historic share prices on the internet for Remec, I haven't found any site where I can download them easily onto my PC in Excel format, rather than tediously copying them manually.

A The best service is provided by **Yahoo Finance**, where you can get daily, weekly and monthly historic stock data (plus dividend data), all of it downloadable in spreadsheet format. Other good historical data services (albeit with charges) are **WSRN** and **Downloadquotes.com**.

L Downloadquotes.com: www.downloadquotes.com

WSRN: www.wsrn.com

Yahoo Finance: chart.yahoo.com/d

YAHOO! FINANCE

Historical Prices - WMT (Wal-Mart Stores Inc)

More Info: Quote | Chart | News |

Start: Feb 18 02
End: May 22 02

- ● Daily
- ○ Weekly
- ○ Monthly
- ○ Dividends

Ticker Symbol: wmt **Get Data**

Date	Open	High	Low	Close	Volume	Adj. Close*
21-May-02	57.90	58.12	56.60	**56.60**	6,376,800	56.60
20-May-02	58.75	58.82	57.70	**57.80**	5,031,900	57.80
17-May-02	58.35	59.30	57.96	**58.33**	7,547,100	58.33
16-May-02	57.65	58.69	57.44	**58.35**	8,016,000	58.35
15-May-02	57.64	58.19	56.64	**56.77**	10,467,000	56.77
14-May-02	57.50	58.25	57.05	**57.39**	12,505,700	57.39
13-May-02	53.84	55.28	53.84	**55.04**	6,421,700	55.04
10-May-02	55.24	55.26	53.61	**53.66**	7,436,000	53.66

Nasdaq stock price downloads

Q Do you know of any sites where I can download closing prices for all Nasdaq stocks on a daily basis?

A I don't think this is possible. If it was, I guess it would be too easy for computer whizzes to automate it and set themselves up in the data provider business. There are sources for historic data (e.g. **Yahoo Finance**), but you can only retrieve data for individual companies one at a time. For multiple companies, the best thing is to set up portfolios with **MSN** or **Yahoo Finance**, where the closing prices of constituent companies can be downloaded as a text file and/or imported into a spreadsheet.

It's probably not possible to include all Nasdaq stocks in the portfolios, but multiple portfolios can be created which should cover a very wide range of the whole market. The only other alternative may be to use an offline portfolio tool, such as **myTrack** or **Portfolio Stock Monitor**. These won't offer much more than MSN's Investor in this case, but the management of very large portfolios of stocks may be easier with these tools, than the purely online browser-based MSN.

L MSN: www.investor.com

myTrack: www.mytrack.com

Portfolio Stock Monitor: www.dtlink.com

Yahoo Finance: finance.yahoo.com

Nasdaq ticker symbols

Q A stock I've been following on Nasdaq has recently changed its ticker symbol. There's now an extra Q letter at the end. What does this mean?

A Unfortunately, a Q indicates that the stock is currently in bankruptcy proceedings. A full list of these fifth letters (sometimes appended to Nasdaq stock symbols) can be found in the Glossary section on the Nasdaq web site (under *Stock symbol*). Some examples: G is for a first convertible bond listing, K indicates non-voting, W for warrants, and Y for an ADR.

L Nasdaq (Glossary): www.nasdaq.com/reference/glossary.stm

Q UK markets seem to be strongly influenced by the release of economic statistics in the US - in fact, the markets seem to have just two modes: reacting to US figures just announced, or waiting for the next set of figures to be released. Is there anywhere on the net where I can find these figures and, importantly, a timetable for their release?

A Yes, if you're looking for those exciting book-to-bill ratios or non-farm payrolls, head straight for the cutely named **The Dismal Scientist** where, among a wealth of economics information, there's a monthly calendar of upcoming figures. It also includes some international statistics.

The Dismal Scientist is a well-designed treasure trove of a site which carries the famous *Stock Market Valuation Calculator*. This calculator uses a couple of assumptions on corporate profit growth and long-term interest rates, and spits out a figure telling you how much the market is currentlyy under/over-valued according to traditional measures. Annoyingly, The Dismal Scientist has become a subscription-only web site, but if you register they will send you a daily email newsletter free of charge.

The official source of much of the data on The Dismal Scientist is the **US Federal Reserve**, a rather large sprawling organisation, but with a good central web site. More accessible might be the web site of the energetic and eponymous **Dr Yardeni**, the Chief Investment Strategist at Prudential Securities, who's created one of the more useful home pages on the web. Besides an impressive list of links to economic data worldwide, there is also daily economics commentary, weekly audio comments and regular polls of institutional investors. Best of all though is a collection of his articles on the economy. Recent gems include a discussion on how companies manipulate their earnings, and the lottery nature of the current technology boom. One thing missing from Dr Yardeni's web site is any mention of Y2K. Strange that, considering the good doctor was one of the most vocal doomsayers of 1999.

Another good source for economic news and a global release calendar is **Economeister**.

L The Dismal Scientist: www.dismal.com

Economeister: www.economeister.com

Federal Reserve: www.federalreserve.gov

Dr Yardeni: www.yardeni.com

The Beige Book

Q What is the 'beige book'?

A The Beige Book is a US report of anecdotal evidence of economic activity collected from the 12 regional districts of the Federal Reserve. Its importance is due to its use in the meetings held every six weeks of the Federal Open Market Committee (FOMC), where interest rate policy is decided.

A summary of previous reports can be read at the web site of the **Federal Reserve**. Commentary on the Beige Book (and other economic figures) can be found at **The Dismal Scientist** (input 'Beige Book' to the search engine to find it quickly), although this is a subscription-based site.

Calendars of upcoming economic releases are at **Briefing.com** and **Nasdaq**. The latter site also has some very good weekly economic US and international reports and a useful reference section that describes all the economic indicators, and what each means to investors (called, rather bluntly, *Why investors care*).

L Briefing.com: www.briefing.com/FreeServices/fs_markcal.htm

The Dismal Scientist: www.dismal.com

Federal Reserve: www.federalreserve.gov/FOMC/BeigeBook/2002/

Nasdaq: www.nasdaq.com/reference/econoday_frameset.htm

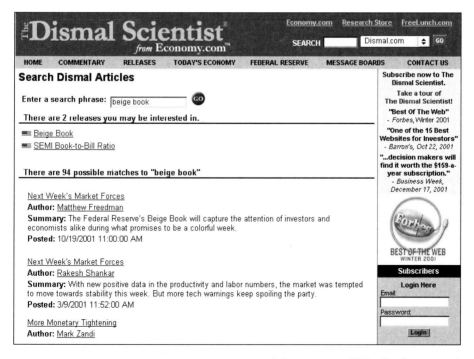

International investing and ADRs

Q I want to invest in some European and Asian shares. Is it possible to open an account with a European online broker and trade these markets?

A A few brokers offer trading of multiple markets from the same account, such as **IMIweb**, but they are limited to a small range of European and US markets. If you are thinking of trading in markets worldwide, it gets complicated - opening accounts with brokers in many different countries. Furthermore, the account opening forms may not be in English, the commissions can be high, and there's the general awkwardness of maintaining multiple accounts in different currencies. In future, the larger online brokers like Schwab or E*Trade will probably offer trading in multiple markets, but we are not there yet.

An alternative is to invest in *American Depository Receipts* (ADRs) in the US market. ADRs are securities issued in the US which are linked to shares in international companies. For example, Ericsson shares are listed on the Stockholm Exchange, but there are also Ericsson ADRs [ERICY] trading in the US. The two securities track each other closely, and the latter can be used as a proxy for investing in the Sweden-listed shares.

There are now over 2,000 ADRs linked to major companies from over 60 countries world-wide. A comprehensive list can be found at the **Bank of New York** web site where you'll also find a good explanation of what ADRs are and how new ones are created. However, note that not all of these ADRs are listed on exchanges; many are traded OTC (over the counter) and are difficult to invest in. The best index of *tradeable* ADRs is at **CNNfn**, while a general description can be seen at the **Motley Fool UK** site.

The advantage of ADRs is that you can **invest in companies from many different countries using one brokerage account**. Other advantages of ADRs are those applying to the trading of any US security, including low commissions, the easy use of trading techniques such as shorting, a well-regulated market, and use of the many advanced US financial web services. For example, company research can be found at **Hoovers** or **Multex**, latest prices at **Lycos Finance** and internet links at **WSRN**. Researching and trading companies like the German SAP [SAP], the Spanish Repsol [REP], the French Alcatel [ALA] or the Italian Gucci [GUC] becomes as easy as investing in Microsoft [MSFT].

Further data and research on ADRs can be found on **JP Morgan's** dreadfully over-engineered web site; **Reuters** produces a daily ADR report, and **worldlyinvestor.com** carries general world markets information.

L
```
Hoovers: www.hoovers.com
JP Morgan (ADRs): www.adr.com
Multext: www.multex.com
Lycos Finance: finance.lycos.com
worldlyinvestor.com: www.worldlyinvestor.com
WSRN: www.wsrn.com
Yahoo Finance (Reuters ADR Report): biz.yahoo.com/rf/
```

ADR information sources

Q I used to be able to get ADR prices from DBC and then CBS MarketWatch, but it seems to be no longer available from those sites. Do you know of another source on the web?

A ADRs (American Depository Receipts) are securities of international companies trading in the US markets. Over 100 UK companies have issued ADRs that trade in the US, including: ARM, Bookham Technology, BP, HSBC, Reuters, Vodafone

CBS MarketWatch does still carry ADR prices, just as it carries all US securities prices, but the section devoted to ADRs has gone. However, input the ticker symbol 'VOD' to their quote box, and the ADR price for Vodafone will be displayed.

Comparing UK and related US ADR prices

To compare Vodafone's ADR price with the price of Vodafone trading in the London market, two conversions must be made.

- First, the **dollar price must be converted to sterling**, at GBP/USD=1.42, this gives a price of £14.59.

- Secondly, the Vodafone ADR has a **conversion ratio** of 10 (i.e. there are 10 London shares to one Vodafone ADR). Hence dividing by 10, gives a sterling equivalent price of £1.459.

At the time of writing, the London shares are actually trading at £1.455. The two Vodafone securities were therefore trading close to each other – as would be expected for a widely followed company like Vodafone. However, for other companies, their UK and US securities prices can sometimes diverge, at which point an arbitrage opportunity arises.

The most focused information source for ADRs is **JP Morgan's** web site. You can search by company name, region or sector, there is market commentary on ADRs, charts, fundamental data and earnings estimates, links to company web sites, and news items. It also lists the most active ADRs in each sector, which is useful as poor liquidity can be a problem with some ADRs.

The best general site for ADRs is that of the **Bank of New York**. It doesn't carry up to date prices, but it does have a huge amount of background information on the topic, including full details on each ADR (with conversion ratios). There's also a *DR Converter* that compares the cost of owning ADRs against direct ownership of the underlying stock in its domestic market.

L Bank of New York (ADRs): www.adrbny.com

CBS MarketWatch: cbs.marketwatch.com

JP Morgan (ADRs): www.adr.com

183

Q In the past you've recommended that investors should consider investing in ADRs trading in the US. Given that these trade in dollars, doesn't this make the investment more complicated as it is necessary to consider both the equity risk and the currency risk at the same time?

A No, this is not necessarily the case. First, let me recap what ADRs are and why they exist.

The US capital markets are among the most efficient in the world. In consequence it is very cheap for companies to raise money there. This applies not just to US companies, but also to international companies, who want to tap the US capital market. There may well be other strategic reasons why companies want to attract US investors, including diversification of their shareholding base, and a raising of their corporate profile in the US.

However, there are frequently restrictions on the activities of US fund managers, a common one being that they can only invest in securities that are listed on a US exchange. Hence, international companies, if they want US funds as shareholders, must list their shares on a US exchange – usually the New York Stock Exchange, or Nasdaq.

The process by which this happens is not terribly important, but briefly, a tranche of the shares of a non-US company are deposited in a US bank as security for a new set of shares issued to US investors. These new shares are called *American Depository Receipts* (ADRs). If you look on **hemscott.NET** at the major shareholders of a company which has ADRs, you'll sometimes see that a high percentage of the shares are owned by the Bank of New York – one of the main depositor banks in the US for ADRs. The ratio of ADRs issued to underlying shares is not normally 1:1. For example, 1 Vodafone ADR trading on the NYSE is equivalent to 10 Vodafone shares trading on the London exchange.

Currencies are not volatile

Now, back to your question about currency exposure. First, let's examine currency volatility itself. A chart of the USD/GBP rate over the last couple of years can be seen at **Pacific Exchange Rates Service**. From this you can see that over a 12 month period the rate has ranged from a high of approx 166 to a low of 144.

Is that volatile? Well, by comparison, the high/low prices for a selection of stocks over the same period are, Marks & Spencer: 428/218, Vodafone: 401/227, Psion: 1510/169, Dixons: 365/60.

A bond investor might find currencies volatile, but the charge is a bit rich coming from an equity investor. Nevertheless there's this abiding belief that currencies (and commodities in general) are volatile. A reason for this may be that commodities are commonly traded on margin (via the futures market), where the investment itself – thanks to huge gearing – can be very volatile indeed, despite only relatively small moves in the underlying asset itself.

No US Dollar exposure

However, I digress, because, there is no US dollar currency exposure anyway for ADR investments, even though the ADRs themselves are priced in dollars. The reason being that the ADR price in the US continually reacts to two influences-

1. the **share price** of the company in its domestic market

2. the **US dollar exchange rate**

Let me illustrate this with a crude example. Suppose UK company XYZ has a share price in London of £1, while its ADR price in the US is $10. If the London price rises to £2, then the ADR will increase to $20 – assuming no change in the USD/GBP rate. But if, over this period, sterling had doubled in value relative to the dollar, then the ADR price would have increased to $40 – to compensate for the weakened dollar. And the force that keeps these prices aligned as such is from arbitrage traders at investment banks.

The result of this is that the returns on £1,000 invested in Vodafone shares in London, or £1,000 invested in the Vodafone ADR in the US, will be the same – regardless of what the USD/GBP exchange rate does.

The general rule here is that **the currency exposure with ADRs is to the currency of the underlying asset**. For example, currency exposure is to the Euro for an investment in Alcatel or Deutsche Telecom ADRs, to the Yen for an investment in Sony ADRs, and to sterling for an investment in BP ADRs. Finally, remember that as soon as you sell an ADR and the proceeds are deposited to your account, you then have a US dollar currency exposure on the net cash.

hemscott.NET (companies info):
www.hemscott.com/equities/compindx.htm

Pacific Exchange Rates Service:
pacific.commerce.ubc.ca/xr/plot.html

Q

Recently in US market reports I've seen mention of something called the VIX. Can you please explain what it is?

A

To understand what the VIX is, you need to know a little about the options markets. The starting point is that options can be traded on market indices as well as on individual stocks. A list of index options trading on the world's largest options exchange, the Chicago Board Options Exchange (CBOE), can be seen at its web site.

History of the OEX

In 1983, the CBOE wanted to introduce an options contract on the broad US market, and created a special index – now called the *S&P100*. This index [symbol: OEX] tracks the broader S&P500 Index [SPX] very closely, as can be seen by checking the charting service at **cbs.marketwatch** or **Silicon Investor**. (Adding the Dow Jones Industrial Index [DJIA], it can be seen how much SPX and DJIA performance has diverged since November 2000). Options on this S&P100 Index (www.cboe.com/micro/oex/) have become some of the most actively traded options in the US – and will often be the instrument of choice when traders want to quickly take a view on the market as a whole.

Volatility index

As such, OEX options can provide a useful **indicator of the immediate market mood**. And, fortunately, this sentiment indicator can be expressed numerically by calculating the implied volatility of the options. In this case, a *volatility index* is calculated by taking a weighted average of the implied volatilities of 8 close-to-the-money call and put options on the OEX. The calculated index is called the *CBOE Volatility Index* – and its symbol is VIX.

Asymmetric behaviour

The VIX can be plotted on any charting site, just like any another other index or stock. It is commonly plotted against the Nasdaq market, or more specifically the Nasdaq 100 Index [QQQ]. If this is done, you can see quite a marked inverse relationship between the two lines. The theory being that as the market rises, traders get optimistic and so bid up the prices of call options (thereby increasing the implied volatility); conversely, as the market falls, traders pile into put options. But the interesting feature is that the **relationship is not symmetrical**: the VIX increases more when the market falls than when it rises. This has been examined in greater detail in an academic paper published in May 2000.

A measure of fear

The VIX can perhaps be regarded as a measure of fear in the market – it rises when traders are fearful. As such, it can be used as a contrary indicator, encapsulated by the saying, *When the VIX is high, it's time to buy; when the VIX is low, it's time to go.* At the time of writing it stands at 35, which, as can be seen from the chart, is historically high. But there's a general feeling that the bottom of this market (the *capitulation*) will not be seen until the VIX hits 60.

Although the VIX was introduced in 1993, there certainly does seem to have been greater mention of it recently. A cynical view might be that after ordinary investors have got used to references to indicators such as RSI, brokers and media commentators have to move on to ever more obscure terms such as the VIX to keep the obfuscation quotient high.

But volatility is definitely a fashionable area. In recent competitive moves to target more specifically the Nasdaq market, the CBOE has introduced the *CBOE Nasdaq Volatility Index* [VXN], while the Amex has created the *QQQ Volatility Index* [QQV].

Academic paper on the VIX:
papers.ssrn.com/sol3/papers.cfm?abstract_id=194288

CBOE: www.cboe.com

CBS marketWatch: cbs.marketwatch.com

Silicon Investor: www.siliconinvestor.com

US stock index futures

Q Bloomberg TV provides constant updates for Nasdaq, S&P and Dow futures. Where are these being traded and do you know a web site where the prices can be accessed?

A The Nasdaq and S&P500 futures trade at the **CME**, while the Dow Jones futures trade at the **CBOT**. Both these exchanges have very good price information services on their web sites. Particularly good is the CME's *flash page*, which displays prices updated every few minutes for indices, currencies and interest rate contracts.

The best page to view all three contracts at once is the futures page at **INO**. Other good sources of futures quotes are **PC Quote** and **TFC**.

Because the futures markets open earlier than the stock markets, the early trading in the index futures can give a useful indication of how the NYSE and Nasdaq will open. Therefore, a good page to look at in the early afternoon (UK time) is **CNN Morning Call**, which lists the early trading in all three index contracts, plus indications of how US stocks have been trading that day in Europe.

L CBOT: www.cbot.com

CME: www.cme.com

CME (flash quotes): www.cme.com/prices/delayed_intraday_quotes/

CNN Morning Call: cnnfn.cnn.com/markets/morning_call/

INO: quotes.ino.com

INO: (futures quotes): quotes.ino.com/exchanges/?c=indexes

PC Quote: www.pcquote.com/futures/

TFC: www.tfc-charts.w2d.com/marketquotes/

Nasdaq futures

Q Is there a web site where I can see the Nasdaq futures?

A Yes. The Chicago Mercantile Exchange (CME) has a very good page on its web site, which gives a snapshot of many of the contracts trading on the Exchange. Besides the Nasdaq futures, it also includes the S&P500, E-50 and the currency and interest rate contracts.

If you're interested in the Nasdaq index the live charts on **Lycos Finance** are very good. They automatically update every few seconds - although the data for the free service is normally delayed by the 15 minutes. At the time of writing they have a special offer of free streaming real-time Nasdaq quotes to new users signing up. This is well worth it – Quote.com's *LiveCharts* (on which the Lycos service is based) is one of the best investment services on the web.

If you want to play the Nasdaq index, but don't like futures, you might like to look at the Nasdaq 100 (ticker: QQQ, sometimes referred to as *cubes*). This is an ETF (Exchange Traded Fund), which trades like any ordinary shares, but gives exposure to the top 100 shares on Nasdaq. Performance can be followed as with any ordinary stock.

L CME (Nasdaq futures): www.cme.com/prices/delayed_intraday_quotes/

Lycos Finance: finance.lycos.com

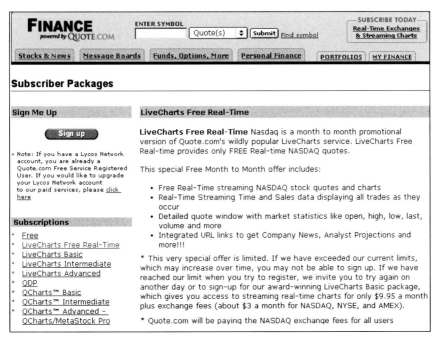

Mutual funds money flow

Q We sometimes hear about the amount of money that is going into, or out of, mutual funds. Is there any updated source for this information online?

A Yes, the two major web sites are **AMG Data Services**, and **TrimTabs Investment Research**. Both of these are subscription services, but they also offer a fair amount of free data on their web sites as well. AMG now tracks over 16,500 share classes representing over $6.3 trillion of money invested in funds. The significance of this is that such a huge sum is seen as a proxy for measuring investor sentiment.

Not surprisingly, analysis of the funds flow of money can be quite complex. And bear in mind that, on occasions, retail investors can be useful **contrary indicators**! For example, retail money can flow into funds at the top of the market, and disappear out quickly at the bottom.

AMG reports that US equity funds saw net cash inflows in April 2001. The net inflow was $14.7 billion, with most coming in the last week. This was counter to the trend in February and March, which saw net outflows.

Trimtabs.com holds that *price is a function of liquidity, having nothing to do with value*, and sets out to monitor the general stock market liquidity, which includes mutual funds flow.

L AMG Data Services: www.amgdata.com

TrimTabs Investment Research: www.trimtabs.com/mffnews.htm

8 International Markets

- Charts of international markets
- Where to get information on companies
- Best sites for research
- How to set up a European trading account
- Indices: the Dow Jones Stoxx index
- Shares listed on Easdaq
- Trading currencies online

World market overview

Q Are there any good web sites that have an overview of all the major markets?

A A good quick overview is the home page of **Bloomberg** which highlights the major equity, currency, interest rate and commodity markets. A more comprehensive view is given in their *World indices* section. Other sources are at **CNNfn** and **Yahoo**, while the most comprehensive coverage is probably at **OnVista**. The CME *flash* page is good for futures contracts; as is the daily closing report from **MRCI**. A more detailed commentary on the markets can be found at **CBS MarketWatch**.

L Bloomberg: www.bloomberg.com

CBS MarketWatch: cbs.marketwatch.com/news/globalmarkets/

CME (flash page): www.cme.com/prices/delayed_intraday_quotes/

CNNfn: cnnfn.cnn.com/markets/world_markets.html

MRCI: www.mrci.com/qpnight.asp

OnVista: indices.onvista.co.uk

Yahoo: quote.yahoo.com/m2?u

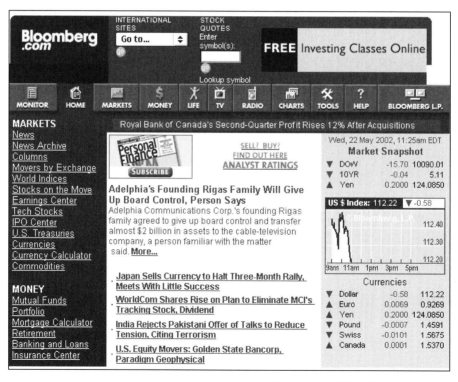

International market charts

Is there anywhere on the web where I can find a page of comparative charts of the major international stock markets?

Good web sites for international market data are: **Bloomberg**, **CNNfn**, **Nasdaq**, **OnVista** and **Reuters**. However, none of these display index performance in a comparative chart format. A possibility is the *Chart Analyser* function in the Portfolio section of **FT Investor**, although the range of indices is limited and the service rather quirky.

An alternative is to create your own web page, with HTML code calling chart images directly from remote web servers. I've created a simple example (*cht-intl.zip*), which can be downloaded from this book's web site. The demonstration page contains small 1-year charts of 20 international market indices, which can be viewed on the one page. All the images are from **Yahoo Finance**, although other good chart sources are **Bloomberg** and **ADVFN**. There are also comparative pages with 5-day charts and performance relative to the S&P500 and FTSE 100 indices. These example pages can be downloaded to your own computer and amended however you like. Further pages could include charts comparing currencies, sectors or stocks within a sector. When editing the HTML code for pages like this, it's sometimes easier to use a spreadsheet; the Excel spreadsheet that was used to create these HTML pages can also be downloaded.

ADVFN: www.advfn.com

Bloomberg: www.bloomberg.com

CNNfn: www.cnnfn.com

FT Investor: www.ft.com/investor

Nasdaq: www.nasdaq.com

OnVista: indices.onvista.co.uk

Reuters: www.reuters.com

Yahoo Finance: finance.yahoo.com

International yield curves

Q Is there anywhere on the web where I can find data for international yield curves?

A The best site is **Bloomberg**, which has yield curves (3 months – 30 years) on the government bonds of Canada, France, Germany, Italy, Japan, UK. and US. A yield curve for the Euro can be found at the **European Union** web site; while links to sources for US bond yield histories can be found at the web site of **Treasury Management Pages**.

L Bloomberg (yield curves): www.bloomberg.com/markets/iyc.html

European Union (Euro yield curve): europa.eu.int/comm/eurostat/

Treasury Management Pages: www.tmpages.com/tmp55.htm

Foreign company information

Q I'm interested in investing in some foreign companies, such as Nokia and France Telecom. Is it possible to get information on these companies on the web?

A Yes, a great deal of information can be found with a little rooting around. The first place to start might be the company's domestic stock exchange. In the case of Nokia, this would be the **Helsinki Exchange**. A full list of global exchanges can be found at **Global-Investor**. In this case, the Helsinki Exchange is not brimming with useful information, but it does at least point you to **Nokia's** own corporate web site.

If you hadn't been able to find the Nokia site through the exchange, you could have gone to **Google** and searched on the keyword 'Nokia'. At that point, you hit a rich seam of information. The Nokia web site has an excellent *Investor Relations* page, comprising their annual reports, press releases, audio conference calls, latest financials and links to the latest prices and charts for Nokia shares trading in Helsinki, New York and Stockholm.

If further information was required, then the search could cross the pond and try the excellent **Wright Investor's Services**, or **Hoovers**. The latter includes summary information on Nokia, financial data and links to the latest news stories on the company. Similar information can also be found at **Zacks**, but they also carry brokers reports and forecasts (in the case of Nokia, 15 brokers are currently recommending it as a strong buy, while none as a strong sell).

If you're a real data fiend, you might like to look at **EDGAR** database which links to any submissions the company has made to the US regulators. A bit hit and miss when it comes to non-US companies, but nuggets can be found here. And, if you'd like to go to just one web site with links to all the above in the US: **WSRN** is it.

L EDGAR database: www.edgar-online.com

Global-Investor: www.global-investor.com

Google: www.google.com

Helsinki Exchange: www.hex.fi

Hoovers: www.hoovers.com

Nokia: www.nokia.com

Wright Investor's Services: www.corporateinformation.com

WSRN: www.wsrn.com

Zacks: www.zacks.com

European research

Q
I've always invested in stocks in the UK, but I'm thinking of making some investments in Europe. Do you have any recommendations for good research sites on European stocks and some simple sites to track performance?

A
You don't have to be a fully paid-up Europhile to appreciate the advantages of diversifying abroad. But if you need convincing, go to the **FT Investor** site, and compare some of the European index performances against the FTSE 100. A good way to do this is to set up a portfolio, and instead of stocks include several indices. As always, the initial problem is finding the right codes, but after a bit of searching I found the following FT Investor codes for some indices-

CAC40 : 1804546

DAX : 1876534

DJ EURO STOXX 50 : 1836572

FTSE 100 : 1805550

techMARK : 1859502

Unfortunately, FT Investor, as yet, only carries the French, German and general European indices. Input those numerical codes into the `Edit Portfolio` page, and leave all boxes relating to trades blank. The resulting `Portfolio View` page is moderately interesting (although the same data is better seen on their pre-configured `Markets/Data > Europe` page); but click the `Chart Analyser` tab and all the indices can be viewed simultaneously in small thumbnail charts. Intraday charts are not so useful for this study, so change the time period to `1-year`. And we get the classic (Economist-approved) misrepresentation of statistics through selective display of the axes range. In other words, it's difficult to compare the charts directly, as the Y-axes are absolute and have different ranges (not starting at zero).

So - select FTSE 100 in the `Compare to index` box, and finally you have something useful. You can see that the FTSE 100 has under-performed all the other indices by quite a large margin over both the last one and two years. Admittedly this does not take currency fluctuations into account. But, despite the seemingly popular impression, currencies are not as volatile as equities; and it would be a rare market when a 30% under-performance of the FTSE 100 against the European market in a year would be compensated for by Sterling appreciation.

After deciding to take the European markets more seriously, where do you go on the web? A good starting point is the web site we've already looked at – FT Investor. The site carries the usual fare: portfolios, share prices, charts and news. The portfolios are quite sophisticated, allowing multi-country portfolios valued in user-defined currencies; the news is adequate, rather too eclectic perhaps, but the stock screener is quite useful. The latter displays rankings of stocks, in the different markets, by percentage increase/decrease, most active, or those stocks hitting 52-week highs or lows.

A decidedly flashier site is **TRADINGCentral.com** - if the internet has done nothing else, it has certainly run amok with ordinary word capitalisation rules - which has been set up by some very enthusiastic ex-traders. The service is not strong on news, but it does carry prices and charts on the major European markets, with the added bonus that it is almost the only European web site offering technical analysis indicators (incl. moving averages, momentum, stochastics and RSI).

Comdirect

Another site to check out is the excellent **Comdirect** – which provides a model for all broker sites. This is one of the few sites which summarises economic, currency, and interest rate data for all the major European markets. Elsewhere, some European data is available on **Bloomberg** (`www.bloomberg.com`).

Bloomberg: www.bloomberg.com

Comdirect: www.comdirect.co.uk

FT Investor site: www.ft.com/investor

TRADINGCentral.com: www.tradingcentral.com

European trading accounts

Q I want to invest in some European stocks, can you recommend an online broker for this?

A A good list of brokers can be found at **BlueSky Ratings**, which shows the top three brokers in each European market. Opening an account with different European brokers though would only be worth it if you intended to be very active in those markets. Better would be to have an account with a pan-European broker such as **IMIweb**, **Comdirect**, or **e-cortal**.

An alternative would be use CFDs or spread betting, the advantage being that they are very simple and, in the case of the latter, multiple accounts can be traded from one Sterling account. Note, though, that these instruments are **more appropriate for short term trading than long term investing** and FSA regulation only allows experienced investors to open CFD accounts. Another alternative for trading short term would be the new *Universal Stock Futures* introduced by **LIFFE**.

L BlueSky Ratings: www.blueskyratings.com

Comdirect: www.comdirect.co.uk

e-cortal: www.e-cortal.com

Imiweb: www.imiweb.co.uk

LIFFE: www.liffe.com

BlueSky
Ratings™

BlueSky's Internet Broker Ratings - Germany - October 2001

| BlueSky's DE Broker Ratings | Trading Cost | Exchanges | Transaction Ability | Research | Information & Contacts | All Countries |

Broker and Site Link	BlueSky Site Usability Rating	Email+ Phone Service Ratings	Overall Rating	
	Trend & Score/100%	Trend & Score/100%	Trend & Position	Trend & Score/100%
1. DAB Bank	▲ 80.59%	▼ 72.75%	▲ 1st in DE	▲ 88.17%
2. Comdirect	▲ 82.94%	▼ 75.01%	▼ 2nd in DE	▼ 87.95%
3. Consors	▲ 77.06%	▼ 60.92%	▲ 3rd in DE	▲ 80.13%
4. maxblue	▲ 78.82%	▲ 63.08%	▼ 4th in DE	▲ 78.53%
5. SBroker	64.12%	76.94%	5th in DE	77.05%
6. Patagon	70.00%	75.20%	6th in DE	75.73%
7. Advance Bank	67.06%	54.73%	7th in DE	63.62%

Link to ratings for: | Germany | France | UK | Spain | Italy

Q Do you know of an internet site which would give me the daily closing price of the Dow Jones Euro Stoxx 50TM Index, together with information on the stocks which are in the Index?

A In 1988 the Deutsche Börse, Dow Jones, SBF-Bourse de Paris and Schweizer Börse got together to create Stoxx Ltd for the purpose of owning and maintaining a new set of stock indices to measure European market performance. The major index is the *Dow Jones STOXX*, which tracks the performance of stocks Europe-wide.

This Index then divides into a bewildering array of sub-indices that try to capture every angle on investing in the European markets. For example, broad indices capturing the wide market, and narrower indices focusing on just the Nordic countries, or Eurozone countries. The UK's prevarication on Euro-membership also provides ample opportunity for indices that include or exclude UK stocks. There's the usual array of indices focusing on sectors, and also a range of indices comprising just blue chip stocks. This latter section includes the Dow Jones STOXX 50, and the Dow Jones EURO STOXX 50 for just Euro-zone stocks.

A good data source on all the Dow Jones STOXX indices is available from the French **Yahoo** site – with quotes, charts and a good table of the EURO STOXX 50 constituent stocks.

A more detailed reference source is at the Finix web site, which includes a list of the 50 constituent stocks. But the definitive reference for the STOXX indices is the **STOXX** web site, where there's a huge amount of information. The most useful sections are those explaining in detail the construction of the indices, and a comprehensive data download area.

Futures and options

The prime purpose of these indices may well be to provide a performance benchmark for funds and portfolios investing in Europe. However, they also spawn a whole sub-industry in derivatives linked to these indices, such as a range of futures and options contracts listed on the EUREX and MONEP exchanges. Such derivatives contracts tend to based on the narrower indices (e.g. the Dow Jones EURO STOXX 50) rather than the broader ones, as it makes arbitrage easier, which adds to liquidity and closer correlation between the derivatives instrument and the underlying index.

Other related instruments

However, besides the standard futures and options contracts, there's also a whole menagerie of other exotic financial animals on offer, including: warrants, certificates, callable protected units, guaranteed units, Rainbow Notes – all linked to the STOXX indices. These other instruments are issued by investment banks, and at base tend to be options dressed up in various disguises to attract investors who wouldn't normally look at investing in options directly. Although frequently the investment pay-off of such instruments can be replicated – more cheaply –

by directly trading exchange-traded futures or options, they can be a convenient method of gaining quick exposure to specific market sectors.

More popular on the continent

It is odd that while these instruments are very popular in Europe (particularly in Germany and France), there is virtually no discussion or coverage of them in the UK. I can't think of any specific reason for this, beyond perhaps a UK regulatory environment superficially designed to protect the consumer, but one that in effect protects a closed industry and stifles innovation. In addition, it must be said, these instruments tend to be highly geared, trade in low volume, and are not necessarily listed on exchanges; therefore they are just extra hassle for the brokers to deal with (who seem to have enough trouble just trading simple LSE listed stocks). There is also little reason for brokers to push such instruments as the commission generated is very low.

Finix: www.finix.at/fin/stoxx_box.html

STOXX: www.stoxx.com

Yahoo (France): fr.finance.yahoo.com/m7.tpl

EURO STOXX 50   long text   constituents   reference

Index

Dow Jones Euro Stoxx 50 Index

Country	Stock	Sector	Weight in %	Number of shares
NV	Royal Dutch Petroleum	Energy	8.62%	2,144,296,000
GER	Allianz AG	Insurance	5.73%	234,775,000
GER	Deutsche Telekom AG	Telecom	4.17%	2,743,700,000
ITA	ENI	Energy	3.72%	7,999,205,000
FRA	France Telecom	Telecom	3.64%	1,000,000,000
NV	ING Groep	Financial Services	3.28%	837,434,000
NV	Unilever Nv (cvaNtfl4)	Food & Beverage	3.02%	640,165,000
GER	Daimler-Benz AG	Auto	2.97%	519,236,000
ITA	Telecom Italia	Telecom	2.86%	5,255,132,000
GER	Deutsche Bank	Bank	2.82%	533,906,000

Easdaq shares

Q I know that Algo Vision shares are not listed in the UK, so where are they listed and how can I find their share price?

A Algo Vision plc is listed on Nasdaq (now incorporating Easdaq). To find the share price, go to the **Easdaq** web site (now branded in Nasdaq colours), and input 'Algo Vision' to the box in the left margin. A page will appear that gives the current share price and also a historic price chart. In addition to this, there are links to recent news stories about the company, key listing data and extracts from the accounts, and a list of market makers in the stock (in this case Beeson Gregory and Winterflood Securities). The web site also has a list of UK brokers that deal on Easdaq, and reminds investors that no stamp duty is payable on stock transactions.

L Easdaq: www.easdaq.com

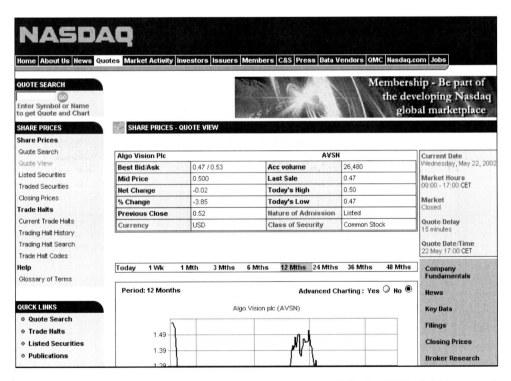

Euro exchange rates

Q Is there a definitive reference source on the web for the fixed conversion rates for the new Euro?

A The most convenient source is the **European Central Bank**. Whereas the home of the Euro can be found at the **European Community** web site, which includes links to other sites, offers graphics of the Euro symbol to download, and informs us that the Euro symbol's parallel lines *represent the stability of the Euro*, which is nice to know.

L European Central Bank: www.ecb.int

European Community site: europa.eu.int/euro/

Q Are there any good internet sites with charts and information on currencies?

A Yes. There's a great currency site called **Oanda**, with a spectacular range of features. One of these is the *FX Map* which represents currency movements over different time periods as a type of *heat map* of the world: green countries have currencies that have risen, while red countries have fallen relative to the specified base currency. There's also a currency trading game, historical rates for download, and a Java tool to analyse multiple currencies graphically. But capping everything is a wonderful *Directional Forecasting* tool: select a currency pair and a future time range, and it calculates the forecast range of values. Simple really. Who cares if it works, it looks great!

For simple currency quotes **Bloomberg** probably has the widest range (i.e. this is where you check the value of those Bhutan Ngultrum you found in your sock after your last holiday). More detailed market quotes (including options) can be found at **INO** which also has interactive charts: plot from 1-60 min bar/candlestick/line charts with specified moving averages.

Further currency charts are available at **ForexATS** and the **Pacific Exchange Rates Service**. The latter are highly configurable: exact time periods can be specified, a range of 50 currencies, moving averages and 60-day volatility with plots on a linear or logarithmic scale.

A fairly serious service is offered by **JP Morgan**, from whose web site you can download proprietary daily trade-weighted currency indices. These measure *nominal exchange rate strength of individual OECD currencies relative to a narrow basket of other OECD currencies*. The indices are weighted to reflect the global pattern of bilateral trade. Hmm, interesting.

Or you might find **Economist's** collection of articles on their *Big Mac Index* more palatable. These are based on PPP (purchase power price), and represent the exchange rate if it were based solely on Big Macs. In other words, Big Macs should cost the same everywhere; and when they don't that represents an over or under-valuation of the currency. Just at the moment, the most under-valued major currency is the Australian Dollar (35% below *McParity*). A full, and updated, table of the BigMac index can be found at the above Oanda web site.

L
Bloomberg (currencies): www.bloomberg.com/markets/currency.html

Economist (Big Mac Index): www.economist.com/markets/Bigmac/

ForexATS: www.forex-ats.com

INO: quotes.ino.com/exchanges/forex/

JP Morgan (currencies):
www.jpmorgan.com/MarketDataInd/Forex/currIndex.html

Oanda: www.oanda.com

Pacific Exchange Rates Service:
pacific.commerce.ubc.ca/xr/plot.html

Trading currencies online

Q Is it possible to trade currencies online?

A Yes, this is quite an active area online. For occasional trading the best option is a spread betting account (many spread betting firms started life as forex brokers). A couple of good ones are **Cantor** and **Finspreads** which allow trading in very small size. Other options would **GNI** or **CMC**.

FX brokers

If you intend to trade currencies more seriously, you might like to open an account with a dedicated forex broker. A popular choice is **SaxoBank.com**, formerly ForexTrading.com. They require a minimum amount of $10,000 to open an account – which is fairly standard among forex brokers. Other online brokers are: **MG Forex**, **Gain Capital**, **GCI Capital** and **Forex Capital Markets.**

FXTrade

Another specialised broker to consider would be **FXTrade**, which is part of the Swiss Oanda group. Whereas some other currency dealers require a large minimum dealing size, with Oanda transactions can be as low as $1. An interesting development here is that they offer a continuous interest payment. This is unlikely to have much impact on an ordinary investor's P & L, but is very significant for the future of financial markets. There is no commission charge, with the cost being borne in the bid-offer spread of 2-3 basis points. For comparison, 20 buy/sell equity trades of £3,000 bargains would attract a cumulative trading cost of around £650. The same size trades in currencies on FXTrade would have a cost of around £12.

BoxOptions

Oanda have just introduced a great new service called **BoxOption**. The best way to understand this is to look at the demo on their home page. Briefly, a chart of, say, GBP/USD is displayed, with an area to the right of the latest price empty. In this area, the user can draw a box with the mouse. The two dimensions of the box are price and time. Click `Price` and the user is given a quote to place an options trade that pays off if the price hits (or alternatively misses) the box. It's a very clever idea, and great way of visually demonstrating straddles and strangles. Oanda also has a **FXGame** which is quite fun.

Futures

An alternative way to trade currencies is via futures, which active traders may prefer if they already have an account with a futures broker. An interesting new broker to consider is **Easy2Trade** which offers direct access futures trading.

Risk

Currencies are commonly thought of as very volatile and thereby risky. This is a misperception. A quick comparison of, say, the two-year GBP/USD chart at the **CurrencyPro** web site against the stock price chart of a Marconi or Energis will quickly reveal the more risky investment. The risk of currency trading does not derive from the underlying asset, but the account gearing (which can be controlled). Personally, I believe all new active traders should start in the currency, and not equity, markets. They'll make all the same mistakes initially, but their transaction costs will be a lot lower.

L

```
BoxOption (Oanda): boxoption.olsen.ch

Cantor: www.cantorindex.com

CMC: www.deal4free.com/forex/

CurrencyPro (GBP/USD): www.currencypro.com/graph.php

Easy2Trade (futures): www.easy2trade.com

Finspreads: www.finspreads.com

Forex Capital Markets: www.fxcm.com

FXGame (Oanda): fxgame.oanda.com

FXTrade (Oanda): fxtrade.oanda.com

Gain Capital: www.gaincapital.com

GCI Capital: www.globalcap.com

GNI: www.gnitouch.com

MG Forex: www.mgforex.com

SaxoBank.com: www.saxobank.com
```

National holidays

Q I occasionally deal in foreign markets, but was caught out recently when a market was closed due to a national holiday. Is there a list of these holidays somewhere?

A JP Morgan used to compile the definitive calendar, but seems to have stopped (perhaps because they thought only wimps took holidays). Stepping into the breach is **The Worldwide Holiday & Festival** site, which has a fairly comprehensive list.

An alternative is the **Bank Holidays of The World** site, which carries extra information on events, such as elections, and a calendar for future years.

L Bank Holidays of The World site: www.national-holidays.com

The Worldwide Holiday & Festival: www.holidayfestival.com

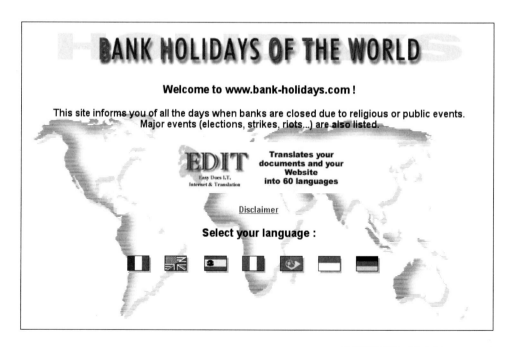

9 Derivatives and Betting

- Traded options
- Warrants and Covered Warrants
- Contracts for Differences (CFDs)
- Fixed odds betting

Traded options

Q

Can you tell me if there is a good web site which will enable me to monitor FTSE 100 traded option prices?

A

The best site is **ThomsonFN**, which is pretty much the same as the old MarketEye site that Thomson bought in 2001, without the premium features such as data download. From the main `Global` page, there's a link for `Options` which gives options prices for UK, European and US options.

Both FTSE 100 options are then displayed, the European style (ESX) and the American style (SEI). For each option there's the choice of viewing the traded prices, the AutoQuote bid/asks or both together.

LIFFE option prices can also be seen on the LIFFE data web site. But the data provider for this service is ThomsonFN, so there's not much more than is found on ThomsonFN's own site (except LIFFE has a greater list of the low activity contracts). LIFFE provides data to many different (albeit mainly US-based) web sites, a list of which can be found on its site.

A non-web-based source of options data is the very good myTrack program available from **myBroker**. This has the advantage over a web page of offering streaming quotes (i.e. prices refresh themselves automatically).

L

LIFFE: www.liffe-data.com

LIFFE (distributors): www.liffe.com/liffedata/realtime/internet.htm

myBroker: www.mybroker.co.uk

ThomsonFN: global.thomsonfn.co.uk

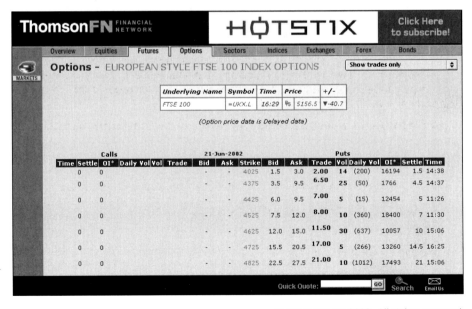

Q Is there a web site that lists company warrants and the particular times in which you have to exercise them, or perhaps the length of warrants lives?

A Warrants remain a rather hidden and obscure corner of the market. The bad news is that it can be difficult to find information about them; the good news is that their very obscurity can lead to inefficiencies in the market that can be exploited by the determined investor.

In the past, a couple of web sites have set up specialising in warrants, but these seem to have faded away - there's still an interesting opportunity for someone to set up an online warrants service. Meanwhile, we have to make do with a hotchpotch of information from different sources.

Investment trust warrants

The majority of warrants in the UK market are issued by investment trusts and an introductory explanation and data for these warrants can be read at the web site of **AITC**. Other good sites are **TrustNet** and the home page **Investment Trust Warrants**.

Non-investment trust warrants

If you're researching a non-IT warrant, such as Luminar, then it becomes a bit more difficult. A potential source of information is the **RNS** archive at **UK-Wire** (there would have been an announcement when the warrants were first issued). However, the Luminar warrants were issued Feb 1999, and the archive does not go back that far. You have to turn, therefore, to the company's own web site. In the case of Luminar, it has an online investors section and the annual report can be downloaded. Neither is very good, but on page 39 of the report you can find that the exercise period of the warrants is Feb 2002 to Feb 2009.

For investors serious about warrants, the bible is the subscription *Warrants Alert* newsletter from **The McHattie Group**. But the easiest, quick reference source for most investors may well be the table of warrant terms that appears periodically in *Investors Chronicle*.

Calculators for valuing warrants can be found on the **Numa** web site.

L AITC: www.aitc.co.uk

Investment Trust Warrants: www.wimb26.freeserve.co.uk/warrants/

McHattie Group: www.tipsheets.co.uk

Numa: www.numa.com

TrustNet: www.trustnet.com

UK-Wire: www.uk-wire.co.uk

Covered warrants

Q Is there any information on the web about covered warrants?

A Your question is well-timed as the London Stock Exchange is expected to launch a covered warrants market in the UK in 2002. Further information on this can be found at in the Technical Library of the LSE web site.

Ordinary warrants have been listed for some time on the LSE, and can be described, crudely, as being long-term options to buy shares in a company. *Covered warrants* are similar, except instead of being issued by the companies themselves, they are **issued by investment banks** – sometimes with the agreement of the underlying company, sometimes not. Covered warrants, however, go well beyond restricting themselves to just stocks. Covered warrants have been issued related to stock indices, baskets of stocks, currencies, commodities and almost anything one can think of.

The UK has been rather left behind in the covered warrant extravaganza. On the continent, especially in the French, German and Italian markets, covered warrants are for some investors more popular than stocks. Examples of European covered warrant web sites are listed below.

Germany	optionsscheine.onvista.de
France	www.oddowarrants.fr
	www.ma-fi.com/portail.htm
	www.boursier.com
	www.firstinvest.com/warrants/
	www.3611bourse.com/warrants/
Italy	www.tradinglab.com
	www.coveredwarrantsonline.com

Although denominated in Euros, the warrants themselves may be linked to almost any stock, including UK and US companies (at the time of writing this, a Euro-denominated warrant on Amazon is up 161% on the day).

Because covered warrants are not listed on one central exchange, information on them can be rather random and scattered. The best sources are often the web sites of the issuing investment banks, a list of which is provided on page 252 of this book.

It will be interesting to see if covered warrants become as popular here as they have been on the continent. We may find that their growth is stunted by the well-established position of spread betting in the UK.

L London Stock Exchange (covered warrants):
www.londonstockexchange.com/techlib/

Contracts for Differences (CFDs)

Q I keep on reading about 'contracts for differences'. What are they?

A Suddenly we're besieged by these things called CFDs – whatever happened to good old shares? When TD Waterhouse first announced that it was going to offer margin trading to clients, there was much head-shaking and disapproval. Now, a short while later, margin trading is in through the back door dressed up in the serious sounding name - *Contracts for Differences*.

A gimmick? Perhaps. But also a decidedly useful tool for short-term traders. So useful in fact that it's **difficult to make a case for trading shares instead of CFDs for holding periods of less than two months**. Beyond that period, the funding cost, on simple long positions, becomes unattractive.

Briefly, CFDs are a kind of futures contract on individual shares. Their attractions are: low dealing costs, no stamp duty, the ability to short, and leverage (gearing) of around 5 times. They've been around for a while in the institutional world, their early use being for hedge funds, but now they're being offered to retail clients. The two leading brokers are **GNI touch** and **CMC Deal4free.com**, but every futures broker and spread better in town is getting in on the act including **Berkeley Futures**, **Cantor**, **City Index**, **Cunningham Asset Management**, **Thomas Grant**, **Halewood International Futures**, **IG Markets**, **Manfinancial** and **Sucden**.

At the moment, the world of CFDs has an energy and excitement that ordinary online share trading has lost. There are certainly many more online share brokers than there were two years ago, but the service is not much more advanced than it was then. Further, all the brokers' services are rather similar. Perhaps it's a matter of regulation. While the share brokers are, or appear to be, operating under sufferance of the regulators and fearful of a crack down at any time, the CFD brokers are expanding like crazy. Ask them if they trade contracts on ..., and they reply *yes* before you've finished the question.

Opening a CFD account is not that straightforward. Funds have to be deposited, and brokers require clients to have previous derivatives experience. For those unwilling, or unable, to open a CFD account, **spread betting may be a better choice**, although it too poses dangers for inexperienced traders.

L
Berkeley Futures: www.bfl.co.uk
Cantor: www.cantorindex.com
City Index: www.cityindex.co.uk
CMC: www.deal4free.com
Cunningham Asset Management: www.camplc.com
GNI Touch: www.gnitouch.com
Thomas Grant & Company: www.thomas-grant.com
Halewood International Futures: www.hifutures.com
IG Markets: www.igshares.com
Manfinancial: www.manfinancial.com
Sucden: www.sucden.co.uk

Fixed odds betting

Q I know there are lots of spread betting firms on the web, but do any offer fixed odds?

A The attraction of fixed odds betting (such as that on horse racing) is that the downside is limited to losing your initial stake. This is different from spread betting where losses can be far higher than your initial stake, although the use of *stop losses* can control this somewhat. However, with fixed odds betting the upside is also limited, and it is therefore better suited to situations that have a yes/no type outcome, rather than a financial market.

Having said that, there are a couple of operations offering fixed odds betting on financial markets. The first is **Blue Square**, a sister company to City Index, which has prices on the daily and year end FTSE 100 Index in addition to other US, European and Asian indices, and currencies and commodities. The other site is **BetonMarkets**, which is a more sophisticated proposition than Blue Square.

Firstly, I would have to say that this is really **only for advanced investors**, and being registered offshore it may carry more risks than a UK registered company. Having said that, it is one of the most fascinating investment sites out there. In essence, the site is a market maker in OTC options; the user logs on, designs their own option parameters and the price of the option is calculated immediately online.

An example option might be: you wish to win $500 if at the close of the market on specific date the FTSE Index is worth more than 5000. At the time of writing, if the date was 300 days forward, the price for that option would be $157. Beyond that, all the great variations of exotic options are possible, including: one-touch, no-touch, barrier range, double touch, up or down.

To re-iterate, this is most definitely not for novice, or even moderately experienced investors. But great fun it is.

L

BetonMarkets: www.betonmarkets.com

Blue Square: www.bluesq.com

10 Miscellaneous

- Economic commentary
- Ethical investing
- Equities vs gilts
- Gilt yields
- Investment clubs
- Heatmaps
- Internet stocks
- Online trading statistics
- Warren Buffett web sites
- Big Mac index
- Compound interest
- Calculating volatility: historic and implied
- Careers in finance

Strategic and economic commentary

Q Can you recommend any sites for good strategic commentary?

A Even a cynic like me is constantly amazed and delighted by what an afternoon's serendipitous web surfing can produce. Proof, if needed, that there is more to online finance than real-time prices, rankings of stock movements and hot tips – all of which carry the subliminal message, *buy, sell, it doesn't matter which, just do something*. I list below ten sources of articles for the thoughtful investor.

Bill Sharpe (www.stanford.edu/~wfsharpe/art/art.htm) – Articles by Nobel Prize winner Bill Sharpe, originator of the Capital Asset Pricing Model.

Samuel Brittan (www.samuelbrittan.co.uk) – A comprehensive collection of articles from FT columnist and author Samuel Brittan. I particularly liked the article, "What is wrong with economics?", which describes economic forecasts, at the popular level, as being part of the entertainment industry. (Unfair to quote out of context like that, but fun nevertheless).

Paul Krugman (web.mit.edu/krugman/www/) - With commendable honesty, the Princeton economist admits that his serious articles on finance are 'pretty well incomprehensible to laymen'. So he sets out to try to communicate with non-economists through articles in *Slate*, *Fortune* and the *NY Times* (www.nytimes.com/pages/opinion/columns/). As a non-economist, I think he succeeds magnificently. ('Supply, demand, and English food' – is brilliant.)

Peter Bernstein (www.peterlbernsteininc.com) – America's "greatest living economist", Peter Bernstein, publishes the journal, *Economics and Portfolio Strategy*, extracts of which can be read at his web site.

Andrew Smithers (www.smithers.co.uk/news.shtml) – Using Tobin's q ratio, Andrew Smithers forecast that the US market was wildly over-valued in April 2000. His site includes an archive of articles written for the *Evening Standard*, including one of 13.3.00, which ends with the despairing aphorism, "The moral is simple. If you want to invest don't be rational and if you want to be rational don't invest."

Jeremy Grantham (www.gmo.com) – A library of articles maintained by US investment managers GMO. Grantham's are the pick of the bunch.

Bank Credit Analyst (www.bcapub.com/public/anthology.asp) – Highlights from the past 50 years of the *Bank Credit Analyst*.

Robert Shiller (www.econ.yale.edu/~shiller/) - Papers from the author of *Irrational Exuberance*, and leading proponent of Behavioral Finance.

Wharton School (knowledge.wharton.upenn.edu) – Collection of articles from The Wharton School, including finance professor Jeremy Siegel, author of the influential *Stocks for the Long Run*.

Gold-Eagle (www.gold-eagle.com/editorials.html) – Although primarily a hard metals web site, its diverse collection of articles covers wider financial markets too.

Ethical investing

Q Are there any good web sites that cover ethical investing?

A Yes, there are pockets of green all over the web. A couple of organisations - with links to further web sites - are the **UK Social Investment Forum** and the **Ethical Investment Association**. The latter is a body of independent financial advisers promoting ethical investment. Quite a few IFAs are active in this area, including: **Gaia**, **Ethical Servives** and **Ethical Partners**. In fact any linguistic derivative of *ethics* and *investing* with a *www.* at the front and *.co.uk* or *.com* at the end will probably throw up a web site.

Over in the US there's **Green Money** and **Good Money** – which compiles a *Good Money Industrial Index*, showing a 2,045% cumulative gain since 1976, against a 1,044% gain in the DJ30 index. For some serious research on corporate misbehaviour, check out **The Multinational Monitor**, a monthly newsletter which tracks corporate activity in the Third World, export of hazardous substances, worker health and safety, labor union issues and the environment. The web site includes plenty of articles with titles like, *When the People Speak, the Corporations Squeak*, but its most useful section is the search engine. Plug in keywords such as 'tobacco' or 'Rio Tinto Zinc' and the search engine goes off like a geiger counter in a plutonium shop, returning in the case of the latter, articles such as, *Pillage in the Pacific*.

Further sites can be found through search engines. Fortunately, in this case, the keywords 'ethical investing' are very specific, such that searches using, **Mirago** (for the UK) or Go.com (international) return highly relevant results. And the ever-useful search engine at the **FT.com's** GlobalArchive can be used for finding articles from many newspapers on this topic.

Before leaving the subject, it has to be said that the general standard of web sites in this sector is shockingly awful – among the worst I've come across. Perhaps investing money in good web design is socially irresponsible. I am normally critical of *over-designed* web sites, but a few hours spent looking at this lot had me running for the hills. If they apply as little innovation and panache to their investing strategies as they do to their web sites, it's not surprising that ethical investment performance leaves something to be desired.

L
```
Ethical Investment Association: www.ethicalinvestment.org.uk
Ethical Partners: www.ethical-partners.co.uk
Ethical Servives: www.ethicalservices.co.uk
FT.com (global archive): globalarchive.ft.com
Gaia: www.gaeia.co.uk
Go: www.go.com
Good Money: www.goodmoney.com
Green Money: www.greenmoney.com
Mirago: www.mirago.co.uk
The Multinational Monitor: www.essential.org/monitor/
UK Social Investment Forum: www.uksif.org
```

Equities vs Gilts

Q I've heard of a study comparing the returns of equities vs gilts over a number of decades. I think this might have been done by Barclays. Is it on the web?

A The Barclay's Equity-Gilt Study is one of the oldest continuous reports in the financial markets – almost deserving the epithet venerable. Now in its 45th year, it provides data and analysis of annual returns in UK equities, government bonds and cash over the period from 1899 to 1999. This year, for the first time, they've added a section on US asset returns since 1925, and increased the analysis of demographics, economic growth and technology.

The online home of the report can be found at the **Barclays Capital** web site, but unfortunately the body of the report is only available to clients of Barclays Capital, or for a fee of £100. However, there's a synopsis of the report, and, more accessible, press releases. The latter contain the report highlights, such as:

- Over the 20th century as a whole the UK equity risk premium has averaged 4.7%.

- £100 invested in equities in 1899, income re-invested, would have grown to £1.28m by end-1999.

- £100 invested in gilts in 1899, without reinvesting income, would have shrunk to less than £1 in real terms by end-1999.

- The probability of equities outperforming gilts even over very short periods is high. Over 2-year periods equities outperform gilts 71% of the time.

There's further comment on the decline in importance of income, as investors focus on long-term wealth accumulation. Funded pension provision is compared with unfunded. There are musings on the durability of the technology revolution. And, commenting on the divergence of equity and bond prices in 1999, they opine (with a hint of self-promotion) *Such occurrences present additional opportunities for profit for the investor who understands the force of long-term trends*.

There's also an **interactive calculator** to find the annualised real return on UK equities over any given time period between 1899-1999. According to this, the annualised real return over the last ten years has been 10.7%.

An alternative to the Barclays study is the one from **Credit Suisse First Boston**. It has the advantage of being free, and being downloadable from the CSFB web site. Also, it covers 130 years, compared with 100 years for Barclays.

These studies can be a wonderful source of trivia: according to CSFB, £100 invested in the equity market in 1869 would now be enough to buy a sizeable house; whereas a similar amount invested in a gilt or cash fund would barely cover the council tax on the same property! They also forecast that if equity returns over the next 30 years match those of the last 130, the FTSE 100 will reach 60,000 by 2030.

L Barclays Capital (Equity-Gilt Study): www.barcap.com/egs/

CSFB (Equity-Gilt Study): www.csfb.com/eqres/eqres_gilt.html

Gilt yields

Q What is the formula used to calculate the yields on gilt issues, as used in the 'Gilt issues - best value v tax status' table printed in the Money FT on Saturdays?

A Bond calculations are not for the faint-hearted, and in the space available here I can only make a start answering this. To illustrate the calculations, I've set up a spreadsheet *(gilt-yield.xls*: download from this book's web site). On *Sheet 1* I've input the price and terms for the Treasury 2007 8.50% gilt.

A gilt's *current yield* (also called *running yield*) is defined as the coupon divided by the bond's price. This is easy to calculate, but not very useful and rarely referred to. The yield calculation more commonly used is the *redemption yield* (also called *yield-to-maturity*), which incorporates the fact that a bond bought at, say, 109 and redeemed at 100, incurs an approximate 10% capital loss. In the spreadsheet, cell B14 calculates the (annual) yield on the capital gain in the bond to redemption. Our first approximation for the redemption yield is then given as the sum of the current yield (on income), and the yield on the capital gain.

The full definition of **redemption yield** is: *the discount rate (interest rate) that equates to the present value of all the bond's cash flows to its current price*. So, to improve the accuracy of our calculation we need to take the present value of the cash flows which is the same thing as an internal rate of return calculation. In *Sheet 2* of the spreadsheet the yield for the same bond is estimated using the pre-configured Excel IRR function. To use the IRR function you have to manually list the cash flows. (Further information on Excel functions can be found in the Excel online Help).

As yet, this is still an approximation because we have not specified the dates for the coupon payments and redemption. This is done on *Sheet 3*. The exact term dates for gilts can be found at the **Government's Debt Management Office** (DMO) web site. Fortunately, Excel provides a function (YIELD), which calculates the redemption yield. If you don't have this in your current list of functions (Insert > Function > Financial), go to Tools > Add Ins and select Analysis ToolPak from the list. The yield values given in *Sheet 3* should correspond to those in the FT pages, and on the DMO web site.

In passing, it must be said that the government's DMO web site is excellent - an essential reference source for all matters concerning gilts. As well as gilt terms, there's background information on the market, historical pricing, lists of market makers and a great explanation for individual investors (The Private Investor's Guide to British Government Stock).

Is that the end of the story? I'm afraid not. Looking further down the FT gilts table, we come across the ominous sounding *index-linked gilts*. To calculate the redemption yield on an index-linked gilt you have to assume a (constant) rate of inflation, at which point the maths becomes more complex. If you want to follow this up, I'd recommend *Bond Market Securities* and *The Bond and Money Markets* both by Moorad Choudhry. Further details of gilt yield calculations can also be found at the DMO site. In fact, I'd recommend looking at their paper on yield equations - if your eyes start to glaze over, bond analysis is not for you.

L Government's Debt Management Office (DMO): www.dmo.gov.uk

DMO (yields): www.dmo.gov.uk/gilts/public/technical/yldeqns.pdf

Investment clubs

Q Are there any web sites specially for investment clubs?

A If there was an appropriate vehicle, I would be a buyer of investment clubs. According to *ProShare*, the leading investment club organisation, there are now over 12,000 of them in the UK, with 300 new ones being created every month. Members come from all walks of life, but apparently 30% work in the education, medical or public sectors. The average monthly contribution to club funds is £25.

Moreover, with the internet, there's no reason to limit yourself to the UK. The US, which has over 60,000 investment clubs, has also spawned the concept of *virtual* clubs, whose members never meet, and where all club discussion takes place online. Even if all the members do live in the same village, a (password-protected) club web site can provide a useful resource for reference material and discussion in the time between physical meetings.

Quite a few financial web sites have realised that meta-communities of clubs may prove more loyal as customers than fickle individuals. So they build a special section for the clubs, providing various services like articles and forums (in effect becoming something of a specialised service targeted at clubs). And then, having got the willing audience, they can sell stuff to them. Well, that's the plan. Admittedly internet companies aren't very good at that second part, but they're certainly busy on stage one.

If you're thinking of setting up a share club, the **ProShare** web site is a good place to start and it's Handbook is also worth getting. It has a joint venture with **hemscott.NET** to provide free web facilities to all ProShare registered clubs. The **Motley Fool** could almost be described as one big investment club. It too has a book - *The Fools Guide To Investment Cubs*. A list of share club web sites can be found at **E-Trader UK**. Quite a few brokers offer special services to share clubs:

> **Barclays**: www.barclays-stockbrokers.co.uk
> **Charles Schwab**: www.schwab-worldwide.com
> **Comdirect**: www.comdirect.co.uk
> **E*Trade UK**: www.etrade.co.uk
> **Hargreaves Lansdown**: www.h-l.co.uk

For novice investors, I can think of no better way to gain experience and confidence than joining a club. On top of that, clubs can be very convivial – 46% of meetings are held in the pub! However, **don't expect to get rich this way**. An argument against clubs is that all investment decisions are made by consensus, which inevitably leads to a herd approach. Successful investors tend to plough their own furrow, and are quite often at odds with the prevailing investment mood. But that doesn't mean they can't enjoy the beer.

L E-Trader UK (lists online clubs): www.e-traderuk.com/invclubs.html
hemscott.NET (share clubs): www.proshareclubs.co.uk
Motley Fool: www.fool.co.uk
ProShare: www.proshare.org

Heatmaps

Q Could you please explain what heatmaps are?

A A couple of years ago **SmartMoney** pioneered a new way of visually representing stock performance within a market with its *Map of the Market*. This technique is now beginning to crop up on other web sites.

The excellent **StockCharts** has a similar map - although they call it a '*Carpet*' which I guess makes it totally different. Besides simple share price movement (as at SmartMoney) the Stock Charts Carpet also offers market views for RSI and Bollinger Bands. And besides the S&P sectors, they also have Carpets for the major averages and also world markets.

Emerging market broker **Brunswick Direct** has a market map which has a good stab at representing a wide range of global markets, although the full service is restricted to clients. A slightly different approach has been taken by **DigitalLook** to represent movements of stocks in the European markets.

L Brunswick Direct: www.brunswickdirect.com

DigitalLook: www.digitallook.com

SmartMoney: www.smartmoney.com

StockCharts (stock carpet): www.stockcharts.com/charts/Carpet.html

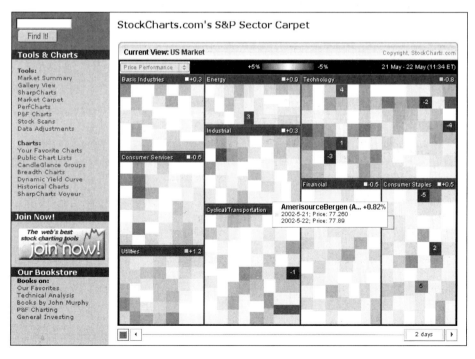

219

Internet stocks

 Where can I find information on internet stocks?

 It's quite a reflection on the bubble nature of the internet boom that in the year 2002, barely two years after the peak, the internet has almost ceased to exist as a stock market sector. Certainly the web sites set up to track the cyber start-ups have all but disappeared, leaving a sorry trail of *Error 404* and *cessation of service* messages. An example is the (previously influential) **Web Report** of investment bank **Robertson Stephens** which has been quietly absorbed back into the parent web site.

The sites that do remain are evolving into general stock, or technology-focused, services. An example is **Internet Stocks Channel**. This is home to the *Internet Stock Index* (ISDEX), a 3-year chart of which can be seen at the WSRN site – and which pretty much says it all!

Part of the Internet.com empire is the **Internet Stock Report**, with news on the sector. The Internet.com sector indices can be seen at **WSRN**. An old-style, internet cheer-leading site is **InternetCap.com**, which modestly claims, *Each month we profile an emerging internet stock with huge upside potential.* Internet stocks are also covered by the more general sites: **CBS MarketWatch**, **CNET** and **MSN Investor**. In the UK one of the few pages still tracking internet stocks is at **Moneyextra**.

Net stocks are naturally one of the most popular topics for discussion on bulletin boards; the best discussion boards can be found at **Raging Bull**, **Silicon Investor** and **Yahoo Finance**.

In 1999, one of the main technology magazines tracking the internet wave, *Red Herring*, published an article (www.redherring.com/mag/issue66/inv-bullet-intro.html), ambitiously titled, *Ten bulletproof Internet stocks - Even if the market suffers a meltdown, these ten companies will survive.* To their credit they didn't do too badly, identifying, among others, eBay, AOL, Charles Schwab and Amazon. Of course, there's a big difference between surviving and actually making money on the investments.

```
CBS MarketWatch: cbs.marketwatch.com
CNET: investor.cnet.com
Internet Stocks Channel: www.internet.com/sections/stocks.html
Internet Stock Report: www.internetstockreport.com
InternetCap.com: www.internetcap.com
Moneyextra (internet stocks): www.moneyextra.com/stocks/internet/
MSN Investor: www.investor.com
Raging Bull: www.ragingbull.com
Robertson Stephens: www.robertsonstephens.com
Silicon Investor: www.techstocks.com
Robertson Stephens Web Report: www.internetstocks.com
WSRN (ISDEX chart): www.wsrn.com/apps/ISDEX/chart.xpl?data=D
WSRN (Internet.com sector indices):
www.wsrn.com/apps/internetstocks/
Yahoo Finance: finance.yahoo.com
```

Internet stock indices

Q Recently you mentioned the Internet Stock Index (ISDEX) on www.internet.com. Can you please tell me how this index is put together, whether or not you think the method chosen for this is a good one, and why?

A Technically, *ISDEX* is a **market capitalisation weighted index**, which is the usual method of calculating an index today (occasionally other methods have been used, such as simple price weighting). Index construction is trickier than it looks, and so, while there are flaws with all methods, this is probably the best balance between simplicity and accuracy.

However, one major problem with indices of non-homogenous groups of stocks can be the great disparity in company sizes. ISDEX comprises 50 stocks (further info at the **KCBT** web site), including Cisco (market capitalisation of many *billions*), and Cybercash (market capitalisation of many *millions*). Obviously a 1% move in the share price of Cisco will have a far greater impact on the index than a similar move by Cybercash. To adjust for this, the index compilers set a maximum weighting for any one stock of 10%.

The question is whether this is valid or not?

The answer depends partly on whether you accept the validity of any index as representing anything useful. Index creation is, and will continue to be, a boom business while the demand exists for benchmarking performance and for providing a reference *security* for derivatives trading. But just because the demand is there, it doesn't necessarily follow that the indices created are logical or sensible. In the specific case of ISDEX, it's clear that the modified market capitalisation weighting method **understates the growth and influence of mega stocks** like AOL and Amazon.

As regards the constituents of ISDEX, the compilers have selected 50 companies whose revenues are derived at least 51% from the internet. But the main justification for the index appears to rest with the fact that Yahoo Finance, and a couple of other web sites, quote it! At this point the obvious questions are: what is an internet stock, and does a well-defined internet sector really exist?

The internet does exist, obviously, but in a short while an 'internet sector' might seem as odd as an index of all companies whose revenues derive from using voice communication. If you are unhappy with ISDEX, there are plenty others to choose from, including the GSTI (Goldman Sachs Internet Index), **Dow Jones Internet Commerce Index** (www.cboe.com/OptProd/index_comp.asp), or the **Wired Index** (www.wired.com).

And if you are still dissatisfied, your local investment bank will be very happy to knock an index up for you. Better still, create your own index, persuade a derivatives exchange to trade futures and options on your index, and you can forget all about investing in the internet – you're in the index compilation business, and have a bright future.

L KCBT (ISDEX info): www.kcbt.com/isdex.htm

Q I am doing some research into the online broking industry, and am trying to find statistics on the number of online accounts in the UK and how many transactions are made through them. Can you point me in the right direction?

A For the UK market some of the most widely quoted figures come from **The Association of Private Client Investment Managers and Stockbrokers** (APCIMS). You should also check the major industry research companies, a list of which is provided below.

There are some sites that collate all the various data. One of the best is **Nua**, while other news sites carrying reports of recent research reports are: **Upside**, **CNET**, **San Francisco Chronicle**, **Internet Stock report** and the **San Jose Mercury**. All the above have search engines for archives of news stories, so use these if looking for specific topics (e.g. 'online accounts').

To be kept abreast of new research reports being released there are several daily email bulletins that collate news reports. This includes the email service from **FT.com**, and also **First Tuesday** and **The Web Report**.

For statistics on internet usage generally, you can see a survey of the number of users online (broken down by language) at **Global Reach**. The size of the internet, as measured by the number of domains, is at **Internet Software Consortium** while general research is at **Cyberatlas**. Also good, for a round-up of recent surveys is the aforementioned Nua.

L
APCIMS: www.apcims.co.uk

CNET: www.cnet.com

Cyberatlas: research.cyberatlas.com

First Tuesday: www.firsttuesday.com

FT.com: www.ft.com

Global Reach: www.glreach.com/globstats/

Internet Software Consortium: www.isc.org/ds/

Internet Stock report: www.internetstockreport.com

Nua: www.nua.ie/surveys/

San Francisco Chronicle: www.sfgate.com

San Jose Mercury: www.mercurycenter.com

Upside: www.upside.com

The Web Report: www.internetstocks.com

Industry research companies
Datamonitor: www.datamonitor.com

Forrester Research: www.forrester.com

Gartner Group: www.gartnerweb.com

Gomez.com: www.gomezadvisors.com

Lafferty Internet Reports: www.lafferty.com

Warren Buffett

Q Does Warren Buffett have a web site?

A No, not directly. But his company, **Berkshire Hathaway** does. The web site is nothing special, resembling not much more than a motley mall of his subsidiary companies: car insurance, annuities, furniture stores, and jewellery. However, there is an archive of his letters to shareholders 1977-1999 and details of the Annual Meetings.

There is also a mini industry in web sites dedicated to the great man. Such as the quirkily named **Warren Buffett meets Sherlock Holmes**, and **Buffett's Tenets**, the latter being a collection of Buffet sayings, including the apposite, *Unless you can watch your stock holding decline by 50% without becoming panic-stricken, you should not be in the stock market.*

For a general study of value investing, look at the valueinvesting.org web site set up by Peter Webb. As well as providing links to Buffett sites, it has an excellent range of resources for value investors, including tools & calculators, explanations of discounting and cash flow analysis, and links to famous value investors.

L Berkshire Hathaway: www.berkshirehathaway.com

Buffetts Tenets: www.angelfire.com/co/simplewealth/buffettips.html

Warren Buffett meets Sherlock Holmes: www.sherlockinvesting.com

Peter Webb's ValueInvesting.org: www.valueinvesting.org

BERKSHIRE HATHAWAY INC.
1440 Kiewit Plaza
Omaha, NE 68131
Official Home Page

- A Message From Warren E. Buffett

- Annual Reports - 1995 - 2001
  Updated March 9, 2002

- Warren Buffett's Letters To Berkshire Shareholders 1977 - 2001
  Updated March 9, 2002
- News Releases
  Updated May 22, 2002

- Interim Shareholder Reports
  Updated May 10, 2002

- Owner's Manual

- Contributions Program Commonly Asked Questions
  Updated October 20, 2000

- 2002 Annual Meeting
  Updated January 17, 2002

- Links to Berkshire Subsidiary Companies
  Updated May 10, 2002

- Charlie Munger's Letters To Wesco Shareholders 1997 - 2001
  Updated April 27, 2002
- Link To EDGAR

- Letter dated November 9, 2001 From Warren E. Buffett To Berkshire Shareholders discussing 2001 Third Quarter Results
- Comparative Rights and Relative Prices of Class A and B Stock

- How To Order Berkshire Activewear
  Updated May 6, 2002

- Legal Disclaimer

Big Mac index

Is the Economist's *Big Mac Index* on the web?

Yes, the Big Mac Index can be found at the **Economist** web site. To recap, this index uses the notion of purchasing-power parity to assess whether currencies are trading at their correct levels, by comparing the price of a Big Mac in each country.

Real-time tracking of the Index can be found at the **Oanda** currency site. As of March 2002, four currencies were 'over-valued' relative to the US Dollar: British Pound, Danish Krone, Israli Shekel and the Swiss Franc.

From *The Economist*, to the *Economy Watch* calculator at **SmartMoney**, which offers a very neat (if also gimmicky) interactive visual display of key US economic indicators; including a good illustration of the rise and fall in earnings growth rates over the last two years.

Economist (Big Mac Index): www.economist.com/markets/Bigmac/

Oanda: www.oanda.com/products/bigmac/bigmac.shtml

SmartMoney: www.smartmoney.com/economywatch/

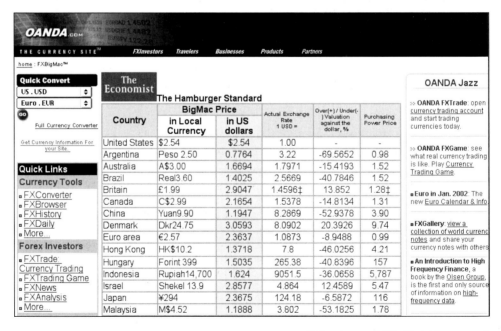

The Hamburger Standard

Country	BigMac Price in Local Currency	in US dollars	Actual Exchange Rate 1 USD =	Over(+) / Under(-) Valuation against the dollar, %	Purchasing Power Price
United States	$2.54	$2.54	1.00	-	-
Argentina	Peso 2.50	0.7764	3.22	-69.5652	0.98
Australia	A$3.00	1.6694	1.7971	-15.4193	1.52
Brazil	Real3.60	1.4025	2.5669	-40.7846	1.52
Britain	£1.99	2.9047	1.4596‡	13.852	1.28‡
Canada	C$2.99	2.1654	1.5378	-14.8134	1.31
China	Yuan9.90	1.1947	8.2869	-52.9378	3.90
Denmark	Dkr24.75	3.0593	8.0902	20.3926	9.74
Euro area	€2.57	2.3637	1.0873	-8.9488	0.99
Hong Kong	HK$10.2	1.3718	7.8	-46.0256	4.21
Hungary	Forint 399	1.5035	265.38	-40.8396	157
Indonesia	Rupiah14,700	1.624	9051.5	-36.0658	5,787
Israel	Shekel 13.9	2.8577	4.864	12.4589	5.47
Japan	¥294	2.3675	124.18	-6.5872	116
Malaysia	M$4.52	1.1888	3.802	-53.1825	1.78

Compound interest

Q I am trying to calculate the future value of my stock market savings scheme in which I invest £200 every month. Assuming that the market rises 14% annually. I can just about work out ordinary compound interest, but the regular payments complicate things. Is there any reference (or ideally a calculator) available on the internet which will do the maths for me?

A Compound interest – what fun! Seriously though, it's all very well punting around in stocks such as Minmet and Motion Media, but people who don't have a thorough understanding of compound interest are liable to have investing careers that are interesting – and brief.

In a concerted attempt to retain readers' attention on this topic, I'll start immediately by trying to explain the power of compound interest, by posing the question: *what if the Wise Men at the birth of Jesus were investment bankers*? What would they be worth today if they had loaned out 1 cent at 6% interest, compounded annually?

The answer is a lot: it's a 1 followed by many zeros (48 in fact). An interesting discussion can be found on the forum at **Colorado University**, where they try to represent how really big this big number is. Quoting liberally, and without checking the figures myself, they say that the resulting *quindectillion, seventy quatrodectillion dollars* would pay for 2.22 x 10 to the 41 tons of gold, which if rolled into a ball would have a radius 2.2 million times that of the earth. Putting this in context, if such a thing is possible, if all of the gold ever mined in 6,000 years of human history was melted down, it would make only an 18-yard cube.

All starting from just 1 cent.

If you are inquisitive and wonder what the Wise Men would be worth now if they hadn't fooled around, and had invested *2 cents* initially instead of 1 – going for some serious money – there's a calculator at www.funk.co.nz/java/jesus-investment.html.

Impressed yet? No wonder when asked, *What do you consider mankind's greatest invention?*, Einstein replied, *Compound interest*.

On the grounds that it is better to teach a person to fish, than merely handing over a fish, we'll work through the process of researching this topic on the web. A useful place to start is what used to be called the Encyclopædia Britannica, but online has the funkier name, **Britannica.com**. Inputting 'compound interest' to the search box displays a list of links to web sites, magazines and Encyclopædia Britannica references. However, in this case there is nothing of much interest to us – besides an historical side note that William Pitt devised a scheme using compound interest to pay for the debts incurred by the American Revolution. Unfortunately the nifty finance plan was upset up by the outbreak of war in 1793 – their equivalent of lastminute.com I suppose.

Another useful reference is **Martindale's Reference Desk**. This is the definitive reference source for online calculators - of all types - with links to over 11,000 web-based calculators. In the field of finance, it covers calculators for economics, stocks, bonds, currencies, options and more. An excellent resource. Remember, on very large web pages like this, it is useful to use the browser's built-in `Find` facility (usually activated with the keys, `Ctrl-F`): search on 'interest' and after a few hits we find a reference to, **How finance works**. This contains very good pages on future and present value, bond yields, annuity payments, and finally, what we're interested in, a page titled *Basic investments*. Here there is a good explanation of the effect of compound interest on regular savings, and there's also a calculator. Unfortunately, though, this calculator assumes regular annual – not monthly – savings. So, we'll have to look elsewhere.

The next place to head for is the search engine at **Go.com**. Of course, there are many search engines that could be used, and all of them have their respective strengths, but I tend to use Go.com first as their references usually seem more relevant. Again, inputting the keywords, 'compound interest' displays a list of links. We'll pass over these for the moment, except to highlight the interest rate calculator at `www.interestratecalculator.com` – it doesn't help us in our current quest, but it does have a great calculator with slide controls and interactive graphics representing principal and interest payments.

The rest of the links listed begin to get to the heart of explaining compound interest. Don't worry that most of the references are to US sites; just mentally change all $ signs to £ signs, and the rest is valid for UK investors. One of the links here is to `www.aarp.org/confacts/money/compinterest.html`, which explains the difference between simple and compound interest, and also describes the latter's effect on regular savings. This page also recommends **Motley Fool** for further information, and if you go to the Fool UK site and input, 'compound interest' you will see several references listed.

First, there's a link to a calculator that does allow for monthly payments, and on the figures in question (£200 monthly at 14% annual return) it produces a figure of £50,600 at the end of 10 years. There's a detailed explanation of compound interest, but the best explanation of the effect it has on regular payments is at: `www.fool.co.uk/personalfinance/personalfinance/2000/pf000111.htm`. The Motley Fool US site has a similar compound interest calculator which you can find at `www.calcbuilder.com/cgi-bin/calcs/SAV2.cgi/themotleyfool`. Using the above parameters this calculates a final value of £52,555. I've created a simple Excel spreadsheet (*compound-interest.xls*: download from this book's web site) to illustrate the calculation for compound interest with regular payments.

Colorado University: csf.colorado.edu/mail/debt/current/0009.html

Encyclopædia Britannica: www.Britannica.com

Go.com: www.go.com

How finance works: www.moneychimp.com/articles/finworks/fmfutval.htm

Martindale's: www-sci.lib.uci.edu/%7Emartindale/RefCalculators.html

Motley Fool (UK): www.fool.co.uk

Calculating historic volatility

Q I've just downloaded a calculator from the internet that values options. How do I calculate volatility?

A Volatility describes the degree of fluctuation of a price over time. A share price with daily moves up or down more than 5% is said to be more volatile than one that rarely moves more than 1%. There are various sources for this data, but it doesn't hurt, if the idea is new to you, to work through the actual arithmetic of the calculation. A good understanding of the method of computation will give you confidence (or otherwise) in knowing how to apply the results. And this is important, as volatility is likely to get an increasingly higher billing in the investment world. Having come to prominence first playing a starring role in the *Black-Scholes* option valuation model, it now also underpins much of risk management theory. **If you don't have a basic comprehension of volatility, you'll be prey to people spouting all sorts of nonsense about it.**

Share volatility - as used in the Black Scholes model - is defined as the standard deviation of the continuously compounded return on a stock. OK, that's the (usual incomprehensible) definition out the way. Let's backtrack, and try to get close to a working model using common sense. To help with this I've downloaded the historic price file for Vodafone from **Yahoo Finance**, and imported this into a spreadsheet (`volatility-vod.xls`: download from this book's web site).

Turning to the spreadsheet (*SimpleCalc* sheet), columns A and B are the date and closing share price respectively. Now, remember that what we are trying to get at is some measure of the fluctuation in share price, so the first thing we'll do is calculate the simple daily return (column C) as the ratio of one day's price over the previous day's. Thus, the first daily return figure is 0.972, representing an approximate 2.8% share price fall from 283.5 (18/11/00) to 275.5 (19/11/00).

The next stage is to calculate the *continuously compounded* returns (column D) by taking the natural log of column C. I'm afraid there isn't space to explain this in detail, but suffice to say it's just a statistical refinement. In practice, we're going to be calculating the variation of figures in column D, but you won't miss anything if you think of these as still just the simple returns in column C. So, we have a column of daily share price returns and you might think (and you'd be right) that it would be useful to calculate the *average* return over the period. This can be found at the bottom of column D, where the average return is calculated to be −0.00029.

This figure we've just calculated is itself quite interesting – being the average daily fluctuation. But it's not quite what we're after. We want a measure that will distinguish between one share whose daily fluctuation range is between −2% to +2%, and another share with a range −15% to +20%, (even though both may have the same *average* daily fluctuation over the whole period). To do this we can take the daily difference between the actual return and the average daily return. If we then sum all these and take their average, we will have a figure that encapsulates the *variation* in daily price fluctuations. A small figure indicates that the daily fluctuations are usually close to the average daily return; whereas a large figure indicates that historically daily returns have deviated widely from the average.

If you follow the above reasoning then that is pretty much all there is to understand about volatility – the rest is just arithmetic, which we will now complete.

When we come to work out the daily difference between a day's actual return and the average, we can't just calculate *return(day n) – average return* as the figures for the days when the market falls will cancel out those for when the market rises; whereas we're interested in the **absolute variation of returns**, regardless of whether they are up or down. The arithmetic device used to calculate this is to take the simple difference and then square it, which guarantees a positive number. And this is what is happening in column E. Then we calculate the average of this column; (but note that we divide the sum by *n-1* data points, not terribly significant just another statistical nicety). The resulting figure, 0.001295, is called the **variance** of the data.

The above calculation was carried out on daily data, but sometimes you may want to use weekly, monthly or some other frequency. That is fine - exactly the same procedure can be used. However, if you want to subsequently compare variance figures, derived from data of different frequencies, you need to normalise the statistic to enable a valid comparison. Normalisation can be done many ways, but the usual way is to express figures in annualised form. In the case of daily data, this means multiplying the variance by 250 (trading days in the year), or by 50 if the data was of weekly frequency. Hence, in this case, the **annualised variance** is 250 x 0.001295 = 0.323688.

We're nearly there.

Remember we squared the daily variations above to calculate Col E? Well, now we'll take the square root of variance, to return the result to units of the original data, and the figure we get is called **standard deviation**. Multiply by 100 and we can express the standard deviation as a percentage – in this case, the 1-year daily returns of Vodafone have a standard deviation, or **volatility**, of 56.89%.

Stop, I hear you cry, I understand the above, leave it at that, no ifs and buts...

Unfortunately, however, it's not quite as simple as that. There is no one definitive way to calculate *historic volatility*; much depends on how the calculated figure will be used. For example, the best estimation for tomorrow's price volatility, is yesterday's volatility; therefore, the time period of the data must be carefully chosen. 1-year data may be too long, or one could think about time-weighting the data. Perhaps one should volume-weight the data so that fluctuations on high volume days have more influence than low volume days. In the computation we calculated the *annualised variance* by multiplying by 250 (as empirical evidence seems to suggest this), but perhaps 350 should be used, or specific to this example 262. The above process assumes the data is *normally distributed* – is this really the case? Also, the data we were using were just closing prices – whereas shouldn't volatility try to capture intra-day price movements as well? And finally, is volatility itself sufficient to measure what we intuitively understand by 'risk'.

Next we'll address some of those questions, make the calculation more efficient by using built in Excel functions, and look at why the Black-Scholes Model was the most dangerous invention of the 20th Century.

Yahoo Finance: chart.yahoo.com/d

Calculating volatility [contd]

We've covered how to calculate the *HV* (historic volatility) of a stock price given a series of periodic data (e.g. daily or weekly closing prices). But, as always, we ended with the usual dispiriting phrase, *however, it's not quite as simple as that*; and I listed some of the qualifications that must be made when making this calculation.

For example, when dealing with daily prices we might want to normalise our calculated figures to express them in an **annualised form** – stock volatility is usually defined as an *annualised* standard deviation. Simple, one might think, just multiply the variance by the number of days in the year. But how many days are there in a year? 365 might seem a reasonable figure. And this is the figure that **Options Direct** uses in its volatility calculation spreadsheet that can be downloaded from its web site. An alternative argument - indeed empirical evidence seems to support this – is that the number of *trading* days in the year should be used. This is usually held to be 250, and I have used that figure in the volatility spreadsheet (`volatility-vod.xls`: download from this book's web site). I suppose a further argument might be that the actual number of trading days in the year should be used. In the example last week for Vodafone, there were in fact 262 trading days in the period we were looking at.

The point of the above is not to say that any particular method is right, but that different approaches are possible. Calculating HV is not an end in itself - knowing that Vodafone has a HV of 58% is not much use, unless that figure is applied somehow. For example, the volatility value may be used in a risk management model, or an options calculation; but its **manner of application should in large part determine its method of calculation**.

Black-Scholes mode

One of the first uses for stock volatility was in the *Black-Scholes model*, devised in the early 1970s to compute a fair value for options. The model, described crudely, estimates a likely range for the stock at a future date (at expiry of the option) using an estimate for the volatility of the stock, and then discounts the option's resulting intrinsic value at the risk-free rate of interest.

The actual Black Scholes formula is not complex, but is sufficiently complicated to deny an immediate understanding of it intuitively. And, as such, it has a strange allure for many. I suspect that people who have the worst problem with the BS formula are engineers, doctors and others with a technical background. Not because they don't understand it, but because they *do*. Or rather, they understand the arithmetic, without appreciating the assumptions and the context within which the formula is used.

Once the formula itself is understood, it is dangerously appealing. It is easy to program into a calculator or spreadsheet, tap in a few values and, hey presto, *fair values* dance before the eyes. One can well understand, after all the *ifs* and *buts* of equity valuation, with their rather simple PE and PEG calculations, the attractions of options with their serious mathematical formulae. But common sense should reason that it can't be as easy as that. If it was, everyone would be calculating the same fair values, and any mis-pricings would disappear immediately. In addition, well-paid researchers in banks spend all their days tweaking the Black Scholes model and variants of it. Recently there was a multi day conference (www.risk-conferences.com) on derivatives modelling, in which one whole day was dedicated to *New advances in forecasting and modelling techniques for volatility and correlation*. Exciting papers were delivered on, *Stochastic volatility correction to Black-Scholes*, and *An eigenfunction approach in two dimensions*. Either this conference was an elaborate cover for a freebie shopping trip to London for the delegates, or there really is something more to volatility calculation and option valuation than a simple spreadsheet computation can encompass.

Up to now we've been using the term *volatility* fairly freely, whereas in fact it has several different meanings.

Firstly, the input value required for Black Scholes is the **forecast volatility** of the stock for the period of the option. We need therefore to make an estimate for what we think the volatility will be in the future. How do we do that? One method is to take the volatility *implied* by the current option price (or a weighted series of option prices) - although there is the obvious danger of a certain circularity here. Another approach, which we have been focusing on so far, is to calculate the *historic* volatility, and to use that as the basis for estimating the future volatility. Or a combination of methods might be used. But a more subtle approach is required than merely calculating a HV figure and banging that into an option calculator.

I mentioned before that we might like to *time-weight* our HV calculation, on the grounds that a price fluctuation yesterday will have more influence on a stock price movement tomorrow, than a daily price fluctuation one year ago. In a similar vein, if we are looking to value an option that expires in 30 days time, the best guide to volatility over the coming 30 days, may be the HV over the previous 30 days. Or, getting rather more sophisticated, we can calculate historic volatility for a rolling 30 day period (somewhat like a 30 day moving average). As an example, I've added a 30-day (and 100-day for good measure) rolling HV to the Vodafone volatility spreadsheet (Sheet: *RollingVol*).

This spreadsheet also makes the HV calculation far more efficient than in the previous deliberately verbose example. In the new spreadsheet, HV has been calculated over a 5-year period, and the results charted, where one can see that 30-day volatility has ranged from 42% to 68% in the last 3 months. Previously we calculated an HV value for Vodafone over the last year of 56%. However, if we were valuing a 30-day Vodafone option on the basis of the chart of the 30-day rolling volatility, we might be tempted to use a volatility figure over 60%.

Options Direct: www.options-direct.co.uk

Calculating *implied* volatility

Q Recently you made a reference to 'implied' volatility. Are there any web sites with a table of these figures, or that allow them to be calculated?

A To recap briefly, there are several types of volatility:

• **historic volatility**, which is calculated from a price data series and measures the fluctuation of prices in the past

• **forecast volatility** as input to the Black Scholes (BS) Model, which is an estimate of future price fluctuations

• **implied volatility**

The BS Model can be used to calculate a theoretical value for an option, based on a few parameters. These include: the underlying stock price, the exercise price of the option, the stock's dividend yield, the risk-free rate, and the stock's estimated volatility over the life of the option. Crudely, the model calculates a probability range for the stock price (at option expiry), from which the option's intrinsic value is derived, and that value is then discounted back to today.

So, given the other terms, a volatility figure can be applied to the BS Model, and a theoretical value of the option can be calculated. This calculated theoretical value can then be compared to the actual current price of the option as it trades in the market. If the theoretical value is above the current option price, the option might be said to be *under-valued*. Or, if the theoretical value of the option was the same as the current option price, the option might be said to be *fairly valued*. In practice, there's a bit more to it than that, but we don't need to go into that here.

The BS Model might therefore be considered a box: input a volatility figure on one side, and out pops a theoretical value on the other side. Fine. However, the calculation can be reversed, whereby a *theoretical value* is input on one side, and out pops a volatility figure on the other. Except, in this case, we don't input a theoretical value but rather we use the **actual trading price** of the option in the market.

OK, you might think warily, we input the actual option trading price, but exactly what is this *volatility* figure we're getting out the other side? What does it mean, how do we use it? Good question. This volatility figure is the volatility value that when input to the ordinary BS Model will calculate a theoretical option value equal to the current option market price. In this reverse operation, the BS Model is being used to infer a volatility level from the actual option price; and, as such, this *backwardly calculated* volatility is termed the *implied volatility*.

Why calculate implied volatility at all?

Options markets operate separately from the underlying stock markets. In many cases the participants are completely different. Due to the nature of the instruments, options tend to be traded, whereas, generally, stocks are for investing in. Options tend to react quicker to changes in short-term views. The two markets react to slightly different influences and can therefore independently relay valuable information on the state of the markets. But whereas with the stock market we have indicators such as long-term stock histories and stock indices to analyse the market, such measures don't exist in the options market. An obvious problem of course is the sheer number of different options contracts related to an individual stock: varying strike prices and expiries, each for calls and puts.

For example, if the premium on a March 50 call option notches up, while the June 45 put option edges down, it can difficult to interpret precisely what that is saying about the market view of the underlying stock.

This is where *implied volatility* comes in. Implied Volatility (IV) can be regarded as a normalising function for options. All the various option parameters (strike price, expiry, option price, call or put) are input to the (reverse) BS Model, and those parameters are summarised in one figure - the implied volatility, which can then be used for comparison with the IV of any other option, or groups of options.

How do we calculate IV?

I said above, rather vaguely, that the IV is calculated by *reversing the BS Model*. Unfortunately, the mathematics of the BS Model don't allow it to be reversed easily. Instead, given an option price, we have to repeatedly input different values of volatility to the ordinary BS Model, until the calculated theoretical value is equal to the current option price – at which point the input volatility is the required IV value. Fortunately, there are various iterative procedures that can be used to speed up the trial and error calculation. But, unfortunately, these can be a bit beyond the capabilities of a simple spreadsheet. Hence, while the calculation of theoretical option values can be fairly easily programmed into a spreadsheet, the calculation of IV is more difficult. At which point we turn to the web.

An index of options calculators can be found at www.freeoptionpricing.com. (Quick note: be wary of bookmarking URLs of the form, www.xxx.edu/~smith/. They are usually the home pages of enthusiastic students, which disappear when the student leaves the college). Unfortunately the majority of online options calculators do not calculate implied volatility. The ones that do are: www.mathfinance.de, www.fintools.net/options/optcalc.html, home.online.no/~espehaug/BlackScholes.html, and www.intrepid.com/~robertl/option-pricer3.html.

My favourite is the one at Mathfinance, but the easiest to use is probably Robert's.

Using Robert's calculator as an example, we can input, volatility=27; stock price=54; strike=50; dividend=1.5; interest rate=2.5; expiration=6 months; for a European call option and find that the theoretical value is 6.38. But, in this hypothetical case, let's say the option is actually trading currently at 7.40. By selecting at the top, Compute volatility and inputting 7.40 into the option price box, we can calculate an implied volatility of 34.61%. This volatility figure could then be compared to the IV of other contracts associated with the same stock, and the relative cheapness, or expensiveness, assessed.

If you'd prefer to play around with a calculator offline, you can download the free calculator at www.snowgold.com/download/downopt.html. We've only scratched the surface of IV here; if you'd like to see how serious it can get take a look at www.ivolatility.com. You might like to input 'VOD' and compare the figures there with those we calculated previously.

Financial careers

Q Are there any good web sites that have information about getting a job in the financial industry?

A Right now may not be the best time to be looking for a job in financial services. Although Laurence Copeland, Finance Professor at Cardiff University, when asked to contribute an investment tip to **Investing-Rules.com** did recommend getting a job as a currency guru, on the grounds that *"The great thing about mission impossible is that nobody expects you to be successful. Failing to work miracles is not adequate ground for dismissal. The pay is good too."*

A good starting point is **eFinancialCareers**, which also manages the career pages on **Bloomberg**. This has a great range of information including job postings and jolly news of all the latest redundancies. There's also a useful section, *Ask the expert* and an intriguingly voyeuristic column, *A Day In The Life…*. If you want to find out what a Securitisation Expert does with his day, here's where to find out.

After that the four best sites are: **Careers-in-Finance**, **JobsInTheMoney**, **Vault.com** and **WetFeet**. The FT also has a careers center at **FTCareerPoint**, although this is not focused uniquely on careers in finance. A fairly comprehensive list of Executive Search Consultants (*headhunters* to you and me) can be found at Numa.com.

L
Bloomberg: www.bloomberg.co.uk/careers/

Careers-in-Finance: www.careers-in-finance.com

eFinancialCareers: www.efinancialnews.com/jobs/

FTCareerPoint: ftcareerpoint.ft.com/ftcareerpoint

Investing Rules: www.investing-rules.com

JobsInTheMoney: www.jobsinthemoney.com

Numa.com: www.numa.com/jobs/

Vault.com: www.vault.com

WetFeet: www.wetfeet.com

Appendix 1: Subject-Ordered List of Web Sites

1. Computers and the internet

Internet statistics
Cyberatlas: research.cyberatlas.com
Global Reach: www.glreach.com/globstats/
Internet Software Consortium: www.isc.org/ds/
Nua: www.nua.ie/surveys/

Computer support
HowStuffWorks (online reference): www.howstuffworks.com
Microsoft (online help): support.microsoft.com
Newsgroups: groups.google.com
PC Medics(telephone tech support): www.pc-medics.co.uk
PCPitstop: www.pcpitstop.com
Tech Tutorials (online reference): www.techtutorials.com

Investment programs for Apple Macs
Metastock: www.equis.com
Paritech: www.paritech.co.uk
Pro Analyst: trendsoft.com/ProAnalyst/
ProTA: www.beesoft.net

Broadband internet
BT Openworld: www.btopenworld.com
Easynet: www.easydial.co.uk
NTL: www.ntl.com
NTL (broadband site): www.broadband-cable.co.uk
Telewest: www.telewest.co.uk

Download programs from the net
Download.com: www.download.com
Tucows: www.tucows.com
ZD Net: www.zdnet.com/downloads/

Search engines
Alltheweb: www.alltheweb.com
Altavista: www.altavista.com
Copernic: www.copernic.com
Dogpile: www.dogpile.com
FT (GlobalArchive): globalarchive.ft.com
Google: www.google.com
HotBot: www.hotbot.com
Lycos: www.lycos.com
Metacrawler: www.metacrawler.com
NorthernLight: www.northernlight.com
Vivisimo: www.vivisimo.com
Yahoo: www.yahoo.com

Anonymous email services

Bigfoot: www.bigfoot.com
Hotmail: www.hotmail.com
Yahoo: www.yahoo.com

Miscellaneous

EditPlus (good text editor): www.editplus.com
Microsoft (keyboard shortcuts):
microsoft.com/enable/products/keyboard/keyboardsearch.asp
Microsoft (Web Queries reference):
officeupdate.microsoft.com/excel/webquery/samples.htm
Paint Shop Pro (good graphics program): www.jasc.com
WinZip (file compression): www.winzip.com

2. Investing basics

News and tips

Company/business news
ADVFN: www.advfn.com/cmn/news/news_list.php
AFXpress: www.afxpress.com
BBC: news.bbc.co.uk/hi/english/business/companies
Bloomberg: www.bloomberg.co.uk/bbn/uk_top.html
Bloomberg world headlines: www.bloomberg.co.uk/bbn/world_top.html
Breaking Views: www.breakingviews.com
BusinessWeek[$]: www.businessweek.com/today.htm
Citywire: www.citywire.co.uk
Evening Standard:
www.thisislondon.co.uk/dynamic/news/business/top_direct.html
Financial Mail: www.financialmail.co.uk
Freequotes: www.freequotes.co.uk
FT Investor www.ftmarketwatch.com/news/headlines.asp
FT: www.ft.com/hippocampus
FT Global Archive Search: globalarchive.ft.com
hemscott.NET: www.hemscott.com/hstoday/index.htm
IHT: www.iht.com/IHT/TODAY/findex.html
Moneyextra: www.moneyextra.com/news/
News Review[$]: www.news-review.co.uk
Telegraph: money.telegraph.co.uk
UK-Wire: www.ukwire.com
Yahoo Business: finance.yahoo.co.uk
Yahoo financial: www.yahoo.co.uk/headlines/financial

Technology company news
AFX Press: www.afxpress.com
Bloomberg: www.bloomberg.co.uk/bbn/technology.html
Citywire: www.citywire.co.uk/previewtechnews/
Equity Investigator: www.equityinvestigator.com
Multex Investor: www.multexinvestor.co.uk
Sharecast: www.sharecast.co.uk
The Register: www.theregister.co.uk

News by email
ADVFN: www.advfn.com
Ample: www.iii.co.uk
Bloomberg: www.bloomberg.co.uk
CityComment: www.citycomment.co.uk
DigitalLook: www.digitallook.com
Economist: www.economist.com
FT Investor: www.ft.com/investor
FT.com: www.ft.com
hemscott.NET: www.hemscott.net
Investors Chronicle: www.investorschronicle.co.uk
The Fetcher: www.thefetcher.com

Economy
Bank of England: www.bankofengland.co.uk
BBC: news.bbc.co.uk/hi/english/business/economy/
CCTA Government Information Service: www.open.gov.uk
Central Office of Information (COI): www.coi.gov.uk/coi
Economist: www.economist.com/markets/indicators
Ed Yardeni: www.yardeni.com
HM Treasury: www.hm-treasury.gov.uk
Institute for Fiscal Studies (IFS): www1.ifs.org.uk
JP Morgan: www.jpmorgan.com/research
Lombard Street Research: www.lombard-st.co.uk
ManDirect: www.mandirect.co.uk/trading-tools/keyevents.cfm

Strategy
Andrew Smithers: www.smithers.co.uk/news.shtml
Bank Credit Analyst: www.bcapub.com/public/anthology.asp
Barry Riley: news.ft.com/news/opinion/columnists
Bill Sharpe: www.stanford.edu/~wfsharpe/art/art.htm
Bloomberg: www.bloomberg.com/columns
Gold Eagle: www.gold-eagle.com/editorials.html
Jeremy Grantham: www.gmo.com/overview/articles.html
Jeremy Siegel: knowledge.wharton.upenn.edu
Paul Krugman: web.mit.edu/krugman/www
Peter Bernstein: www.peterlbernsteininc.com
Peter Martin: news.ft.com/news/opinion/columnists
Philip Coggan: news.ft.com/news/opinion/columnists
Robert Shiller: www.econ.yale.edu/~shiller
Samuel Brittan: www.samuelbrittan.co.uk

Share tips
Bloomberg Money Flow: www.bloomberg.com/uk/tv/moneyflow/index.html
Citywire: www.citywire.co.uk/previewcitywireinsider/
Financial Mail: www.financialmail.co.uk
Share of the Day: www.sharepages.com
T1ps.com: www.t1ps.com
Tipsheets: www.tipsheets.co.uk
Tipswatcher: a1.digitallook.com/pages/tips_watcher.html
Watshot.com: www.watshot.com
Yahoo screener: uk.biz.yahoo.com/screen/i_ftse100.html
Zak Mir TA: www.citycomment.co.uk/columns

Companies

Ticker symbol lookup
Bondscape (bonds): www.bondscape.net
Reuters: www.reuters.co.uk
ThomsonFN: global.thomsonfn.co.uk/
Wright Investors' Service: profiles.wisi.com
Yahoo Finance: finance.yahoo.co.uk/lookup.html

New issues
EO.net: www.eo.net
Financial Mail: www.financialmail.co.uk/newissues.htm
FT: www.ipo.com/ipoinfo/ipoinfo.asp?p=FTFT
HemScott: businessplus.hemscott.net/eprofile/eprofile.dll/ipo-eye
Ample: www.iii.co.uk/newissues
newissues-ipo.com: www.newissues-ipo.com
nothing-ventured.com: www.nothing-ventured.com
selectipo: www.selectipo.com
Wit Capital: www.witcapital.com
Yahoo: uk.biz.yahoo.com/334

New issue prospectuses
hemscott.NET: www.hemscott.net
London Stock Exchange: www.londonstockexchange.com/newissues/
UK-Wire: www.uk-wire.co.uk

AIM companies
hemscott.NET: www.hemscott.net
London Stock Exchange: www.londonstockexchange.com
Reuters: www.reuters.co.uk
Yahoo Finance: finance.yahoo.co.uk

OFEX companies
Durlacher: www.durlacher.co.uk
EO.net: www.eo.net
OFEX: www.ofex.co.uk
Unquoted.co.uk: www.unquoted.co.uk

Value investing
Jim Slater: www.global-investor.com/slater
Berkshire Hathaway: www.berkshirehathaway.com
Peter Webb's web site: www.valueinvesting.org
Value Investor's Workshop: members.aol.com/WCrimi/workshop.html

Exchanges and Regulation

Exchanges
Easdaq: www.easdaq.be
Global-Investor: resources.global-investor.com/pages/exchanges.htm
Jiway: www.jiway.com
LIFFE: www.liffe.com
London Stock Exchange: www.londonstockexchange.com
Nasdaq (UK): www.nasdaquk.com
OFEX: www.ofex.co.uk

Regulation
American Association of Individual Investors (AAII): www.aaii.com
Assoc. for Investment Management and Research (AIMR): www.aimr.com
Commodity Futures Trading Commission (CFTC): www.cftc.gov
National Assoc. of Investors Corp (NAIC): www.better-investing.org
Securities & Exchange Commission (SEC): www.sec.gov
Securities and Futures Authority (SFA): www.fsa.gov.uk/sfa/
Securities And Investment Board (SIB): www.sib.co.uk

Investor compensation
FSA: www.fsa.gov.uk
FSA (Consumer help): www.fsa.gov.uk/consumer/consumer_help/
The Financial Services Compensation Scheme: www.the-ics.org.uk

Scams
SamSpade (domain tools): samspade.org/t/
Securities & Exchange Commission (SEC): www.sec.gov
Securities And Investment Board (SIB): www.sib.co.uk
UXN spam combat (domain tools): combat.uxn.com

Funds

Funds
Assoc. of Investment Trusts Companies (AITC): www.aitc.co.uk
Assoc. of Unit Trusts & Investment Funds: www.investmentfunds.org.uk
Fundfact.com: www.fundfact.com
Funds S&P: www.funds-sp.com
HSW: www.hsw.co.uk/UT/UTindex.html
Micropal: www.funds-sp.com
Morningstar: www.morningstar.co.uk
Splitsonline: www.splitsonline.co.uk
TrustNet: www.trustnet.com
Trustnews.co.uk: www.trustnews.co.uk

Fund holdings
Citywatch: www.citywatch.co.uk
Gartmore: www.gartmore.co.uk
Morningstar: www.morningstar.co.uk

Investment trusts
AITC: www.aitc.co.uk
Ample: www.iii.co.uk
DigitalLook: www.digitallook.com
Lipper: www.lipperweb.com
Micropal: www.funds-sp.com
Moneyextra (ITs): www.moneyextra.com/funds/invtrusts/itlist.htm
TrustNet: www.trustnet.com

Exchange traded funds
iShares (Barclays): www.ishares.net/index2.html
Investors Chronicle: www.ic-community.co.uk/etfs/

Tax

Tax information
AccountingWeb: www.accountingweb.co.uk/tax/
Ample: www.iii.co.uk/tax/
Digita: www.digita.com
FTYourMoney: www.ftyourmoney.com
Inland Revenue: www.inlandrevenue.gov.uk
Inland Revenue CGT intro: www.inlandrevenue.gov.uk/leaflets/c4.htm,
Inland Revenue CGT 1998 reform: www.inlandrevenue.gov.uk/cgtreform/
Inland Revenue CGT calc: www.inlandrevenue.gov.uk/pdfs/cgt1_9.htm
Moneyextra: www.moneyextra.com/tax/
This Is Money: www.thisismoney.com/undated/tx3146.html
Yahoo Finance (tax): uk.biz.yahoo.com/tax/home.html
Yahoo Finance (CGT guide): uk.biz.yahoo.com/tax/taxguide/cgt.html

CGT programs
Fairshares: www.updata.co.uk
Inland Revenue: www.inlandrevenue.gov.uk
Sharescope: www.sharescope.co.uk

Miscellaneous

Online portfolios
ADVFN: www.advfn.com
Ample: www.iii.co.uk/portfolio
FT Investor www.ftmarketwatch.com
Moneyextra: www.moneyworld.co.uk/stocks/portfolio
MSN UK: money.msn.co.uk/Investing/
Yahoo Finance: finance.yahoo.co.uk

Bulletin boards
ADVFN: www.advfn.com
Ample: www.iii.co.uk
hemscott.NET: www.hemscott.net
IRD: www.ird.com
Motley Fool: www.fool.co.uk
Sharepages: www.sharepages.com
Trade2Win: www.Trade2Win.co.uk
Digital Look (BB reference): www.digitallook.com

3. Data sources

Data downloads
ADVFN [$]: www.advfn.com
Downloadquotes.com [$]: www.downloadquotes.com
FTSE International: www.ftse.com
Moneyextra: www.moneyextra.com/stocks/data_downloads.html
Paritech [$]: www.paritech.co.uk
Prestel [$]: www.finexprestel.com
Sharescope [$]: www.sharescope.co.uk
Yahoo Finance: chart.yahoo.com/d

4. Fundamental analysis

Company reports
Company Annual Reports Online (Carol): www.carol.co.uk
Corporate Reports: www.corpreports.co.uk
Yahoo (WILink): yahoouk.ar.wilink.com

Company profiles
hemscott.NET: www.hemscott.co.uk/equities/index.htm
Hoovers: www.hoovers.com/uk/
Wright: profiles.wisi.com/profiles/UnitedKingdom.htm
Yahoo: uk.biz.yahoo.com/p/ukie/a

Company research
Equity Development [$]: www.equity-development.co.uk
Equity Growth Research (EGR): www.equitygrowth.net
Equity Investigator [$]: www.equityinvestigator.com
Growth Company Investor: www.growthcompany.co.uk
ICC[$]: www.icc.co.uk
Investor Information: www.investorinformation.co.uk
Investors Chronicle: www.investorschronicle.co.uk
iTruffle [$]: www.itruffle.com
MoneyGuru [$]: www.moneyguru.co.uk
Ovum Holway: www.holway.co.uk
RedSky Research: www.redskyresearch.com
t1ps.com [$]: www.t1ps.com
techMARK Research: www.techmarkresearch.com
thewrongprice [$]: www.thewrongprice.com

Diary/company announcements
BBC: news.bbc.co.uk/hi/english/business/business_diary
Companies House: www.companies-house.gov.uk
hemscott.NET: www.hemscott.net
Yahoo: uk.biz.yahoo.com/172

Company results calendars
ADVFN: www.advfn.com
Ample: www.iii.co.uk
hemscott.NET: www.hemscott.net
Hemscott (results): www.hemscott.com/hstoday/week_aheadndex.htm
nothing-ventured.com: www.nothing-ventured.com

Earnings estimates
Ample: www.iii.co.uk
FT.com (analyst forecasts): news.ft.com/news/companynews/multex/
hemscott.NET: www.hemscott.net
Motley Fool: www.fool.co.uk
MSN Money: uk.moneycentral.msn.com/investor
Yahoo Finance: finance.yahoo.co.uk

Online conference calls

Best Calls: www.bestcalls.com
Itruffle: www.itruffle.com
Microsoft: www.microsoft.com/msft/speech.htm
Motley Fool (Reg FD): www.fool.com/Specials/2000/sp001212b.htm
RAWfinancial.com: www.rawfinancial.com
Yahoo Finance US (conference call calendar): biz.yahoo.com/cc/
Yahoo Finance UK (conference call calendar): uk.biz.yahoo.com/140/

CEO interviews

t1ps.com: www. t1ps.com
Yahoo Finance (TWST interviews): uk.biz.yahoo.com/171/

Directors' dealings

Citywatch [$]: www.citywatch.co.uk
Citywire: www.citywire.co.uk/previewdirectorsdealings/
DigitalLook: www.digitallook.com
hemscott.NET: www.hemscott.NET
Investor Ease: www.investorease.com
UK-Wire: www.uk-wire.com

Stock screeners

ADVFN: www.advfn.com
DigitalLook: www.digitallook.com
iTruffle: www.truffle.com
MSN UK: uk.moneycentral.msn.com/investor/finder/custstoc.asp
OnVista: www.onvista.co.uk
Sharescope: www.sharescope.com
Yahoo Finance: uk.biz.yahoo.com/screen/i_ftse100.html

Model portfolios

Ample: www.iii.co.uk/iiianalyst/
Motley Fool UK: www.fool.co.uk/portfolios.htm

5. Technical analysis

Online charts

Ample: www.iii.co.uk
Bloomberg: www.bloomberg.co.uk
Downloadquotes.com: www.downloadquotes.com
FT Investor: www.ft.com/investor
Nothing-ventured.com: www.nothing-ventured.com
OnVista: www.onvista.co.uk
Yahoo: finance.yahoo.co.uk

Streaming charts

IRD: www.ird.com
Lycos Finance: finance.lycos.com

myTrack: www.myBroker.co.uk
Proquote: www.proquote.net
Sharepages: www.sharepages.com
Updata: www.updata.co.uk

Sector charts

ADVFN: www.advfn.com
Ample: www.iii.co.uk
Comdirect: www.comdirect.co.uk
FT Investor: www.ft.com/investor

Long-term charts

Cross Currents: www.cross-currents.net
Decision Point: www.decisionpoint.com
Dr Edward Yardeni: www.yardeni.com/finmkts.asp
LongWaves: csf.colorado.edu/forums/longwaves/
Lowrisk: www.lowrisk.com
Martin Capital: www.martincapital.com/charts.htm
Moore Research Center (long-term charts): www.mrci.com/pdf/
StockCharts.com (Historical Chart Gallery):
stockcharts.com/charts/historical/
TradingCharts.com (commodity charts): www.tfc-charts.w2d.com/chart/
TradingCharts.com (Dow Jones technical chart):
futures.tradingcharts.com/chart/DW/W

Chart alerts

ADVFN (chart breakouts): www.advfn.com/cmn/tl/movers.php3
AIQ: www.aiqsystems.com
AvidTrader: www.avidinfo.com
Barchart.com: www.barchart.com
Investtech: www.investtech.com/uk/
Omnitrader: www.omnitrader.com
Sixer.com: www.sixer.com
The Security Blanket: www.thesecurityblanket.com/tradingideas/
Updata: www.updata.co.uk

Technical analysis commentary

Chartanalysts: www.chartanalysts.com
CityComment: www.citycomment.co.uk
David Schwartz: www.schwartztrends.com
Financial Spreads: www.finspreads.com
FT Investor: www.ft.com/investor
GNI TA commentary (onewaybet.com): www.onewaybet.com
GNI: www.gni.co.uk
Investtech.com: www.investtech.com/uk/
Sharecast: www.sharecast.co.uk
ShareStar: www.sharestar-uk.com
t1ps.com: www.t1ps.com
TRADINGCentral.com: www.TradingCentral.com

Trading systems

AIQ Systems: www.aiqsystems.com
Barchart.com: www.barchart.com
Indigo Investor: www.indigoinvestor.com
Investtech.com: www.investtech.com
Metastock: www.equis.com
OmniTrader: www.omnitrader.com
Paritech: www.paritech.co.uk
Sixer.com: www.sixer.com
TC2000: www.tc2000.com
Trade2Win: www.trade2win.co.uk

Tutorials

Ample: www.iii.co.uk
Chart Patterns: www.chartpatterns.com
FT Investor: www.ft.com/investor
MetaStock: www.equis.com
Stock Charts (TA columns): www.stockcharts.com/commentary/
Stock Charts: www.stockcharts.com

6. Trading

Brokers

Ample: www.iii.co.uk/sharedealing/
Charles Schwab: www.schwab-worldwide.com/Worldwide/Europe
Comdirect: www.comdirect.co.uk
DLJ direct UK: www.dljdirect.co.uk
E*Trade UK: www.etrade.co.uk
Halifax: www.halifax.co.uk/sharedealing
Hargreaves Lansdown: www.h-l.co.uk
iDealing: www.idealing.com
Imiweb: www.imiweb.co.uk
Nothing-Ventured: www.nothing-ventured.com
Selftrade: www.selftrade.co.uk
Sharepeople: www.sharepeople.co.uk
StockAcademy: www.stockacademy.com
Stocktrade: www.stocktrade.co.uk
TD Waterhouse: www.tdwaterhouse.co.uk

Reference

APCIMS: www.apcims.org
BlueSky: www.blueskyratings.com
FTYourMoney (Brokerfinder): ftyourmoney.ft.com/FTym/brokerfinder
Motley Fool:
www.fool.co.uk/personalfinance/discountbrokers/discountbrokers1.htm

Market snapshot

ADVFN: www.advfn.com
Ample: www.iii.co.uk
BBC (market data): news.bbc.co.uk/hi/english/business/market_data/
Bloomberg: www.bloomberg.co.uk
Comdirect: www.comdirect.co.uk
FT Investor: www.ft.com/investor
Moneyextra: www.moneyextra.com
Motley Fool: www.fool.co.uk
Sharepages: www.sharepages.com
Yahoo Finance: finance.yahoo.co.uk

Delayed share prices

ADVFN: www.advfn.com
Ample: www.iii.co.uk/quotes/search/?
Sharepages: www.sharepages.com
Yahoo: finance.yahoo.co.uk

Real-time share prices

ADVFN: www.advfn.com
Ample [$]: ww.iii.co.uk
City Comment: www.citycomment.co.uk
LondonMoneyMarket [$]: www.londonmoneymarket.com
myTrack [$]: www.mytrack.com
ProQuote [$]: www.proquote.net
RealTimeShares.com: www.realtimeshares.com
Teletext [$]: www.teletext.co.uk

Level II

ADVFN: www.advfn.com/cmn/level2.php
E*Trade: www.etrade.co.uk
GNI: www.gni.co.uk
Proquote: www.proquote.net

UK major movers

Bloomberg: www.bloomberg.co.uk/markets/
hemscott.NET: www.hemscott.co.uk/equities/stats/
Yahoo: uk.finance.yahoo.com/a02?u

UK closing prices

Financial Mail: www.thisismoney.com/ftse.asp

UK market report

FT Investor: www.ftmarketwatch.com/news/pulse.asp
Moneyextra: www.moneyextra.com/stocks/stockrep.htm
Motley Fool: www.fool.co.uk/DailyFool/dailyfool.htm
Telegraph: portal.telegraph.co.uk

Sector performance
ADVFN: www.advfn.com/cmn/tl/sectors.php3
Ample: www.iii.co.uk/ukequity/?type=sectors
Comdirect: focus.comdirect.co.uk

Market comment
Lex: news.ft.com/news/opinion/lex
Motley Fool: www.fool.co.uk/news/marketnews

Market outlook
Cantor Index: www.cantorindex.com/fayre/todaysfayre.cfm

Normal market size
ADVFN: www.advfn.com
LSE: www.londonstockexchange.com/techlib/nms_default.asp

Times & Sales price data
ADVFN: www.advfn.com
Ample: www.iii.co.uk
hemscott.NET: www.hemscott.net
Motley Fool BB:
boards.fool.co.uk/Message.asp?id=2010001011075000&sort=id
Sharepages: www.sharepages.com

Trade definitions
ADVFN: www.advfn.com
hemscott.NET: www.hemscott.net
LSE: www.prices.londonstockexchange.com/glossary.asp#tradetypes

Email alerts
ADVFN: www.advfn.com
Ample: www.iii.co.uk
Moneyextra: www.moneyextra.com

Email newsletters
Brunswick Direct: www.brunswickdirect.com
Growth Company Investor: www.growthcompany.co.uk
Michael Walters: www.michaelwalters.com
Motley Fool: www.fool.com
Multex: www.multexinvestor.com
T1ps.com: www.t1ps.com

Day trading
ADVFN (Level II explanation): www.advfn.com/cmn/help/level2.php
DayTradingStocks.com: www.daytradingstocks.com
DirectAccessTrader: www.directaccesstrader.com
GNItouch: www.gnitouch.com

myTrack: www.mytrack.com
Proquote: www.proquote.net
Raging Bull: www.ragingbull.com
The Rookie DayTrader: www.rookiedaytrader.com

Trading simulation and competitions

CityComment: www.citycomment.co.uk
Cybertrader: www.cybertrader.com
FinSpreads: www.finspreads.com
FXTrade: fxtrade.oanda.com
Nasdaq (Head Trader): www.academic.nasdaq.com/HeadTrader/
SimVest Solution: www.simvesting.com

7. US markets

Brokers

Ameritrade: www.ameritrade.com
Charles Schwab: www.schwab.com
Datek: www.datek.com
E*Trade: www.etrade.com
Swiftrade: www.swiftrade.com
TD Waterhouse: www.waterhouse.com

Reference

Gomez Advisors: www.gomezadvisors.com
Keynote (speed comparisons): www.keynote.com/measures/brokers
Motley Fool:
www.fool.com/Media/DiscountBrokerageCenter/SelectingABroker.htm
Smart Money: www.smartmoney.com/brokermeter/

Day trading brokers

CyberTrader: www.cybertrader.com
Datek: www.datek.com
DirectAccessTrader: www.directaccesstrader.com
myTrack: www.mytrack.com
Tradecast: www.tradecast.com
Tradescape.com: www.tradescape.com

Hybrid brokers

Datek: www.datek.com
E*Trade: www.etrade.com
Interactive brokers: www.interactivebrokers.com

Ticker symbol lookup

Quicken: www.quicken.com/investments/tickersearch
Yahoo: finance.yahoo.com/l

Historic price data

Downloadquotes.com: www.downloadquotes.com
WSRN: www.wsrn.com
Yahoo Finance: chart.yahoo.com/d

Real time stock prices

Datek: www.datek.com
FreeRealTime: quotes.freerealtime.com
IQ Chart [$]: www.iqchart.com
Island: www.island.com
Lycos Finance [$]: finance.lycos.com
Wall Street City: www.wallstreetcity.com
Money.net [$]: www.money.net

Level II stock prices

3D StockCharts: www.3dstockcharts.com
Island: www.isld.com

Stock index futures

CBOT: www.cbot.com
CME (www.cme.com)
CME (flash quotes): www.cme.com/prices/delayed_intraday_quotes/
CNN Morning Call: cnnfn.cnn.com/markets/morning_call/
INO: quotes.ino.com
INO: (futures quotes): quotes.ino.com/exchanges/?c=indexes
PC Quote: www.pcquote.com/futures/
TFC: www.tfc-charts.w2d.com/marketquotes/

Market comment

CBS MarketWatch: cbs.marketwatch.com/news/commentary/
Quicken: www.quicken.com/investments/columns
RealMoney: www.realmoney.com
TheStreet.com: www.thestreet.com

Commentators

Adam Lashinsky: money.cnn.com/commentary/bottomline/
Bernie Schaeffer:
www.schaeffersresearch.com/schaeffer/bernie_schaeffer.asp
Herb Greenberg: www.thestreet.com/comment/
Jim Jubak: moneycentral.msn.com/content/data/jubakjournal.asp
John Dorfman: www.bloomberg.com/columns/
John Murphy: www.stockcharts.com/commentary/Murphy/
Ken Fisher: www.forbes.com/columnists
Thom Calandra: cbs.marketwatch.com

Share tips

Hulbert Financial Digest: www.hulbertdigest.com
InvesTools: www.investools.com/cgi-bin/IT/advisory/home
John Dorfman (Bloomberg): www.bloomberg.com/columns/

248

```
Jim Jubak: moneycentral.msn.com/content/data/jubakjournal.asp
SmartMoney: www.smartmoney.com/smmovers/
Validea.com [ $]: www.validea.com
Wall Street Guru: www.wallstreetguru.com
```

Company profiles
```
EDGAR Online: www.edgar-online.com
Hoovers: www.hoovers.com
Market Guide: www.marketguide.com/MGI
Multex: www.multexinvestor.com
Yahoo: quote.yahoo.com
Zacks: www.zacks.com
```

Stock screeners
```
Hoovers StockScreener: www.stockscreener.com
MarketGuide: www.marketguide.com
MarketPlayer: www.marketplayer.com
Quicken: www.quicken.com
StockTables: www.stocktables.com
```

News by email
```
CNET: www.news.com
Lycos Finance: finance.lycos.com
Marketwatch: cbs.marketwatch.com
Moneynet: www.moneynet.com
Motley Fool: www.fool.com
NewsPage: www.newspage.com
Real Money: www.realmoney.com
Reuters' Moneynet: www.moneynet.com
Silicon Investor: www.siliconinvestor.com
Sixer.com: www.sixer.com
Upside: www.upside.com
```

Economic releases
```
The Dismal Scientist: www.dismal.com
Economeister: www.economeister.com
Federal Reserve: www.federalreserve.gov
Dr Yardeni: www.yardeni.com
```

Model portfolios
```
Motley Fool: www.fool.com
SmartMoney: www.smartmoney.com
```

Online portfolios
```
DBC: portfolio.marketwatch.com/portfolio
Quicken: www.quicken.com/investments/portfolio/?pid=686504459547908
Reuters MoneyNet: www.moneynet.com
SmartMoney: www.smartmoney.com/portfolio/
StockTools: www.stocktools.com
```

Bulletin boards

Raging Bull: www.ragingbull.com
Silicon Investor: www.siliconinvestor.com
Yahoo Finance: messages.yahoo.com/yahoo/Business_Finance/

Mutual funds money flow

AMG Data Services: www.amgdata.com
TrimTabs Investment Research: www.trimtabs.com/mffnews.htm

Exchange traded funds

ETFZone: www.indexfunds.com/ETFzone.htm
HOLDRS: www.holdrs.com
Morningstar: www.morningstar.com/Cover/ETF.html

ADRs

Bank of New York (ADRs): www.adrbny.com
CBS MarketWatch: cbs.marketwatch.com
Hoovers: www.hoovers.com
JP Morgan (ADRs): www.adr.com
Lycos Finance: finance.lycos.com
Multex: www.multex.com
Worldlyinvestor.com: www.worldlyinvestor.com
WSRN: www.wsrn.com
Yahoo Finance (Reuters ADR Report): biz.yahoo.com/rf/

VIX

Academic paper: papers.ssrn.com/sol3/papers.cfm?abstract_id=194288
CBOE: www.cboe.com
CBS MarketWatch: cbs.marketwatch.com

8. International markets (excluding UK and US)

International brokers

BlueSky Ratings: www.blueskyratings.com
Brunswick Direct: www.brunswickdirect.com
Comdirect: www.comdirect.co.uk
e-cortal: www.e-cortal.com
IMIWeb: www.imiweb.co.uk
Interactive Brokers: www.interactivebrokers.com

World markets overview

Bloomberg: www.bloomberg.com
CBS MarketWatch: cbs.marketwatch.com/news/globalmarkets/
CME (flash page): www.cme.com/prices/delayed_intraday_quotes/
CNNfn: cnnfn.cnn.com/markets/world_markets.html
MRCI: www.mrci.com/qpnight.asp
OnVista: indices.onvista.co.uk
Yahoo: quote.yahoo.com/m2?u

European Markets
Bloomberg: www.bloomberg.com
Comdirect: www.comdirect.co.uk
FT Investor: www.ft.com/investor
TRADINGCentral.com: www.tradingcentral.com

International market charts
Bloomberg: www.bloomberg.com
CNNfn: www.cnnfn.com
FT Investor: www.ft.com/investor
Nasdaq: www.nasdaq.com
OnVista: indices.onvista.co.uk
Reuters: www.reuters.com
Yahoo Finance: finance.yahoo.com

International yield curves
Bloomberg (yield curves): www.bloomberg.com/markets/iyc.html
European Union (Euro yield curve): europa.eu.int/comm/eurostat/
Treasury Management Pages: www.tmpages.com/tmp55.htm

Company information
EDGAR database: www.edgar-online.com
Global-Investor: www.global-investor.com
Hoovers: www.hoovers.com
Wright Investor's Services: www.corporateinformation.com
WSRN: www.wsrn.com
Zacks: www.zacks.com

European research
Bloomberg: www.bloomberg.com
Comdirect: www.comdirect.co.uk
FT Investor: www.ft.com/investor
TRADINGCentral.com: www.tradingcentral.com

Currency information
Bloomberg (currencies): www.bloomberg.com/markets/currency.html
Economist (Big Mac Index): www.economist.com/markets/Bigmac/
ForexATS: www.forex-ats.com
INO: quotes.ino.com/exchanges/forex/
JP Morgan: www.jpmorgan.com/MarketDataInd/Forex/currIndex.html
Oanda: www.oanda.com
Pacific Exchange Rates Service:
pacific.commerce.ubc.ca/xr/plot.html

Trading currencies online
BoxOption (Oanda): boxoption.olsen.ch
Cantor: www.cantorindex.com
CMC: www.deal4free.com/forex/
CurrencyPro (GBPUSD): www.currencypro.com/graph.php

Trading currencies online (contd.)

```
Easy2Trade (futures): www.easy2trade.com
Finspreads: www.finspreads.com
Forex Capital Markets: www.fxcm.com
FXGame (Oanda): fxgame.oanda.com
FXTrade (Oanda): fxtrade.oanda.com
Gain Capital: www.gaincapital.com
GCI Capital: www.globalcap.com
GNI: www.gnitouch.com
MG Forex: www.mgforex.com
Saxo Bank: www.saxobank.com
```

National holidays

```
Bank Holidays Of The World: www.national-holidays.com
The Worldwide Holiday & Festival: www.holidayfestival.com
```

9. Derivatives and betting

Futures

```
Easy2Trade: www.easy2trade.com
Berkeley Futures: www.bfl.co.uk
LIFFE: www.liffe.com
Man Futures: www.manfutures.com
```

Options

```
LIFFE (data): www.liffe-data.com
LIFFE (distributors): www.liffe.com/liffedata/realtime/internet.htm
Man Financial (broker): www.manfinancial.com/home.cfm
myBroker (broker): www.mybroker.co.uk
Options Direct (broker): www.options-direct.co.uk
ThomsonFN (data): global.thomsonfn.co.uk
```

Warrants

```
AITC (investment trust warrants): www.aitc.co.uk
Investment Trust Warrants: www.wimb26.freeserve.co.uk/warrants/
McHattie Group (Warrants Alert newsletter): www.tipsheets.co.uk
Numa (warrant calculator): www.numa.com
TrustNet (investment trust warrants): www.trustnet.co.uk
```

Covered warrants

Issuing banks
```
ABN Amro: www.derivates.abnamro.com
Bank Leu: www.leutrading.com
```

Bank Vontobel: www.vontobel.ch
BNP Paribas: warrants.bnpparibas.com
Citibank: warrants.citibank.com
Commerzbank: www.warrants.commerzbank.com
Credit Lyonnais: www.clwarrants.com
Dredsner Kleinwort Wasserstein: www.warrants.dresdner.com
Goldman Sachs: www.gs.com/warrants
Lehman Brothers: www.lehmanlive.com
Société General: www.warrants.socgen.com
UBS: quotes.ubs.com/quotes/
UBS Warburg: ubswarburg.com/warrants/I

UK
London Stock Exchange: www.londonstockexchange.com/techlib/

France
Oddo Warrants: www.oddowarrants.fr
Ma-Fi: www.ma-fi.com/portail.htm
Boursier.com: www.boursier.com
First Invest: www.firstinvest.com/warrants/
3611 Bourse: www.3611bourse.com/warrants/

Germany
OnVista: optionsscheine.onvista.de

Italy
TradingLab: www.tradinglab.com
CoveredWarantsOnline: www.coveredwarrantsonline.com

CFDs
Deal4free: www.deal4free.com
GNITouch: www.gnitouch.com
IFX: www.ifx.co.uk
ManDirect: www.mandirect.co.uk
Sucden: www.equitycfd.co.uk

Spread betting
Cantor Index: www.cantorindex.com
City Index: www.cityindex.co.uk
Deal4free: www.deal4free.com
Financial Spreads: www.finspreads.com
IFX: www.ifx.co.uk
IG Index: www.igindex.co.uk
Spreadex: www.spreadex.co.uk
Onewaybet.com (research): www.onewaybet.com
TheSpreadTrader.com (research): www.thespreadtrader.com

Fixed odds betting
BetonMarkets: www.betonmarkets.com
Blue Square: www.bluesq.com

10. Miscellaneous

Share clubs

E-Trader UK (list of online share clubs):
www.e-traderuk.com/invclubs.html
Hemscott (share clubs): www.proshareclubs.co.uk
Motley Fool: www.fool.co.uk
ProShare: www.proshare.org

Equity-Gilt studies

Barclays Capital (Equity-Gilt Study): www.barcap.com/egs/
CSFB (Equity-Gilt Study): www.csfb.com/eqres/eqres_gilt.html

Internet stocks

Internet Stocks Channel: www.internet.com/sections/stocks.html
InternetCap.com: www.internetcap.com
Moneyextra (internet stocks): www.moneyextra.com/stocks/internet/
MSN Investor: www.investor.com
Raging Bull: www.ragingbull.com
Robertson Stephens: www.robertsonstephens.com
Silicon Investor: www.techstocks.com
WSRN (ISDEX chart): www.wsrn.com/apps/ISDEX/chart.xpl?data=D
WSRN (Internet sector indices): www.wsrn.com/apps/internetstocks/

Ethical investing

Ethical Investment Association: www.ethicalinvestment.org.uk
Ethical Partners: www.ethical-partners.co.uk
Ethical Services: www.ethicalservices.co.uk
FT.com (global archive): globalarchive.ft.com
Gaia: www.gaeia.co.uk
Good Money: www.goodmoney.com
Green Money: www.greenmoney.com
The Multinational Monitor: www.essential.org/monitor/
UK Social Investment Forum: www.uksif.org

Bonds

Bondscape.net: www.bondscape.net

Online calculators

FT P/E Calculator: www.ft.com/cgi-bin/pft/pecalc.pl?basic
Motley Fool PEGulator: www.fool.com/Pegulator/Pegulator.htm
Numa options calculator:
www.numa.com/derivs/ref/calculat/option/calc-opa.htm
Numa CB calculator:
www.numa.com/derivs/ref/calculat/cb/calc-cba.htm

Online trading statistics

APCIMS: www.apcims.org
CNET: www.cnet.com
First Tuesday: www.firsttuesday.com
FT.com: www.ft.com
Internet Stock report: www.internetstockreport.com
Nua: www.nua.ie/surveys/
San Francisco Chronicle: www.sfgate.com
San Jose Mercury: www.mercurycenter.com
Upside: www.upside.com
The Web Report: www.internetstocks.com

Industry research companies

Datamonitor: www.datamonitor.com
Forrester Research: www.forrester.com
Gartner Group: www.gartnerweb.com
Gomez.com: www.gomezadvisors.com
Lafferty Internet Reports: www.lafferty.com

Careers in finance

Bloomberg: www.bloomberg.co.uk/careers/
Careers-in-Finance: www.careers-in-finance.com
eFinancialCareers: www.efinancialnews.com/jobs/
FTCareerPoint: ftcareerpoint.ft.com/ftcareerpoint
JobsInTheMoney: www.jobsinthemoney.com
Numa.com: www.numa.com/jobs/
Vault.com: www.vault.com
WetFeet: www.wetfeet.com

Appendix 2: Alphabetical List of Web Sites

A
3611 Bourse: www.3611bourse.com
3D StockCharts: www.3dstockcharts.com
ABN Amro: www.derivates.abnamro.com
AccountingWeb: www.accountingweb.co.uk
ADVFN: www.advfn.com
AFX Press: www.afxpress.com
AIQ: www.aiqsystems.com
AITC: www.aitc.co.uk
Alltheweb: www.alltheweb.com
Altavista: www.altavista.com
American Association of Individual Investors (AAII): www.aaii.com
Ameritrade: www.ameritrade.com
AMG Data Services: www.amgdata.com
Ample: www.iii.co.uk
Andrew Smithers: www.smithers.co.uk/news.shtml
APCIMS: www.apcims.org
Association for Investment Management and Research (AIMR): www.aimr.com
Association of Investment Trusts Companies (AITC): www.aitc.co.uk
Association of Unit Trusts and Investment Funds (AUTIF): www.investmentfunds.org.uk
AvidTrader: www.avidinfo.com

B
Bank Credit Analyst: www.bcapub.com
Bank Holidays Of The World site: www.national-holidays.com
Bank Leu: www.leutrading.com
Bank of England: www.bankofengland.co.uk
Bank of New York (ADRs): www.adrbny.com
Bank Vontobel: www.vontobel.ch
Barchart.com: www.barchart.com
Barclays Capital (Equity-Gilt Study): www.barcap.com/egs/
BBC: news.bbc.co.uk
Berkshire Hathaway: www.berkshirehathaway.com
Best Calls: www.bestcalls.com
BetonMarkets: www.betonmarkets.com
Bigfoot: www.bigfoot.com
Bill Sharpe: www.stanford.edu/~wfsharpe/art/art.htm
Bloomberg: www.bloomberg.com
Blue Square: www.bluesq.com
BlueSky Ratings: www.blueskyratings.com
BNP Paribas: warrants.bnpparibas.com
Bondscape: www.bondscape.net
Boursier.com: www.boursier.com
BoxOption (Oanda): boxoption.olsen.ch
Breaking Views: www.breakingviews.com
Brunswick Direct: www.brunswickdirect.com
BT Openworld: www.btopenworld.com
BusinessWeek: www.businessweek.com

C
Cantor Index: www.cantorindex.com
Careers-in-Finance: www.careers-in-finance.com
CBOE: www.cboe.com
CBOT:www.cbot.com
CBS marketWatch: cbs.marketwatch.com
CCTA Government Information Service: www.open.gov.uk
Central Office of Information (COI): www.coi.gov.uk/coi
Charles Schwab Europe: www.schwab-worldwide.com/Worldwide/Europe
Charles Schwab: www.schwab.com
Chart Patterns: www.chartpatterns.com
Chartanalysts: www.chartanalysts.com
Citibank: warrants.citibank.com
City Comment: www.citycomment.co.uk
City Index: www.cityindex.co.uk
CityComment: www.citycomment.co.uk
Citywatch: www.citywatch.co.uk
Citywire: www.citywire.co.uk
CMC: www.deal4free.com/forex/
CME (www.cme.com)
CNET: www.news.com
CNNfn: www.cnnfn.com
Comdirect: www.comdirect.co.uk
Commerzbank: www.warrants.commerzbank.com
Commodity Futures Trading Commission (CFTC): www.cftc.gov
Companies House: www.companies-house.gov.uk
Company Annual Reports Online (Carol): www.carol.co.uk
Copernic: www.copernic.com
Corporate Reports: www.corpreports.co.uk
CorporateInformation: www.corporateinformation.com
CoveredWarantsOnline: www.coveredwarrantsonline.com.
Credit Lyonnais: www.clwarrants.com
Cross Currents: www.cross-currents.net
CSFB: www.csfb.com
CurrencyPro: www.currencypro.com
Cyberatlas: research.cyberatlas.com
CyberTrader: www.cybertrader.com

D
Datamonitor: www.datamonitor.com
Datek: www.datek.com
David Schwartz: www.schwartztrends.com
DayTradingStocks.com: www.daytradingstocks.com
DBC: portfolio.marketwatch.com/portfolio
Deal4free: www.deal4free.com
Decision Point: www.decisionpoint.com
Digita: www.digita.com
DigitalLook: www.digitallook.com
DirectAccessTrader: www.directaccesstrader.com
Dismal Scientist: www.dismal.com
DLJ direct UK: www.dljdirect.co.uk
Dogpile: www.dogpile.com
Download.com: www.download.com
Downloadquotes.com: www.downloadquotes.com
Dr Edward Yardeni: www.yardeni.com

Dredsner Kleinwort Wasserstein: www.warrants.dresdner.com
Durlacher: www.durlacher.co.uk

E   Easdaq: www.easdaq.be
Easy2Trade (futures): www.easy2trade.com
Easynet: www.easydial.co.uk
Economeister: www.economeister.com
Economist: www.economist.com
e-cortal: www.e-cortal.com
EDGAR Online: www.edgar-online.com
EditPlus: www.editplus.com
eFinancialCareers: www.efinancialnews.com/jobs/
EO.net: www.eo.net
Equity Development : www.equity-development.co.uk
Equity Growth Research (EGR): www.equitygrowth.net
Equity Investigator: www.equityinvestigator.com
ETFZone: www.indexfunds.com/ETFzone.htm
Ethical Investment Association: www.ethicalinvestment.org.uk
Ethical Partners: www.ethical-partners.co.uk
Ethical Servives: www.ethicalservices.co.uk
E*Trade UK: www.etrade.co.uk
E*Trade: www.etrade.com
E-Trader UK: www.e-traderuk.com
European Union: europa.eu.int
Evening Standard: www.thisislondon.co.uk

F   Fairshares: www.updata.co.uk
Federal Reserve: www.federalreserve.gov
Fetcher: www.thefetcher.com
Financial Mail: www.financialmail.co.uk
Financial Services Compensation Scheme: www.the-ics.org.uk
Financial Spreads: www.finspreads.com
First Invest: www.firstinvest.com
First Tuesday: www.firsttuesday.com
Forex Capital Markets: www.fxcm.com
ForexATS: www.forex-ats.com
Forrester Research: www.forrester.com
Freequotes: www.freequotes.co.uk
FreeRealTime: quotes.freerealtime.com
FSA (Financial Services Compensation Scheme):
www.fsa.gov.uk/consumer/consumer_help/
FSA: www.fsa.gov.uk
FT (GlobalArchive): globalarchive.ft.com
FT Investor: www.ft.com/investor
FT.com: www.ft.com
FTCareerPoint: ftcareerpoint.ft.com/ftcareerpoint
FTSE International: www.ftse.com
FTYourMoney: www.ftyourmoney.com
Fundfact.com: www.fundfact.com
Funds S&P: www.funds-sp.com
FXGame (Oanda): fxgame.oanda.com
FXTrade (Oanda): fxtrade.oanda.com
FXTrade: fxtrade.oanda.com

G Gaia: www.gaeia.co.uk
Gain Capital: www.gaincapital.com
Gartmore: www.gartmore.co.uk
Gartner Group: www.gartnerweb.com
GCI Capital: www.globalcap.com
Global Reach: www.glreach.com
Global-Investor: www.global-investor.com
GNI: www.gni.co.uk
GNItouch: www.gnitouch.com
Go: www.go.com
Gold Eagle: www.gold-eagle.com
Goldman Sachs: www.gs.com
Gomez Advisors: www.gomezadvisors.com
Good Money: www.goodmoney.com
Google: www.google.com
Green Money: www.greenmoney.com
Growth Company Investor: www.growthcompany.co.uk

H Hargreaves Lansdown Stockbrokers: www.h-l.co.uk
Hemmington Scott: www.hemscott.co.uk
hemscott.NET: www.hemscott.net
HM Treasury: www.hm-treasury.gov.uk
HOLDRS: www.holdrs.com
Hoovers UK: www.hoovers.com/uk/
Hoovers: www.hoovers.com
HotBot: www.hotbot.com
Hotmail: www.hotmail.com
HowStuffWorks: www.howstuffworks.com
HSW: www.hsw.co.uk
Hulbert Financial Digest: www.hulbertdigest.com

I ICC: www.icc.co.uk
iDealing: www.idealing.com
IFX: www.ifx.co.uk
IG Index: www.igindex.co.uk
IMIWeb: www.imiweb.co.uk
Indigo Investor: www.indigoinvestor.com
Inland Revenue: www.inlandrevenue.gov.uk
INO: quotes.ino.com
Institute for Fiscal Studies (IFS): www1.ifs.org.uk
Interactive Brokers: www.interactivebrokers.com
International Herald Tribune (IHT): www.iht.com
Internet Software Consortium: www.isc.org
Internet Stocks Channel: www.internet.com/sections/stocks.html
InternetCap.com: www.internetcap.com
InvestIN: www.investin.co.uk
Investment Trust Warrants: www.wimb26.freeserve.co.uk/warrants/
InvesTools: www.investools.com/cgi-bin/IT/advisory/home
Investor Ease: www.investorease.com
Investor Information: www.investorinformation.co.uk
invest-o-rama:
www.moneynet.com/content/INVESTORAMA/Ptracker/default.asp
Investors Chronicle: www.investorschronicle.co.uk

Investtech.com: www.investtech.com
IQ Chart: www.iqchart.com
IRD: www.ird.com
iShares (Barclays): www.ishares.net
Island: www.isld.com
iTruffle: www.truffle.com

J   Jeremy Grantham: www.gmo.com/overview/articles.html
Jeremy Siegel: knowledge.wharton.upenn.edu
Jim Slater: www.global-investor.com/slater
Jiway: www.jiway.com
JobsInTheMoney: www.jobsinthemoney.com
John Dorfman (Bloomberg): www.bloomberg.com/columns/
JP Morgan (ADRs): www.adr.com
JP Morgan: www.jpmorgan.com

K   Keynote (speed comparisons): www.keynote.com
Killik: www.killik.co.uk

L   Lafferty Internet Reports: www.lafferty.com
Lehman Brothers: www.lehmanlive.com
LIFFE (data): www.liffe-data.com
LIFFE: www.liffe.com
Lipper: www.lipperweb.com
Lombard Street Research: www.lombard-st.co.uk
London Stock Exchange: www.londonstockexchange.com
LondonMoneyMarket : www.londonmoneymarket.com
LongWaves: csf.colorado.edu/forums/longwaves/
Lowrisk: www.lowrisk.com
LSE: www.londonstockexchange.com
Lycos Finance: finance.lycos.com

M   Ma-Fi: www.ma-fi.com
Man Financial: www.manfinancial.com
ManDirect: www.mandirect.co.uk
MarketGuide: www.marketguide.com
MarketPlayer: www.marketplayer.com
Marketwatch: cbs.marketwatch.com
Martin Capital: www.martincapital.com
Martin Currie: www.martincurrie.com
McHattie Group (Warrants Alert newsletter): www.tipsheets.co.uk
Metacrawler: www.metacrawler.com
Metastock: www.equis.com
MG Forex: www.mgforex.com
Michael Walters: www.michaelwalters.com
Micropal: www.funds-sp.com
Microsoft (online help): support.microsoft.com
Mirago: www.mirago.co.uk
Moneyextra: www.moneyextra.com
MoneyGuru: www.moneyguru.co.uk
Moneynet (Reuters): www.moneynet.com
Moore Research Center: www.mrci.com

Morningstar UK: www.morningstar.co.uk
Morningstar: www.morningstar.com
Motley Fool UK: www.fool.co.uk
Motley Fool: www.fool.com
MRCI: www.mrci.com
MSN Money UK: money.msn.co.uk
MSN Money: moneycentral.msn.com
Multex Investor UK: www.multexinvestor.co.uk
Multex Investor: www.multexinvestor.com
Multex: www.multex.com
myBroker: www.mybroker.co.uk
myTrack: www.mytrack.com

N Nasdaq (Head Trader): www.academic.nasdaq.com/HeadTrader/
Nasdaq (UK): www.nasdaquk.com
Nasdaq: www.nasdaq.com
National Assoc. of Investors Corporation: www.better-investing.org
newissues-ipo.com: www.newissues-ipo.com
News Review: www.news-review.co.uk
Newsgroups: groups.google.com
NewsPage: www.newspage.com
NorthernLight: www.northernlight.com
nothing-ventured.com: www.nothing-ventured.com
NTL (broadband site): www.broadband-cable.co.uk
NTL: www.ntl.com
Nua: www.nua.ie
Numa: www.numa.com

O Oanda: www.oanda.com
Oddo Warrants: www.oddowarrants.fr
OFEX: www.ofex.co.uk
OmniTrader: www.omnitrader.com
Onewaybet.com: www.onewaybet.com
OnVista UK: www.onvista.co.uk
OnVista: www.onvista.de
Options Direct: www.options-direct.co.uk
Ovum Holway: www.holway.co.uk

P Pacific Exchange Rates Service: pacific.commerce.ubc.ca/
Paint Shop Pro: www.jasc.com
Paritech: www.paritech.co.uk
Paul Krugman: web.mit.edu/krugman/www
PC Medics: www.pc-medics.co.uk
PC Quote: www.pcquote.com
PCPitstop: www.pcpitstop.com
Peter Bernstein: www.peterlbernsteininc.com
Philip Fisher: www.forbes.com/fisher
Prestel : www.finexprestel.com
Pro Analyst: www.trendsoft.com/ProAnalyst/
Proquote: www.proquote.net
ProShare UK: www.proshare.org
ProTA: www.beesoft.net

Q   Quicken: www.quicken.com
       Quote.com: finance.lycos.com

R   Raging Bull: www.ragingbull.com
       RAWfinancial.com: www.rawfinancial.com
       RealMoney.com: www.realmoney.com
       RealTimeShares.com: www.realtimeshares.com
       RedSky Research: www.redskyresearch.com
       Reuters UK: www.reuters.co.uk
       Reuters: www.reuters.com
       Robert Shiller: www.econ.yale.edu/~shiller/
       Robertson Stephens: www.robertsonstephens.com
       Rookie DayTrader: www.rookiedaytrader.com

S   SamSpade: samspade.org/t/
       Samuel Brittan: www.samuelbrittan.co.uk
       San Francisco Chronicle: www.sfgate.com
       San Jose Mercury: www.mercurycenter.com
       Saxo Bank: www.saxobank.com
       Securities & Exchange Commission (SEC): www.sec.gov
       Securities and Futures Authority (SFA): www.fsa.gov.uk/sfa/
       Securities And Investment Board (SIB): www.sib.co.uk
       Security Blanket: www.thesecurityblanket.com
       selectipo: www.selectipo.com
       Selftrade UK: www.selftrade.co.uk
       Sharecast: www.sharecast.co.uk
       Sharepages: www.sharepages.com
       Sharepeople: www.sharepeople.co.uk
       Sharescope: www.sharescope.co.uk
       ShareStar: www.sharestar-uk.com
       Silicon Investor: www.siliconinvestor.com
       SimVest Solution: www.simvesting.com
       Sixer.com: www.sixer.com
       SmartMoney: www.smartmoney.com
       Société General: www.warrants.socgen.com
       Splitsonline: www.splitsonline.co.uk
       Spreadex: www.spreadex.co.uk
       StockAcademy: www.stockacademy.com
       StockCharts: www.stockcharts.com
       StockTables: www.stocktables.com
       StockTools: www.stocktools.com
       Sucden: www.equitycfd.co.uk
       Swiftrade: www.swiftrade.com

T   t1ps.com: www. t1ps.com
       TC2000: www.tc2000.com
       TD Waterhouse UK: www.tdwaterhouse.co.uk
       TD Waterhouse: www.waterhouse.com
       Tech Tutorials: www.techtutorials.com
       techMARK Research: www.techmarkresearch.com
       Telegraph (money): money.telegraph.co.uk
       Teletext : www.teletext.co.uk
       Telewest: www.telewest.co.uk

TFC: www.tfc-charts.w2d.com
The Multinational Monitor: www.essential.org/monitor/
The Register: www.theregister.co.uk
TheSpreadTrader.com: www.thespreadtrader.com
TheStreet.com: www.thestreet.com
thewrongprice : www.thewrongprice.com
ThomsonFN (global): global.thomsonfn.co.uk
ThomsonFN: www.thomsonfn.com/
Tipsheets: www.tipsheets.co.uk
Trade2Win: www.Trade2Win.co.uk
Tradecast: www.tradecast.com
Tradescape.com: www.tradescape.com
TRADINGCentral.com: www.tradingcentral.com
TradingCharts.com: www.tfc-charts.w2d.com
TradingLab: www.tradinglab.com
Treasury Management Pages: www.tmpages.com
TrimTabs Investment Research: www.trimtabs.com
TrustNet: www.trustnet.com
trustnews.co.uk: www.trustnews.co.uk
Tucows: www.tucows.com

U   UK Social Investment Forum: www.uksif.org
     UBS Warburg: ubswarburg.com
     UK-Wire: www.uk-wire.co.uk
     unquoted.co.uk: www.unquoted.co.uk
     Updata: www.updata.co.uk
     Upside: www.upside.com
     UXN spam combat: combat.uxn.com

V   Validea.com: www.validea.com
     Value Investor's Workshop: members.aol.com/WCrimi/workshop.html
     Vault.com: www.vault.com
     Vivisimo: www.vivisimo.com

W   Wall Street City: www.wallstreetcity.com
     Wall Street Guru: www.wallstreetguru.com
     watshot.com: www.watshot.com
     Web Report: www.internetstocks.com
     WetFeet: www.wetfeet.com
     WinZip: www.winzip.com
     Wit Capital: www.witcapital.com
     worldlyinvestor.com: www.worldlyinvestor.com
     Worldwide Holiday & Festival: www.holidayfestival.com
     Wright Investors' Service (company profiles): profiles.wisi.com
     Wright Investors' Service: www.wisi.com
     WSRN: www.wsrn.com

Y   Yahoo Finance UK: finance.yahoo.co.uk
     Yahoo Finance: finance.yahoo.com

Z   Zacks: www.zacks.com
     ZD Net: www.zdnet.com

Appendix 3: LSE Trade Definitions

The London Stock Exchange defines a number of different types of trade. Every trade that occurs on the Exchange must be designated with one of these trade types, which will usually be relayed at the time of the trade along with the price and time. The table below summarises the trade types defined by the Exchange.

Code	Trade type	Description
AI	Automated Input	If reporting that a member firm has disabled its automated input facility in response to a request from the Exchange.
AT	Automatic Trade	An automatic trade generated by the SETS system through the order book.
	Average Price	The transaction was effected at a price based on a volume weighted average price over a given period.
	Bargain Conditions Apply	Certain conditions were agreed between the two participants at the time of trading.
K	Block Trade	The transaction was reported using the block trade facility, which is ≥75 times the NMS for a security with an NMS of 2,000 shares OR ≥50 times the NMS for a security with an NMS of 1,000 shares.
B	Broker to Broker	The transaction was between two member firms where neither firm is registered as a market maker in the security in question and neither is a designated fund manager. Brokers may also apply this indicator when buying or selling domestic equity market securities through a broker, which is not a member firm.
CT	Contra Trade	The trade was reported for a transaction previously automatically executed through the order book.
	Correction	This covers any corrections made to trade reports.
X	Cross	The transaction was effected as an agency cross or a riskless principle trade between two member firms at the same price and on the same terms.

		Currency Conversion	The trade was executed in one currency but converted for trade reporting.
EU		Euro Automated Trades	
ER		Euro Trades	
L		Late Reported Trade	Late trades, as the name implies, are trades that are reported to the Stock Exchange some time after the trade has been executed. There can be a number of reasons for this. If a trade is executed that is six times the Normal Market Size then the market makers, for stocks traded on the full list, do not have to report the trade for one hour after the trade was executed. Once reported, this would show as a Late Trade. A trade would also show as being late if the bargain had to be amended for any reason, like an alteration to the settlement date. Once the bargain was amended, the amended bargain would show up as a late trade.
LC		Late Trade Correction	A correction submitted more than 3 days after the trade date, or where deferred publication is permitted at any time after the trade report was submitted to the Exchange reporting system.
M		Market Maker to Market Maker	The transaction was between two market makers registered in the security in question. This may also include those executed through an inter-dealer broker or a public display system.
N		Non Protected Portfolio	A non-protected portfolio transaction or a fully disclosed portfolio transaction. Normally a transaction of a number of stocks dealt with by one market maker at an agreed discount to the market price.
NR		Non-Risk Trade	These trades are the same as Ordinary Trades but specifically for SEATS based segments only (i.e. SEQ1, AIM, SEAT).
NM		Not to Mark	A transaction where the Exchange has granted permission for non-publication.

O	Ordinary Trade	A standard trade made through the Market Makers and dealt at normal settlement date. (System will delay if over six times NMS)
	Overnight Trade	The transaction was reported after 17h15 and before 07h15 the following day.
PC	Post Contra	Used when reporting a Contra Trade when the contra date is not the trade date.
P	Protected Portfolio	A protected portfolio transaction or a trade resulting from a worked principal agreement for a portfolio transaction. Like a non-protected portfolio, but the price dealt at can be amended if the market maker manages to make a profit.
PA	Protection Applied	Protected transaction at the time that protection is applied.
RC	Regulatory Conformance	This is a test segment for which no trade reports will be disseminated.
RO	Result of Exercising Option	A transaction reported as a result of exercising a traditional option or a negotiated option.
	Result of Stock Swap	The transaction was reported as a result of a stock swap or stock switch (one report is required for each line of stock swapped or switched).
RT	Risk Trade	The transaction was reported by a market maker registered in either a SEATS security, an AIM security or a covered warrant market security.
R	Riskless Principal	A riskless principal transaction with two non members, where the two transactions are executed at different prices or on different terms (this requires two separate trade reports). This happens often on a trade where commission is not charged. Instead of paying commission, the client will pay extra for their shares.

ST	SEAQ Trade	This is used for the single uncrossing trade, detailing the total executed volume and uncrossing price as a result of a SEAQ auction
T	Single Protected Trade	The trade was reported as a result of a single protected transaction. A protected transaction occurs when a large order is going through the market. The buyer (or seller) may wish to keep the order anonymous from the rest of the market as the size of the order could greatly alter the price of the stock. With a protected transaction, the dealer will put the trade through in small quantities rather than in one go. The entire transaction is reported once the deal is completed. The LSE is notified at the start and at the end of the transaction. However, the market as a whole isn't told until the end, thus the order is protected.
SW	Stock Swap	Transactions comprised in a stock swap or stock switch (one report is required for each line of stock swapped or switched).
TS	Test Security	If using a test security to test trade reporting.
UT	Uncrossing Trade	This is used for the single uncrossing trade, detailing the total executed volume and uncrossing price as a result of a SETS auction.
VW	Volume Weighted Average Price	A transaction that was effected at a price based on a volume weighted average price over a given period.
WN	Worked Principal	The Exchange is notified that a member firm has entered into a worked principal agreement for a single security.
PN	Worked Principal Portfolio Notification	A Member firm has agreed to take on a worked principal agreement for a portfolio transaction.
WT	Worked Principal Trade	The reported trade was from a worked principle agreement for a single security.

Source: ADVFN, London Stock Exchange

Appendix 4: List of Downloadable Spreadsheets

The spreadsheets below can be downloaded free of charge from this book's web site: http://www.global-investor.com/onlineinvesting.

Related Q&A in this book	page #	File name
Build your own bookmark page	18	links-v2.htm
Prices direct to a spreadsheet	33	uk_adr_trac.xls
Excel Web Queries	34	ic_quote.iqy
On Balance Volume	118	obv.xls
Coppock Indicator	124	ftse100-coppock.xls
Rebasing charts vs the FTSE 100	128	tsco_ftse100.xls
Stocks for day trading	154	ftse100-daytrading.xls
International market charts	193	cht-intl.zip
Gilt yields	217	gilt-yield.xls
Compound interest	226	compound-interest.xls
Calculating historic volatility	227	volatility-vod.xls

DISCLAIMER OF LIABILITY:

Neither the author nor the publisher can accept liability for any loss that results to a user from downloading and/or using the spreadsheets. Downloads are undertaken and the spreadsheets used entirely at the user's risk.

A

ADRs
Advantages of: 182
Currency exposure: 184
Information sources: 183

American markets: see US Markets

Association of Investment Trust Companies (AITC): 74

Alternative Investment Market (AIM): 51

American Depository Receipts: See ADRs

B

Beta values: 69

Block Trades: See Trade Definitions

Bonds and Gilts
Equities vs Gilts: 216
Gilt yields: 217
Bond price quotes: 45

Brokers
Commission charges: 140
Delayed settlement: 161
ECNs: 175
European accounts: 198
Expatriate accounts: 135
Order execution: 139, 146
Regulation: 136
Research from: 104, 172
Running two accounts: 137, 138
Types of order: 150, 151

Buffett, Warren: 223

Bulletin Boards
Best boards: 68
Newsgroups: 36

Buy and sell volumes: 148

C

Candlestick charting: 116

CFDs: See Contracts for Differences

Charting: See Technical Analysis

Company Analysis
Best and worst performers: 57
Cash flow statements: 98
CEO interviews: 108
EPS forecasts: 99, 100, 101, 172
Email news bulletins: 67
EPIC, TIDMN & ISIN codes: 43, 44
European research: 196
Foreign companies: 195
Fundamental data: 94
Online conferences calls: 107
PEG ratios: 63, 100
Registrars: 96
Reporting dates: 97
Research: 104, 106
SEDOL codes: 44
Share issues: 46
Share splits: 70, 71
Stock screeners: 55
US companies: 168
Web addresses: 95

Company reports & accounts: 98

Compound interest: 225

Computers
Apple Macs: 4
Finding lost files: 29
Keyboard shortcuts: 22
Laptops & internet: 3
Support: 2

Contracts for Differences (CFDs): 156, 211

Coppock Indicator: 124

Covered warrants: 210

Currencies/Exchange Rates
Charting of: 203
Euro exchange rates: 202
Risk of trading: 205
Trading currencies: 204

VOLATILITY — COMDIRECT + LOOK AT —daytrading.xlst
SHARE SCOPE